Legacy of Valour

*for Kerry
in her new house

love
Gren*

Daniel G. Dancocks
Legacy of Valour
The Canadians at Passchendaele

Hurtig Publishers
Edmonton

Copyright ©1986 by Daniel G. Dancocks

All rights reserved. No part of this book may be reproduced or transmitted in any form by any means, electronic, electrical, mechanical, chemical, optical, or otherwise, including photocopying and recording, or by any information storage or retrieval system, without written permission from the publishers, except for brief passages quoted by a reviewer in a newspaper or magazine.

Hurtig Publishers Ltd.
10560-105 Street
Edmonton, Alberta
Canada T5H 2W7

Canadian Cataloguing in Publication Data

Dancocks, Daniel G. (Daniel George), 1950–
    Legacy of valour

ISBN 0-88830-305-X

1. Ypres, 3rd Battle of, 1917. 2. World War, 1914-1918 - Campaigns - Belgium - Ieper. 3. World War, 1914-1918—Participation, Canadian. I. Title.
D542.Y72D3 1986   940.4'31   C86-091283-3

Printed and bound in Canada
by John Deyell Company

Contents

Introduction / ix

PART ONE: **Genesis**

1 / Soldiers and Statesmen / 3
2 / War at the Top / 17
3 / "Correct Principles" / 39

PART TWO: **Flanders**

4 / Wipers / 51
5 / Rain, Mud, and Blood / 63
6 / "A Battle of Attrition" / 70
7 / More Mud and Blood / 79

PART THREE: **The Canadians**

8 / Professional Amateurs / 89
9 / Preparations / 99
10 / Ready and Waiting / 115
11 / "A Truly Magnificent Performance" / 125
12 / Another Step Closer / 140
13 / "At All Costs" / 155
14 / Bayonets and Bombs / 162
15 / "They Are Wonderful Troops" / 171
16 / Farewell to the Salient / 178
17 / Death Struggle / 184

PART FOUR: **Consequences**

18 / Watershed / 187
19 / "Irregular Warfare" / 190
20 / The Feud Continues / 209
21 / Currie: Glory and Tragedy / 222

Conclusion / 231
Appendix 1: Order of Battle, Canadian Army Corps / 241
Appendix 2: Canadian Corps Instructions for the Offensive / 245
Acknowledgments / 255
Notes / 257
Bibliography / 273
Index / 279

*For Andy and Betty McCarroll
and in the memory of
Private Allan Faulds Kerr,
Royal Scots Fusiliers,
killed in action,
Passchendaele,
22 October 1917*

> ...　*I died in hell—*
> *(They called it Passchendaele). My wound was slight,*
> *And I was hobbling back; and then a shell*
> *Burst slick upon the duck-boards: so I fell*
> *Into the bottomless mud, and lost the light.*
>
> (Siegfried Sassoon, "Memorial Tablet")

Introduction

Passchendaele was the most controversial battle of the Great War of 1914-18. Officially known as the Third Battle of Ypres, and composed of eight separate engagements,* it was fought between 31 July and 12 November 1917 in Flanders, in western Belgium. Passchendaele derived its name from a ruined village atop a hardly noticeable ridge which became the focal point of the fighting.

Even today, seven decades later, the debate still rages over the merits of this apparently tragic and futile offensive which was the inevitable by-product of a long and bitter dispute between, on the one hand, politicians who sought a painless path to victory and, on the other hand, generals who were determined to win a war of attrition. Passchendaele's detractors are legion. It was, in the words of Britain's wartime prime minister, David Lloyd George, one of the "most gigantic, tenacious, grim, futile and bloody fights ever waged in the history of war." Another statesman, Winston Churchill, called it "a forlorn expenditure of valour and life without equal in futility." The verdict of military historians is no less critical. "Third Ypres was the blindest slaughter of a blind war," commented A.J.P. Taylor, while Sir Basil Liddell Hart labelled it "the gloomiest drama in British military history.... So fruitless in its results, so depressing in its direction was this 1917 offensive, that 'Passchendaele' has come to be... a synonym for military failure—a name black-bordered in the records of the British Army." These comments are typical, reflecting the viewpoint of the overwhelming majority of observers, who contend that Passchendaele was pointless. This book will attempt to demonstrate that they are wrong.[1]

Passchendaele is synonymous not only with military failure but with mud. Much of the campaign was waged in conditions that almost defy description. Indeed, it may be safely stated that no battle has ever been fought under worse conditions. The unprecedented shell fire turned the locale into a lunar landscape, innumerable craters that obliterated virtually every landmark and destroyed the

---

* The eight battles that comprise Third Ypres:
    Pilckem, 31 July-2 August
    Langemarck, 16-18 August
    Menin Road, 20-25 August
    Polygon Wood, 26 September-3 October
    Broodseinde, 4 October
    Poelcappelle, 9 October
    First Passchendaele, 12 October
    Second Passchendaele, 26 October-10 November

delicate drainage system: combined with above average rainfall, the battlefield turned into a vast bog. Soupy, sticky, smelly mud became a fact of life—and death. It clogged rifles. Food tasted of it. Guns sank in it. Soldiers slept in it, floundered in it, drowned in it. Unfortunately, this sad situation has tended to overshadow the achievements of the men who fought in Flanders.

Canada is linked inextricably with Passchendaele. This bloodletting, with its attendant horror and heartbreak, stands as an unparalleled feat of arms in Canadian military history. Although they were innocent bystanders in the feud between British politicians and generals—it must be remembered that Canada, though a self-governing dominion, was for all intents and purposes a colony of Britain and had no say in the military conduct of the war—the Canadians succeeded where all others had failed, in the face of overwhelming odds and a skilful, determined, and confident enemy. Employing "brilliant organization and method," according to John Terraine, the leading authority on the Great War, the Canadian Corps captured Passchendaele in "a triumph of what might be called aquatic engineering." It was a breathtaking accomplishment. Heroism was commonplace: in less than two weeks at Passchendaele, Canadians won nine Victoria Crosses, almost as many as won by Canadian soldiers—ten—during the whole of World War II.[2]

I make no apology for making the focus of this book the Canadian role at Passchendaele. Previous publications have, for the most part, given the Canadians short shrift, and not surprisingly: most condemn and castigate the British high command for its conduct of the battle, and the Canadian success tends to undermine their criticism. But, as a result, Canadians today are largely ignorant of the splendid part played by their fathers, grandfathers, and great-grandfathers. In focusing on the Canadians, I do not mean to belittle the efforts and sacrifices of the other British Empire forces who participated. Rather, it is my intention to pay long overdue tribute to the magnificent performance of the Canadian Corps in this grim struggle.

For others, Passchendaele may be a name of shame and infamy. For Canadians, it is an incredible tale of courage and endurance. Passchendaele is proof—if any is needed—that there is no glory in war, but it can be, nonetheless, a source of justifiable pride. That, for Canadians, is the legacy of Passchendaele.

Part One: Genesis

1 / Soldiers and Statesmen

It was the summer of 1917. The great European war which had begun in August 1914 was now nearing the end of its third exhausting year. Three Christmases had come and gone—few experts had expected the war to last beyond the first Christmas. Already, millions of men had been killed or maimed in this colossal tragedy, and no one could predict when it might end.

To an impartial observer, it must have seemed that the Central Powers—Germany and her allies, Austria-Hungary, Turkey, and Bulgaria—were winning. They had more than held their own against the superior numbers of the Triple Entente—Great Britain and her Empire, France, and Russia—and allied powers that included Romania, Italy, and, most recently, the United States of America. The entry of the U.S. into the war, in April 1917, had been, for the Central Powers, a disturbing development, but it would be many months before the Americans could field an effective force, and there were several offsetting factors. Russia, with her vast but ill equipped and poorly led armies, was now a doubtful partner in the Triple Entente, following the overthrow of Czar Nicholas II in March. Romania, declaring war in late 1916, had been all but crushed. Italy's warlords, meantime, were setting records for futility and incompetence in a conflict notable for both—the Italians, battering their heads against powerful Austrian positions in the southern Alps, would fight the Eleventh Battle of the Isonzo this summer, and it would be no more successful than the previous ten. France, her armies bled white and in a mutinous mood, was war-weary and teetering on the brink of collapse. Indeed, only the British Empire stood between Kaiser Wilhelm II and his goal of German hegemony over Europe.

However, British leadership was deeply divided. The reason for this rift was the Western Front. Here, the opposing sides held virtually the same positions as they had in the autumn of 1914, when the brief war of movement congealed into stagnant and stultifying trench warfare on a 400-mile front stretching from Switzerland to the North Sea. Both sides appeared powerless to break the deadlock. Because the Germans occupied most of Belgium and much of northern France, which had fallen in the first weeks of the war, they practised a defensive strategy, attacking on just a few occasions. When they did attack, they had no more success than the British and French: trenches and other field fortifications, barbed wire, machine-guns, and modern artillery proved too much for human flesh to overcome. The very size of the armies, numbering in the millions, was a factor, too; despite great advances in technology, Great War generals were handicapped by limited transportation facilities and primitive communications, making it difficult for an attacker to capitalize on success. It was much easier for a defender to plug a hole in his line than for the attacking side to exploit the opening, thus giving rise to the dangerous myth that defensive fighting was easier, and therefore less costly, than the offensive. What cannot be questioned, though, is that the butcher's bill in this siege warfare, twentieth-century style, was enormous.

Verdun symbolized the futility of this strange, new war. The Germans attacked here in February 1916. Code-named *Gericht,* "place of execution," Verdun was a coldly calculated battle of attrition, the sector having been selected by the German high command in the knowledge that the French, who considered it to be hallowed ground, would defend it to the last man if necessary. This grim battle lasted months. The French saved Verdun, but at the cost of half a million casualties: "L'infanterie française n'existe plus," wept one of their generals.[1] At the same time, the Germans lost 400,000 men they could ill afford to lose.

The British experienced their first wholesale slaughter in the summer of 1916. To be sure, their losses had been heavy enough prior to this, but they had been a mere fraction of those suffered by the French and Germans, both of whom had been, until then, employing much larger forces on the Western Front. On 1 July 1916 the British Expeditionary Force, a million men strong, attacked on either side of the River Somme in north-central France. It was the first test for the civilian volunteers and conscripts assembled by Lord Kitchener, Britain's secretary of state for war. By the time the fighting ended in November, British casualties totalled 419,654—including a staggering 57,470 on the *first day*—with only a few square miles of muddy, pockmarked real estate of no military importance to show for the sacrifice.

The Somme had come as a shock to the British public. Although the actual numbers of dead were withheld until after the war, the censors could not conceal the mourning that took place in every city, town, village, and hamlet in the United Kingdom. Anger and frustration accompanied the tears, and people began to wonder whether this war was worthwhile. One of the most prominent people to express such doubts was Lord Landsdowne who, in mid-November 1916, circulated a private memorandum among cabinet ministers.

Lansdowne sought assurances that the war could be brought "to an effectual conclusion within a reasonable space of time." The cost, he maintained, was intolerable, in both human and financial terms.

> Our own casualties already amount to over 1,100,000.... We are slowly but surely killing off the best of the male population of these islands.... The financial burden...is almost incalculable. We are adding to it at the rate of over £5,000,000 per day. Generations will have to come and go before the country recovers from the loss which it has sustained in human beings, and from the financial ruin and the destruction of the means of production which are taking place.[2]

Because most of these heartbreaking losses were being incurred on the Western Front, it was only natural that it should be the focal point of a renewed and bitter debate over British military strategy. Three men personified this dispute: one was a politician, the other two were soldiers.

The politician was the energetic and enigmatic David Lloyd George, a leading member of Prime Minister Herbert Asquith's Liberal government and, arguably, the outstanding orator of his day. With bushy eyebrows and snow-white hair highlighting a friendly face, and displaying a tendency toward rumpled suits, Lloyd George looked like an absent-minded professor. But his appearance masked a complex personality, as Walter Page, the American ambassador in wartime London, perceptively observed: "he is changeable—mercurial. He reaches quick conclusions by his emotions as well as his reason—he reasons with his emotions.... He is the one public man in the Kingdom who has an undoubted touch of genius. He has also the defects of a genius. He has vision and imagination, and his imagination sometimes runs away with him.... He compels admiration and permits, but does not compel, complete confidence."[3]

English-born but Welsh-raised, a lawyer by training, Lloyd George had entered Parliament in 1890, winning a by-election in Carnarvon Boroughs, a riding he represented for fifty-five years. Associated with the radical wing of the Liberals, he acquired a reputation as a pacifist and social reformer. Prime Minister Asquith appointed Lloyd George to his cabinet in 1908, giving him the post of chancellor of the exchequer, which he retained until January 1915. At that time, with a major European war on his hands, Asquith was forced to form a coalition with the Conservatives, and Lloyd George found himself minister of munitions in the reorganized cabinet. Performing capably, he succeeded, in July 1916, the late Lord

Kitchener as secretary of state for war, an ironic appointment, in view of Lloyd George's leading role in cutting military and naval spending on the eve of the war.

Disillusionment set in quickly. In February 1916, Lloyd George's mistress, Frances Stevenson, commented in her diary: "D. is heartily sick of the present Government. He says it would be laughable if it were not tragic." As early as May, Lloyd George had confided to a colleague, Sir Maurice Hankey, that "he was seriously thinking of leaving the Government, as he thought he might do more good outside than inside."[4]

Much of his frustration stemmed from what he called "a feeble and shaky cabinet." Prime Minister Asquith presided over an unwieldy and inefficient decision-making process which involved his full cabinet in lengthy deliberations on even the most minor matters, to Lloyd George's disgust. "If we pull through," he complained to Sir George Riddell in February 1916, "it will be the nation who will accomplish the feat in spite of the Government." He bluntly blamed Asquith, lamenting that "the P.M. never moves until he is forced, and then it is usually too late."[5]

Lloyd George was equally disenchanted with the military. "I am the butcher's boy who leads the animals to the slaughter," he raged in July 1916, shortly after his appointment as secretary for war. "When I have delivered the men my task in the war is over." He was indignant that the soldiers, both at the War Office and on the Western Front, were unwilling to accept his advice, or that of other politicians, on how to go about winning the war. "He is very dissatisfied regarding the conduct of the war," Riddell wrote in his diary on 11 July 1916, "and thinks... our failures inexcusable, as we have men, guns, and ammunition. He considers that we have no brains at the top." This belief blossomed into an obsession. By October, Sir Maurice Hankey noted that Lloyd George had become "very depressed, very disappointed with the lack of imagination of the General Staff, and very disgusted at the heavy losses involved in the offensive on the Somme as contrasted with the relatively small successes achieved." In early November he told Hankey that he "considered that the Somme offensive had been a bloody and disastrous failure; he was not willing to remain in office, if it was to be repeated next year."[6]

In David Lloyd George's opinion, there was only one man who could save the situation: David Lloyd George. Looking over the list of possible competitors to succeed Asquith as prime minister, he could only conclude, "There *is* no one." His ambition was poorly concealed. When he was named secretary of state for war, Asquith's wife, Margot, commented privately that "it can only be a question of time now when we shall have to leave Downing Street." Her prediction was realized in less than six months. In December 1916, in the midst of a Lloyd George-precipitated cabinet crisis, Asquith resigned. He was succeeded as prime minister by fifty-four-year-old David Lloyd George.[7]

The new prime minister was fiercely determined to win the war. "Time is the least vital factor," he had thundered in response to Lord Lansdowne's memorandum. "It took England twenty years to defeat Napoleon, and the first fifteen of these years were bleak with British defeat. It will not take twenty years to win this war, but whatever time is required it will be done!" But he was not willing to win at all costs, as the British army and its leaders seemed intent on doing. Lloyd George brought to 10 Downing Street a suspicion of the military: he had been only too ready to believe rumours of a conspiracy involving, according to the diary of his mistress, "certain members of the Army in high places to get rid of L.G." in October 1916. His evident paranoia fuelled the fires of his discontent with the generals entrusted with the direction of the war. "L.G. says our generals lack vision," Sir George Riddell remarked in his diary. "They are able, industrious, brave, and thorough, but have no genius." The prime minister was considerably more caustic in his post-war memoirs. "Seniority and Society were the dominant factors in Army promotion," he wrote. "Deportment counted a good deal. Brains came a bad fourth." Lloyd George would also grumble that "I had to contend not with a profession but with a priesthood, devoted to its chosen idol."[8]

That idol, of course, was the Western Front. It was no coincidence that Lloyd George had been one of the first to advocate its abandonment. On 1 January 1915 he had circulated among his fellow cabinet ministers a memorandum in which he foresaw "an eternal stalemate" on the Western Front, and suggested the withdrawal of all but token British forces from France. "A clear definite victory which has visibly materialized in guns and prisoners captured, in unmistakable retreats of the enemy's armies, and in large sections of enemy territory captured, will alone satisfy the public that tangible results are being achieved by the great sacrifices they are making...." To achieve this, he argued in favour of operations "which would have the common purpose of bringing Germany down by the process of knocking the props under her." There were two options: "an attack upon Austria, in conjunction with the Serbians, Roumanians and the Greeks," or "an attack upon Turkey."[9]

This marked the beginning of the so-called "side-shows." Lloyd George found an eloquent ally in First Lord of the Admiralty Winston Churchill, who convinced the cabinet to approve an attack on Turkey via the Dardanelles, a naval thrust to capture Constantinople and open a direct link with Russia. The resulting fiasco at Gallipoli cost Churchill his cabinet post. But far from discrediting Lloyd George and his supporters, who sought an alternative to the Western Front, it was merely one of several side-shows in the Mediterranean theatre. In co-operation with the French, an expedition was also dispatched to Salonika, Greece; it tied up 400,000 British troops, to no useful purpose. A like number was eventually committed to Mesopotamia, while 1,192,511 British soldiers served in Palestine by the end of the war. In rescuing these thousands from the slime and slaughter of the Western Front, Lloyd George and his ilk condemned them to a misery of a different sort: the stifling heat and debilitating diseases of the Middle East. Of the half-million British casualties in this theatre, fewer than 10 per cent were due to enemy action. And their sacrifice had little or no appreciable impact on the war's outcome.

Lloyd George's plan for "bringing Germany down by the process of knocking the props under her" was patently ridiculous. It was Germany which propped up Austria-Hungary and Turkey, not vice versa. Killing Austrians and Turks might have made Lloyd George, and the British public, feel as if much was being accomplished, but the truth is that precious resources, human and material, were being squandered in the side-shows. Lloyd George failed to grasp the essential fact that the war would not, and could not, end until Germany and her powerful armies had been defeated. The majority of these forces were located on the Western Front, and it was there that the war must be decided. The only possible justification for the side-shows would have been the presence of sizeable German formations, but that condition was not fulfilled; there were very few German troops opposing the British adventures. (Interestingly, a similar situation arose during World War II, with the campaigns in North Africa and Italy. However, unlike the Great War, these sideshows involved substantial German forces, and the killing and capturing of Germans contributed in a meaningful way to the war effort. Nevertheless, no knowledgeable person can argue that the defeat of Italy, in 1943, knocked the props from under Germany.)

David Lloyd George was not a stupid man—far from it. But he had a very naïve view of war. And he was, above all, a politician. When politicians apply themselves to a problem—military, economic, social, whatever—more problems usually result. They tend to seek the easy way out of difficulties, and Lloyd George was no exception: he sought a cheap, relatively painless path to victory, and to win that victory with, preferably, the blood of Russians, Italians, and, ultimately, Americans. Lloyd George did not understand—did not *want* to, perhaps—that there is no easy way to win a war, particularly in modern times, given the massive manpower and technology available to industrialized nations.

His iconoclastic views were opposed by the military as a whole and by two soldiers in particular. They were Sir William Robertson, the chief of the Imperial General Staff (CIGS) and the cabinet's military adviser, and Sir Douglas Haig, commander-in-chief of the British Expeditionary Force (BEF) fighting in France and Flanders.

Robertson, whose nickname was "Wully," had had a remarkable career. A native of Lincolnshire, he had enlisted as a private in 1877, at the age of twenty-seven, and would retire after the Great War as a field-marshal, the highest rank in the British army. Commissioned in 1888, Robertson became the first officer from the ranks to graduate from the Staff College at Camberley, Surrey. A superb administrator, he later returned as commandant of the college. When the war broke out in August 1914, Robertson was named quartermaster-general of the BEF, and in early 1915 became chief of staff to the force's first commander-in-chief, Sir John French. Robertson's appointment as the CIGS came in December 1915.

Witty and intelligent but moody and ill-mannered, Robertson was often incapable of articulate expression, sometimes managing no more than a "series of grunts." When angry or excited he would drop his h's, and he had a standard retort when confronted with an argument he was unprepared for: "I've 'eard different." He also disliked and distrusted politicians. In early January 1916, less than two weeks after becoming the CIGS, Robertson wrote: "It is deplorable the way these politicians fight and intrigue against each other. They are my great difficulty here. They have no idea how war must be conducted in order to be given a reasonable chance of success, and they will not allow professionals a free hand." In another letter he complained that "much of my time is taken up in *talking*, and in explaining what these people cannot understand and sometimes do not wish to understand." As his confidence grew, so did his disdain for politicians, and he came to look upon his dealings with them as some sort of high-stakes game, "that one had to manage these politicians, to give way on small points, to postpone larger questions which were awkward, and to temporise if the politicians were promoting them. In this manner time was gained, and it was also 7 to 4 that the politician went off at a tangent on some other lay, or entirely forgot about the first affair." He bluntly told Colonel Charles Repington, the war correspondent for *The Times* of London, "that he did not intend to lose the war by giving in to the politicians."[10]

In Robertson's opinion, the politicians were a lot like Britain's allies—more of a hindrance than a help. The CIGS was a francophobe; "a peculiar lot," he called the French. "The great thing to remember in dealing with them," he once said, "is that they are Frenchmen and not Englishmen, and do not and never will look at things in the way we look at them." (The French had a nickname for Robertson, "Général Non Non," a reference to his typical response to anything and everything they proposed.) The Italians and Russians fared little better. Robertson had no use whatever for the Italians, complaining that their "senior generals were too old and guns were too few." The Russians he dismissed as good for little "except music and dancing and tommy-rot love stories."[11]

Wully Robertson was totally dedicated to winning the war on the Western Front. "It is one of the first principles of war," he later wrote, "that all available resources should be concentrated at the 'decisive' point—that is, at the place where the main decision of war is to be fought out." Robertson had believed for a long time that only the Western Front filled the bill. In November 1915, before he became the CIGS, he had written a memorandum to Prime Minister Asquith, arguing that the only way to win the war was "to defeat decisively the main German armies, which are still on the Western Front.... Each successive offensive of the Allies in the West is regarded as a failure unless it produces a decisive result. But the decisive defeat of 2,000,000 men on a front of 400 miles can only be brought about by prolonged effort, and cannot in the most favourable circumstances be the consequence of one battle." He correctly insisted that "we and the French have gained positive results on the Western Front [to date], and if the task before us there is serious and progress slow, there is no shorter cut to victory in sight. That being so, France and Flanders must continue to be the principal theatre of war, and on it our main efforts must be concentrated."[12]

Sir Douglas Haig concurred completely. The Western Front, Haig maintained, "is the decisive point: bring all the strength of the Empire to this point and beat the enemy. Then all else will be ours for the picking up," he wrote in the summer of 1915. "Defeats of Bulgarians and Turks in Mesopotamia, on the Egyptian Frontier and in Greece cannot seriously shake Germany's position or even her influence over her Allies, so long as she shows herself able to hold her own on the main front. If Germany wins in the end, her Allies will win with her: if Germany is beaten, they are lost."[13]

Haig's opinion carried considerable weight. Born to a wealthy Edinburgh family of whisky-distilling fame, he had connections with the élite of British society, including King George V. A cavalryman by training, Haig had graduated from the Staff College, seen action in the Sudan and in South Africa, and served as an aide-de-camp to King Edward VII, George's predecessor on the throne. Along the way, Haig had written the standard textbook of the day on cavalry tactics, worked at the War Office—where he had helped draw up Britain's mobilization plans in the event of a European war, and come to realize the enormous manpower reserves that could be summoned by all nations—and commanded at Aldershot, the British army's main training centre. Lord Haldane, the pre-war secretary of state for war, called Haig "the most highly equipped thinker in the British Army."[14] A corps commander when the war began, Haig rose quickly in stature. In December 1915, at the same time as Wully Robertson was named the CIGS, Haig succeeded Sir John French as commander-in-chief of the BEF.

He was an unusual man, this Douglas Haig. In superb physical condition for a man in his early fifties, he took good care of himself, being a non-smoker and devoted to what we today would call fad diets, a reflection of his fear of infirmity and old age. His only physical defect, if it can be called that, was colour-blindness. Strikingly handsome, his features highlighted by "luminous blue eyes," flawlessly attired and groomed, Haig gave the impression "of a cultured, gracious and peace-loving country squire." But he had few friends. Innately shy, he was dour, stolid, and very reserved, "always dignified in manner," according to his devoted subordinate, Brigadier-General John Charteris. "D.H.'s greatest asset," observed Charteris, "is that nobody can conceive that any action of his is not prompted by the highest motives." Haig was, in short, every inch an officer and a gentleman.[15]

He was also deeply religious. "I feel that every step in my plan has been taken with the Divine help—and I ask daily for aid, not merely in making the plan, but in carrying it out, and this I hope I shall continue to do until the end of all things which concern me on earth," he once wrote. "I try to do no more than 'do my best and trust to

God'." On another occasion he confessed: "I *know* I am sustained in my efforts by the Great Unseen Power, otherwise I could not be standing the strain as I am doing."[16]

Haig shared some of Sir William Robertson's characteristics. Like the CIGS, he had a poor estimate of his French allies. "I began with a readiness to believe the best of the French—as was only natural for a Scot with memories of the old Alliance; but events were too much for me," he later admitted. The first few months of the war convinced him that France's martial might had been vastly overrated, that this ally was, at best, unreliable. "What a wretched lot the majority of the French are!" is one of several such outbursts to be found in his personal diary.[17]

Haig also shared Robertson's contempt for elected officials. "'Politician' with Douglas Haig is synonymous with crooked dealings and wrong sense of values," commented General Charteris. "You can't trust anyone who has ever been in Parliament," Haig confided to Charteris, another time declaring, "Our greatest danger is not in Serbia, or the Dardanelles, or here in France, but in Westminster."[18]

And, like Robertson, he was remarkably inarticulate. Haig, recalled Charteris, "had contracted a habit of breaking off a sentence and leaving the rest to the imagination of his listeners. Even if the sentence did chance to have an end, as often as not he would have omitted the verb. Only Staff Officers who thoroughly understood their Commander's mind could grasp his meaning from his spoken word." The result of Haig's verbal fumbling could be quite comical at times. He once addressed the winners of an inter-regimental cross-country competition: "I congratulate you on your running. You have run well. I hope you will run as well in the presence of the enemy." Haig had no more luck on the rare occasions he spoke to individual soldiers. "And where did you start the war?" he asked a private. "Nowhere, sir," came the predictable reply, "I didn't start the war." Ironically, Haig became fluent in French and could, according to Charteris, "express himself far more coherently and accurately in French than in English." Although Haig, like Robertson, was competent at composing written statements, the ramifications of his shortcomings as a speaker were immense. While able to make himself understood by soldiers when speaking on simple subjects, he was at a complete loss when dealing with laymen, trying to explain the complexities of modern war to politicians.[19]

Haig had clear ideas about this war. As early as 1906 he had foreseen the coming conflict. "We may well be fighting Germany in the next few years," he had told associates. "In battle with troops as brave and efficient as the Germans, we shall have to fight long and hard before we can hope for a decision. It will be dangerous to attempt a decisive blow until we have worn down the enemy's power of resistance." The war, he believed, would unfold in several distinct phases:

> The manoeuvre for position.
> The first clash of battle.
> The wearing-out fight of varying duration.
> And the eventual decisive blow, which would give victory.

Above all, one precept governed Haig's actions once the war was under way. "We cannot hope to win," he wrote in March 1915, "until we have defeated the German Army."[20]

When war finally came in August 1914, Charteris noted that Haig was one of the very few who did not expect it to end by Christmas. "Sir Douglas Haig was already quite convinced," Charteris remarked, "that the war in some form or other would last for several years...it was in his opinion a fight for existence between us and Germany. Neither could survive defeat. Neither would give in until beaten to the knees, and in no circumstances could this be accomplished in one or even two years."[21] Haig would be proven correct, on this as on many other points, in the final analysis, though Britain and her Empire would pay dearly.

Sir Douglas Haig was not a cold-blooded butcher, as history has tended to portray him. Indeed, he was devoted to the men under his command, as revealed by a letter to his wife in April 1917:

> I have myself tremendous affection for those fine fellows who are ready to give their lives for the Old Country at any moment. I feel quite sad at times when I see them march past me, knowing as I do how many must pay the full penalty before we can have peace.

At about the same time, the famed artist Sir William Orpen arrived at General Headquarters (GHQ) to paint Haig's portrait. "Why waste your time painting me?" Haig asked Orpen. "Go and paint the men. They're the fellows who are saving the world, and they're getting killed every day." And when, soon after the armistice in November 1918, he was congratulated for winning the war, Haig replied, "Oh! you mustn't congratulate *me*," and, pointing to a nearby veteran, said, "It is fellows like him who deserve congratulations."[22]

But there can be no question that Haig was unfazed by heavy casualties. These, he realized, were an unfortunate but unavoidable element of modern war. For example, British losses during the first month of fighting on the Somme totalled 164,909, or, as Haig calmly asserted, "about 120,000 more than they would have been had we not attacked. They cannot be regarded as sufficient to justify any anxiety as to our ability to continue the offensive"—and the offensive continued for three more agonizing months. And Haig certainly did not share the prevailing despair over the outcome of the Somme campaign. It had played an important part in what he liked to call "the wearing-out fight"; as a result of the Somme, he insisted, "an appreciable proportion of the German soldiers are now practically beaten men, ready to surrender if they could find opportunity, thoroughly tired of the War, and hopeless of eventual success." This was typical of another characteristic of Haig's: he was an incurable optimist.[23]

Personal animosities played a prominent part in the developing dispute over the Western Front. Lloyd George felt nothing but contempt for his generals. He recalled a 1916 remark by a French premier, Aristide Briand: "This war is too important to be left to military men"—Lloyd George wished he had said it, because it perfectly reflected his own thoughts. The soldiers, he believed, were "running the country on the rocks," and the worst offender was Sir Douglas Haig. "Haig does not care how many men he loses," Lloyd George told his mistress. "He just squanders the lives of these boys. I mean to save some of them in the future. He seems to think they are his property. I am their trustee. I will never let him rest. I will raise the subject again & again until I *nag* him out of it—until he knows that as soon as the casualty lists get large he will get nothing but black looks and scowls and awkward questions."[24]

As time passed, Lloyd George cultivated an almost psychopathic dislike of Haig. He bitterly joked: "We could certainly beat the Germans if only we could get Haig to join them. The German armies would then be a pushover for us—with Haig leading them." Later, Lloyd George described Haig as "a painstaking professional soldier with a sound intelligence of secondary quality.... I never met any man in a high position who seemed to me so utterly devoid of imagination." The prime minister did not appreciate Haig's tongue-tied speech, either, noting that "in my experience a confused talker is never a clear thinker."[25]

Lloyd George had mixed feelings about Wully Robertson, once calling him "a splendid fellow," and admitting as late as December 1917, when they were barely on speaking terms, that "I like him personally. He can be very amusing. He has many good stories."

But, ultimately, Lloyd George's verdict was harsh. "A mistaken loyalty to Sir Douglas Haig fettered his common sense," the prime minister later wrote, contending "that Haig dominated, over-awed and almost bullied" Robertson, whose "mind was sound but commonplace. He was cautious to the point of timidity." It was a cruel indictment of a faithful and skilful soldier.[26]

Haig and Robertson reciprocated Lloyd George's feelings. Meeting him for the first time in January 1916, Haig commented in his diary that "Lloyd George seems to be astute and cunning, with much energy and push but I should think shifty and unreliable." That initial impression did not change. Months later, Haig remarked that "he seems to me to be so flighty—makes plans and is always changing them and his mind." Haig complained that "with Lloyd George I can feel no confidence, and far from meeting my wishes and supplying my wants, he places every obstacle in my way, and in fact he hampers the conduct of the War." A frustrated Haig would eventually declare: "It is, indeed, a calamity for the country to have such a man at the head of affairs in this time of great crisis. We can only try and make the best of him."[27]

An incident in September 1916 confirmed Haig's opinion of Lloyd George, who, as secretary of state for war, had visited GHQ. Haig was hardly impressed, as he told his wife:

> L.G.'s [visit] has been a huge "joy ride"! Breakfast with newspaper men, and posings for the Cinema Shows, pleased him more than anything else. No doubt with the ulterior motive of catching votes. From what I have written, you will gather that I have no great opinion of L.G. *as a man or leader*.

But the episode did not end there. Lloyd George, after departing GHQ, had travelled to the headquarters of a French general, Ferdinand Foch. Later, Foch told a shocked Haig that Lloyd George "wished to know why the British who had gained no more ground than the French, if as much, had suffered such heavy casualties....* LG also asked his opinion as to the ability of the British Generals.... Unless I had been told of this conversation personally by Gen. Foch," a seething Haig told his diary, "I would not have believed that a British Minister could have been so ungentlemanly as to go to a foreigner and put such questions regarding his own subordinates."[28]

---

* This is a reference to the early fighting on the Somme, when the small contingent of French troops enjoyed initial success, compared to the disaster that befell the British. It was one of the few occasions in the entire war in which the French outperformed their British counterparts.

Robertson shared Haig's views on Lloyd George. "He is a real bad 'un," Sir William said of the prime minister. The CIGS was regularly infuriated by his dealings with Lloyd George, who "would unfairly belittle British military efforts as compared with the German, and the attempt on my part to put the other point of view... would be met with the reply that the same sort of thing had been said many times before, and that we were still as far from winning the war as ever."[29]

It was in this less than congenial atmosphere that the crucial decisions affecting British military strategy were being made. Of course, personality conflicts such as these were not unique to the Great War, and with a little effort and goodwill could have been relegated to the background where they properly belonged. Sad to say, Lloyd George, in a shocking show of irresponsibility, chose to escalate his animosity toward Haig and Robertson in what can only be called a vendetta. Thus, personalities became the dominant factor in the British conduct of the war, with sorry results.

2/War at the Top

By the time Lloyd George was sworn in as prime minister on 7 December 1916, Allied strategy for the following year had seemingly been settled. At a mid-November conference at Chantilly, outside Paris, Allied political and military leaders had agreed that "the Armies of the Coalition will be ready to undertake joint offensives from the first fortnight of February 1917 with all the means at their disposal." It was felt, and reasonably so, that simultaneous attacks by the Russians in the east, the Italians in the south, and the British and French on the Western Front would "give a decisive character to the campaigns of 1917."[1]

These generalities determined, it was left to the British and French commanders-in-chief—Sir Douglas Haig and Joseph Joffre, respectively—to work out the details of their joint offensive. Haig and Joffre worked well together. Although there was no unified command structure on the Western Front, the British and French armies operating as separate entities, Haig accepted—initially, at least—Britain's status as junior partner, declaring: "I am *not under* General Joffre's orders, but that would make no difference, as my intention was to do my utmost to carry out General Joffre's wishes on strategical matters, as if they were orders."[2] It helped, certainly, that they saw eye-to-eye on just about everything. However, by late 1916, the British army was nearly as large as the French, and Haig, eager to secure his ally's recognition of British equality in their partnership, was ready to shoulder a larger share of the burden. Notwithstanding the British experience on the Somme, the French had been shattered by the prolonged bloodshed at Verdun in 1916. In order to give the French time to recover, Haig and Joffre agreed that the BEF would carry out the primary operations during 1917.

Their plans were formulated amicably and quickly. A joint attack would take place in February, in northern France, with the British striking between Bapaume and Vimy and the French between the Oise and Somme rivers. This blow would be followed by what Haig considered "should be the main operation of the British in the entire summer," an offensive in Flanders. "Its objective," noted Haig, "is the capture of the Belgian coast by a combined operation of the British Army and Fleet.... This is practically the scheme at which I have aimed for the past twelve months."[3]

Actually, Haig and others had had their eyes fixed on Flanders for much more than a year. The British affinity for Flanders is easily explained. Aside from valid strategical considerations, it must be remembered that Britain had gone to war ostensibly to avenge the violation of Belgium's neutrality, which had been guaranteed by international treaty in 1831. As early as 5 August 1914, the day after the British Empire declared war on Germany, Haig had attended a council of war at 10 Downing Street, the prime minister's residence in London, and presented "a memorandum which he had prepared on the various possibilities of employing the British [Expeditionary] Force in Flanders." One of the most enthusiastic advocates of an operation along the Belgian coast in the fall of 1914 was, ironically, the Admiralty's Winston Churchill, who feared that unless the Germans were driven from the ports of Ostend and Zeebrugge "the whole transportation of troops across the Channel will be seriously and increasingly compromised."* In early 1915, John Charteris, serving as Haig's intelligence chief at First Army headquarters, observed that GHQ was "discussing proposals for attacks along the Belgian coast. . . . But the operation would require many more troops and artillery than we have available." These plans came to naught, but the idea of a Flanders campaign proved remarkably resilient. In late 1915, Haig, now installed as commander-in-chief of the BEF, received a visit from Vice-Admiral Sir Reginald Bacon, who "discussed the co-operation of the Fleet with my Armies on the Belgian coast," as Haig noted in his diary. "He said that the front from Zeebrugge to Ostend was of vital importance to England because the Germans command the east end of the Channel from there and threaten England."[5]

Serious consideration was then given to a Flanders offensive in 1916. As Charteris remarked, the choice for the main British effort that year was between Flanders and the Somme. Charteris, writing on 26 January 1916, personally favoured "Flanders. Strategically there is no doubt about that being the best place for us to attack. It strikes direct at the main railway communications of all the German armies. The Germans could not even make good their retreat. A victory, however great, on the Somme would still let them get back to the Meuse." But Charteris admitted that Flanders did have drawbacks. "Tactically the ground is more difficult. Most important of all is the weather. An attack in Flanders must be delivered in the early summer. June at the latest."[6]

It was the French commander-in-chief, Joffre, who steered the

---

* Churchill, however, soon changed his mind. "Are there not other alternatives," he wondered in a December memo to Prime Minister Asquith, "than sending our armies to chew barbed wire in Flanders?"[4] His own proposal was the ill-fated Dardanelles expedition.

British away from Flanders. Drafting his own offensive plans for the year, Joffre told Haig that "l'offensive française serait grandement favorisée par une offensive simultanée des forces britanniques entre la Somme et Arras." Haig, who believed that Flanders offered "an objective of great political and naval as well as military importance," which the Somme could not match, felt obliged to defer to Joffre's wishes. But the British commander-in-chief did so reluctantly: "Operations to clear the Belgian coast must be kept in view, but it is still doubtful how best they can be fitted into the programme." A compromise was reached at Chantilly on 14 February 1916: Haig consented to co-operate with Joffre's cherished attack on either side of the River Somme, after which Joffre conceded that the British could campaign in Flanders if they wished to do so.[7]

Then the Germans upset the Allied applecart. Just a week after the Chantilly conference, the enemy launched their Verdun offensive and drew the French armies into a bloodbath of unprecedented proportions. As a result, the Somme offensive, which Haig was so reluctant to undertake, became primarily a British show, designed to relieve the intense pressure on the French fighting at Verdun. The Somme did, indeed, save the French, though at terrible cost to the BEF. But Haig lacked the resources to mount two major operations at the same time. His Flanders offensive, first scheduled for 15 July, was rescheduled for 31 July, before finally being postponed indefinitely.

German naval activity on the coast of Belgium led to renewed interest in Flanders before the end of the year. This was what Prime Minister Asquith referred to as "the submarine menace," the U-boat campaign that eventually led to unrestricted sinkings and brought the United States into the war, besides coming perilously close to its goal of strangling the British Isles, which were so reliant on naval supremacy. In late November 1916, Asquith composed a memorandum, one of his last as prime minister, in which he stated: "There is no operation of war to which the War Committee [of cabinet] would attach greater importance than the successful occupation, or at least the deprivation to the enemy, of Ostend, and especially Zeebrugge." The CIGS, Sir William Robertson, was deeply impressed by Asquith's memo and duly informed Joffre that "my Government desire that the occupation of Ostend and Zeebrugge should form one of the objectives of the campaign next year." Haig, meanwhile, had received another visit from Admiral Bacon, who warned that "the situation in the Channel is much less satisfactory than it was. The German sailors," wrote Haig, "... can interfere with our communications without much danger or difficulty."[8]

Two unrelated events in December 1916 relegated Flanders to the back burner once again. One of these was the dismissal of Joseph Joffre. The rotund, fatherly Joffre had become a liability to the French government, which held him responsible for the horrific losses suffered at Verdun. His successor was Robert Nivelle, one of Verdun's heroes. Nivelle had thrilled the nation with his defiant words, "Ils ne passeront pas," and his brilliant counter-attacks in October and early December had recaptured most of the ground lost by the French at the beginning of the battle. Although a relatively junior general—he had begun the war as an artillery colonel—Nivelle had a lot going for him. Not only was he "good-looking, smart, plausible and cool," he was supremely self-confident, even cocksure. And he enjoyed a considerable advantage over rival French officers, not to mention Haig and Robertson: he was fluent in English, having had an English mother. Haig's early impression of the new French commander-in-chief says much. "I am sorry for poor old Joffre," he commented, "but from what I have seen of Nivelle up to date I think he is the more energetic man."[9]

The other December development that affected the proposed Flanders operation was, of course, the appointment of David Lloyd George as prime minister of Britain. Lloyd George took office grimly determined to change the direction of the war, and immediately "decided to explore every possibility before surrendering to a renewal of the horrors of the Western Front." Soon after Lloyd George moved into 10 Downing Street, Wully Robertson noted with alarm that "there is a very dangerous tendency becoming apparent for the War Cabinet to direct military operations." Robertson dispatched a warning to Haig: "Our new P.M. is well on the move. He...wants to get to Jerusalem." However, this was merely one of several ideas running through Lloyd George's active mind. He was also attracted, according to Sir Maurice Hankey, by the prospect of "a big military coup in Syria." But by late December he had made up his mind to throw British support behind a grand offensive in Italy, in a bid to knock Austria-Hungary out of the war. Haig called the very suggestion "the act of a lunatic," but Lloyd George was a formidable foe. To pursue the proposal, the prime minister arranged for an inter-Allied conference in early January 1917.[10]

The conference, held in Rome, was a bitter disappointment for Lloyd George. Neither the French nor the Italians would endorse his plan, and the prime minister left for home "irritable and in a thoroughly bad temper."[11]

But he was in a much better mood by the time he arrived back in London. En route, he had stopped briefly in Paris and met the new

French commander, Nivelle. Lloyd George was most impressed. Dazzled by Nivelle's immense personal charm, the prime minister was delighted by his insistence that he could end the deadlock on the Western Front, provided "that we do not attack it at its strongest point, and that the operation is carried out by a sudden surprise attack, and is not extended beyond twenty-four or forty-eight hours."[12] There was something else Lloyd George liked about the Frenchman: the shape of his head. An amateur phrenologist, the prime minister believed that a man's cranium revealed much about him. At the conclusion of their meeting, he invited Nivelle to come to London to explain his strategy in detail.

Sir Douglas Haig was well aware of Nivelle's plans. They had met on 20 December and subsequently had exchanged considerable correspondence. Nivelle envisioned a gigantic clash conducted in three phases:

> The first, in the course of which we will endeavour to immobilize the greatest possible number of enemy reserves, while obtaining tactical results which can be extensively developed. The second, in which the principal mass of the French Armies will be engaged in order to break through the enemy's front and defeat the forces remaining at his disposal. And finally the third, in the course of which the British and French Groups of Armies will undertake the large-scale exploitation of the success previously obtained, and will pursue the enemy.[13]

Nivelle had made significant changes to the offensive planned by Haig and Joffre. Not only had he considerably widened the front that would be attacked, but he intended to make his main effort with the French army, the BEF being restricted to a supporting role, undoubtedly the aspect that Lloyd George liked best.

There were doubts at Haig's headquarters. "Nivelle certainly sees big!" remarked Charteris. "The French are to do the main attack, *not* alongside of us. We are to attack to help them. This means a complete change in all our schemes.... D.H. is sceptical about the French being able to deliver a decisive attack. If it fails we shall be back at the position of a year ago, with all the advantages of the Somme thrown away."[14]

Haig expressed his concerns in a letter to Nivelle. Reminding the French commander-in-chief "that you estimated a period of 24 to 48 hours as sufficient to enable you to decide whether your decisive attack had succeeded or should be abandoned," Haig, with one eye on Flanders, warned that "the first two phases of the battle cannot be of une durée prolongée.... If these two phases are not so successful as to justify me in entering on the third phase, then I must transfer my main forces to the north...the clearance of the Belgian Coast is of such importance to the British Government that it must be fully provided for before I can finally agree to your proposals."[15]

Nivelle soon tired of Haig's repeated references to Flanders. "C'est une idée fixe," he complained privately, while patiently explaining to Haig that the plan "does not exclude the possibility, if the need arises, of an operation for the conquest of Ostend and Zeebrugge.... If our great offensive succeeds, it is certain that the Belgian coast will fall into our hands as a consequence of the retreat of the German Armies, without having to be directly attacked. If, on the other hand, our attack fails, it will always be possible when the fine weather comes to carry out the projected operation in Flanders."[16]

More conferences and correspondence ensued. By 13 January 1917, Haig could write: "We are agreed on nearly every point." But, as he confided in his diary, he was not entirely happy with the arrangement for Nivelle's offensive:

> We willingly play a second rôle to the French, that is, we are making a holding attack to draw in the enemy's reserves so as to make the task of the French easier. We shall at any rate have heavy losses with the possibility of no showy successes, whereas the French are to make the decisive attack with every prospect of gaining the fruits of victory.[17]

More unhappiness was in store for the British commander-in-chief. On 15 January, he travelled to London for a conference to finalize the Nivelle offensive. Things went badly for Haig, beginning with a stormy private meeting with Lloyd George at the prime minister's Downing Street residence. According to Haig's diary,

> the P.M. proceeded to compare the successes obtained by the French during the past summer with what the British had achieved. His conclusions were that the French Army was better all round, and was able to gain success at less cost of life.* That much of our losses on the Somme was [sic] wasted, and that the country would not stand any more of that sort of thing. That to win, we must attack a soft front, and we would not find that on the Western Front.[18]

Yet, within hours, Lloyd George had pulled one of those surpris-

---

* Obviously, Lloyd George was ignorant of the Verdun battle.

than the French would or could provide. Although discussions between the two had ironed out most of their differences—as late as 16 February, Haig had declared that "I was much pleased with the result of our meeting"—Lloyd George used this issue as an excuse to convene an Anglo-French conference that would later be described as "the high-water mark of ineptitude of civilian interference with the conduct of military operations."[25]

Lloyd George set his plan in motion on Saturday, 24 February, two days before the scheduled conference. That day, he held a meeting of his war cabinet, deliberately excluding Sir William Robertson who, as the government's chief military adviser, normally attended these gatherings. Lloyd George then persuaded the cabinet to accept his proposed adjustment of the command structure in France, though he carefully avoided going into details. But his intentions were perfectly plain, as he confided to his mistress later in the day. "It is a very ticklish corner that I have to turn. It practically means putting Haig under Nivelle, & it will be a hard fight, but I mean to have my way."[26]

The Anglo-French conference was convened at Calais on 26 February, in the appropriately shabby surroundings of the second-rate Hôtel de la Gare Maritime. Lloyd George, Robertson, and Haig were the key British representatives; the French delegation was led by Premier Aristide Briand, Minister of War Louis Lyautey, and Nivelle. To begin with, there was a brief—"barely an hour," according to Haig[27]—discussion of the railway dispute that was ostensibly the reason for the conference. Lloyd George impatiently suggested that technical experts for both sides work out the problem among themselves elsewhere. The conference, apparently headed nowhere, then broke for tea.

After tea, Nivelle outlined his plans for the April offensive and the preparations to date. When he concluded, Haig later noted in his diary, "L.G. said 'that is not all—I want to hear everything' and to Briand he said, 'Tell him to keep nothing back' and so forth 'as to his disagreements with Marshal Haig.' This was quite a surprise to me...."[28] There would be more surprises in store for the field-marshal.

Nivelle could offer only one point of contention, a minor one at that, with Haig: Vimy Ridge. Nivelle wanted the British to ignore it, while Haig argued that it would secure his left flank: "I regarded the Vimy ridge as a very important position for us to hold from a defensive point of view." At Haig's insistence, the ridge remained on the list of British objectives in the forthcoming offensive. This was followed by a discussion of tactics, which clearly did not interest Lloyd George in the least. Finally, at 6:45 P.M., he abruptly ended the meeting by asking "the French to draw up their proposals for a *system of command,*" as a surprised Haig commented in his diary. If he and Robertson wondered what the prime minister meant, they would soon find out.[29]

Later in the evening, Sir Maurice Hankey, in his capacity as the war cabinet's secretary, was summoned to Lloyd George's room. The prime minister handed him a document and asked, "What do you think of it?" Hankey, scanning the paper, was appalled. "It fairly took my breath away, as it practically demanded the placing of the British Army under Nivelle; the appointment of a British 'Chief of Staff' to Nivelle, who had powers practically eliminating Haig and his Chief of the General Staff, the scheme reducing Haig to a cipher." Lloyd George, observed Hankey, "really seemed rather to like the French scheme. I warned him that it was quite impossible...."[30]

A copy of the proposal was subsequently delivered to Wully Robertson. The CIGS was infuriated. "Get 'aig!" he roared at an aide. Haig, arriving a few moments later, found Robertson "most excited." The field-marshal was "aghast" at the proposed command structure, and he and Robertson rushed up to Lloyd George's room to register their protests. A stormy scene ensued. Haig bluntly declared that "it would be madness to place the British forces under the French, and that I did not believe our troops would fight under French leadership." Robertson warned that "it would be extremely unwise to entrust the command of our armies to a foreign General about whose qualifications so very little was known. I reminded him that officers and men preferred to fight under their own commanders; that the Dominion Governments might object to having their troops placed under a foreigner; and that in point of fact no British soldier could constitutionally be put under the *orders* of anyone not holding His Majesty's Commission."[31]

These arguments made no impression on Lloyd George, who "was extraordinarily brutal to Haig," according to Hankey. He savagely told his commander-in-chief, "Well, Field-Marshal, I know the private soldier very well. He speaks very freely to me, and there are people he criticises a good deal more strongly than Gen. Nivelle!" As Hankey recalled, Lloyd George "more than hinted that Haig would have to resign, if he didn't come to heel."[32]

Shaken, the two soldiers returned to Robertson's room. They were joined by a sympathetic Hankey who, Haig later remarked, "further added to our dissatisfaction by saying that 'L.G. had not received full authority from the War Cabinet' for acting as he was doing." Haig and Robertson sat up late that night, mulling over the possibility of resigning—indeed, Haig later offered his resignation to the King, who refused it—or of flatly refusing to co-operate and risking a court-martial. "And so we went to bed," wrote an unhappy Haig, "thoroughly disgusted with our Government and the politicians."[33]

Haig had calmed down by morning. Rising early, he had composed for Robertson a memorandum, in which he coolly assessed the proposed alteration in the Allied high command. It would, he said, "involve the disappearance of the British Commander-in-Chief and G.H.Q..... So drastic a change in our system of command at a moment when active operations on a large scale have already commenced seems to me to be fraught with the gravest danger." Robertson, on the other hand, was still in a rage. "He was in a terrible state," observed Hankey, "and ramped up and down the room, talking about the horrible idea of putting the 'wonderful army' under a Frenchman, swearing he would never serve under one, nor his son either, and that no one could order him to."[34]

It was Hankey who saved the day. He proposed a compromise— "my little scrap of paper," he called it[35]—that seemed acceptable to all concerned: Haig would be subordinated to Nivelle's command only for the duration of the coming operations. In addition, Haig was given the right of appeal to London if he received orders which he believed would endanger the BEF.

Not surprisingly, Sir Douglas Haig was displeased with the outcome of the Calais conference. He scrawled across his copy of the final agreement: "Signed by me as a correct statement, but not as approving the arrangement. D. Haig." As he later explained, he signed it merely to show "that I would loyally do my best to carry out its provisions *not* that I thought such a paper to be desirable or necessary." Its purpose, "the closest co-operation of French and British," was something he had always striven to achieve. Ever optimistic, Haig foresaw that "no great difficulty will occur in carrying on just as I have been doing *provided* there is not something behind it." Of course, there was much behind it: Lloyd George's heightening hostility toward him.[36]

Years later, in his *War Memoirs,* the prime minister would lamely justify his astonishing behaviour at Calais, ascribing it to an attempt to realize "unity of commandment in the West," something "I never ceased to work for." This is always a problem in coalition warfare, and failure to resolve it is not unusual. And it was clear, both at the time and with the benefit of hindsight, that the Calais agreement was no satisfactory solution. Lloyd George had not unified the Allied command; he had merely subordinated the British army to the French, in effect handing over to a foreign power the greatest force Britain and her Empire had ever amassed. It was Haig who first discerned the dangerous flaw in this arrangement, "because General Nivelle is a loyal servant of his Government, and does their bidding." The British army was now, thanks to Lloyd George, for all intents and purposes an instrument of French policy.[37]

Lloyd George had won a Pyrrhic victory, and a short-lived one, at that. He had forever sacrificed the confidence and co-operation between soldiers and statesmen so essential for a smooth-running war machine. He was even less than candid with his own war cabinet, as an astonished Robertson recorded for Haig's benefit at the first post-Calais meeting:

> He accused the French of putting forward a monstrous proposal, and yet you and I know that he was at the bottom of it.... I can't believe that such a man as he can remain for long head of any Government. Surely *some* honesty and truth are required.

Haig was in a similar frame of mind. "All would be so easy if I only had to deal with Germans," he lamented privately, while on another occasion sighing: "It is too sad at this critical time to have to fight with one's Allies and the Home Government, in addition to the enemy in the Field."*[38]

In the short term, Lloyd George's meddling produced an unprecedented strain in Anglo-French military relations. For this, Nivelle was chiefly responsible. On 27 February, with the Calais conference barely concluded, Nivelle sent a letter to Haig instructing him to "communicate to me as soon as possible the orders which you have given to your Army Commanders, as well as the steps taken by

---

* Interestingly, Haig absolved Nivelle of any blame in the Calais affair. "The Calais conference was a mistake," he would write, "but it was not Nivelle's fault." That was incorrect. In fact, the proposals for revamping the command structure on the Western Front had been drafted, with Lloyd George's blessings, at Nivelle's headquarters. And, prior to the conference, Nivelle had made his intentions quite clear in a conversation with the French president, Raymond Poincaré, who wrote in his diary:

> Nivelle believes that if Douglas Haig remains at the head of the British Army, the relations will always remain courteous, but that we shall not obtain a real subordination of the British Army to the French Command. He believes a change in the command to be necessary.

It is little wonder that Nivelle and Lloyd George worked so well together.[39]

the latter to carry out your orders." It was an ill-advised and needlessly callous blunder, and Haig was deeply offended at this blatant interference. Nivelle's message, he fumed,

> is a type of letter which no gentleman could have drafted, and it also is one which certainly no C. in C. of this great British Army should receive without protest. By the Calais agreement I only come under his orders after the Battle commences, and then only for operations in the sector assigned to me already. I intend to send a copy of the letter with my reply to the War Committee, with a request to be told whether it is their wishes that the C. in C. of this British Army should be subjected to such treatment by a junior *foreign* Commander.[40]

But Haig, too, was working to undermine the agreement he had "loyally" promised to uphold. And he was aided by the Germans who, in late February and early March, carried out a major withdrawal along virtually the entire front Nivelle proposed to attack, retiring behind the massive fortifications of the newly built Hindenburg Line; in doing so, the Germans gave up ground of no military importance while at the same time considerably shortening their overall line and therefore increasing their reserve forces. Haig seized upon this withdrawal to urge Nivelle to revise his plans, arguing that the BEF's assigned objectives were no longer "feasible." He convinced himself that the Germans were assembling their extra divisions to mount an offensive against the British in, of all places, Flanders.* Haig's own intelligence chief, Brigadier-General Charteris, could find no sign of such an impending attack—as late as 14 March, Charteris wrote that "all our information from the front line, and our photographs, do not show any of the signs which we generally get prior to a large offensive"—but Haig warned Nivelle that, unless the Frenchman changed his plans, "I have to consider the possibility of finding myself no longer free to deal adequately with such an emergency." In that event, he said, he would appeal to London, as per the Calais agreement.[41]

Haig's motives were made plain in his diary. "I am therefore in favour of at once going on with our preparations for attacking near Ypres. This may not suit the French!"[42]

Nivelle probably suspected as much, and he was becoming in-

---

* In fairness to Haig, it should be pointed out that eight enemy divisions did move into Belgium, but they were there merely as a safeguard against Holland's possible entry into the war, as a result of unrestricted submarine warfare which began on 1 February.

creasingly annoyed with the British commander. Stubbornly, he rejected the warning from Haig, insisting that "the 'Hindenburg' Line is so situated that our principal attacks both in the British and in the French Zones could outflank and take it in rear. On this account the German withdrawal will, even if it becomes general, be to our advantage...." And then he made a serious error. Perceiving Haig's position as a refusal to co-operate, Nivelle complained to Premier Briand, who responded by sending a telegram to London, protesting that "Marshal Haig's repeated tendency to avoid the instructions which have been given to him . . . would render the co-operation of the British forces illusory and would make the exercise of a unified command impossible."[43]

The Briand telegram produced a mixed reaction in the British capital. Most members of the war cabinet were appalled and angered: they now realized what the Calais agreement had done, to the disadvantage of the BEF, and clamoured for another conference to repair the damage.

Lloyd George's response was, predictably, quite different. He was becoming obsessed with "the question of whether or no[t] he should get rid of Haig," observed Sir Maurice Hankey on 10 March.

> That evening he asked me to give him my views next morning.... I sat up until past midnight writing out my views... weighing all the pros and cons and winding up strongly in favour of Haig. He didn't like it, as he wanted me to report the other way, and argued and contested my points hotly.... But I met him on every point and stuck to my guns.

Nevertheless, word of a possible shake-up reached Lord Bertie, Britain's dreary and pessimistic ambassador in Paris. "I hear rumours," Bertie wrote on the tenth, "of [General Sir] Henry Wilson taking the place of Robertson, who does not see eye to eye with Lloyd George. [General Sir Hubert] Gough's name is mentioned in French quarters as a possible successor to Haig."[44]

The prime minister, unable to summon the courage to deal with either Haig or Robertson, bowed to the wishes of his war cabinet and convened another conference with the French. It was held on 12 March, in London. Nivelle, who felt that the whole thing was "both unnecessary and inopportune," fared poorly. Absent was his chief political ally, Premier Briand, who remained in Paris to deal with a burgeoning crisis that would soon bring down his government. Louis Lyautey, the French war minister, blamed Nivelle for the strained relations between the British and French high commands and sympathized with Haig's complaints about the 27 February letter from Nivelle and its "somewhat dictatorial language."[45]

The London conference mended many of the fences torn asunder at Calais. Haig urged "that the Calais agreement...should now be so clearly defined as to prevent any future misunderstanding," and the British and French representatives hammered out a new agreement that both clarified and modified the previous arrangement. Haig and the BEF were to be subordinated to Nivelle's command for the duration of the offensive, but the British were not to be treated as such; Haig personally appended to his copy of the new deal a clause stating that "the British Army and its Commander-in-Chief will be regarded by General Nivelle as allies and not as subordinates."[46] Equally important, Haig was to be given free rein over tactical planning in his sector. Moreover, the validity of the pre-Calais command structure was endorsed, and it was to be restored promptly upon the conclusion of the coming campaign.

Before leaving London, Haig laid out his plans for the benefit of the war cabinet. At a 14 March meeting, he explained that if the Nivelle offensive succeeded, he intended to "exploit with all reserves and the cavalry"; if it failed, he would "launch attacks near Ypres [in Flanders] to clear the Belgian coast." Flanders remained near and dear to Haig's heart, and no one in cabinet, least of all Lloyd George, uttered a word of opposition. Indeed, four days later, Hankey noted that the prime minister "seems, for the present at any rate, to have got over his aversion and contempt for Haig." It was, of course, a temporary condition.[47]

Nivelle, in the meantime, had plenty of problems of his own. The Briand government fell on 19 March, and the new régime—eighty-year-old Alexandre Ribot as premier and Paul Painlevé as war minister—was plagued with doubts about Nivelle's proposed operations, which were to be under way within weeks. Nor were Nivelle's difficulties strictly political. Many French generals—more than a few of them envious at their colleague's rapid rise through the ranks and resentful of being placed under the command of a younger man—openly questioned their commander-in-chief's competence. They did so with justification: a capable army commander, Nivelle was out of his league leading several groups of armies. As late as 7 April, practically on the eve of his attack, Nivelle was forced to defend his plans before worried government leaders. "I will not, under any pretext, get involved in another Battle of the Somme," he assured them.[48]

And so his offensive proceeded. The first phase, the British diversionary attack in the Arras area, was a striking success, highlighted by the Canadian capture of the hitherto impregnable bastion of Vimy Ridge—which, it will be recalled, Nivelle had urged Haig to ignore—on Easter Monday, 9 April. All of France was thrilled by the taking of Vimy, as Lord Bertie recorded in his diary: "The French newspapers of all shades of politics are loud in praise of the victory."[49] But the French operations, a week later along the River Aisne, were a profound disappointment. They did not, in retrospect, have much chance to succeed, for surprise had been forfeited: the offensive was common talk throughout France, and the Germans had captured copies of plans for the attack. Though it was a modest success, by Great War standards, the French attack fell far short of expectations, merely denting the mighty Hindenburg Line, at very heavy cost in lives, and despair swept the French nation. The failure cost Nivelle his job: on 15 May he was replaced by Henri Pétain.

Haig would have preferred to retain Nivelle as the French commander-in-chief. He feared that it might be demoralizing to the French army to get rid of Nivelle after less than six months. Privately, he believed that "the devil you know is better in any event than the devil you do not know," but he sincerely sympathized with Nivelle. "The great error," Haig wrote, "was that N and his staff gave out that they were going to advance a long way very quickly. Hence there is a feeling of disappointment everywhere in France at the results of Nivelle's operations." It was, surprisingly, a mistake that Haig was doomed to repeat.[50]

Sir William Robertson felt no remorse at the Frenchman's failure. He told Haig that

> Nivelle's prophecy of doing the trick in 24 to 48 hours and then pushing up a lot of other divisions was always to my mind most ridiculous.... It was a very silly theory for him to have advanced and he seems to have entirely wasted the lessons of the last two years and a half.... I cannot help thinking that Nivelle has attached too much importance to what is called "breaking the enemy's front." The best plan seems to me to go back to one of the old principles, that of defeating the enemy's army... and that means inflicting heavier losses upon him than one suffers oneself. If this old principle is kept in view and the object of breaking the enemy's army is achieved the front will look after itself, and the casualty bill will be less. I apologize for breaking out in this manner into a sort of Staff College lecture....[51]

Naturally, no apology was necessary, for Haig's beliefs mirrored Robertson's.

How did Lloyd George feel? He was, according to his mistress, "very sick" at the outcome of the Nivelle offensive. No doubt. Years later, he bitterly remarked that "General Nivelle in December [1916] was a cool and competent planner. By April he had become a crazy plunger." His confidence in the superiority of the French military had been shaken, as Lord Esher observed in a letter to Haig on 21 April:

> He has entirely changed his point of view as to the respective merits of the chiefs of the Allied Army, their staffs, and powers of offence. It is almost comic to see how the balance has turned. For the moment I do not think *you* could do wrong.

For the moment, Lloyd George was confused and disheartened. Convinced that victory on the Western Front was impossible, he had allowed himself to be sweet-talked by the silver-tongued Nivelle, who had betrayed him. The lesson was not lost on the prime minister: by the end of May, he would be more resolute than ever that there had to be an alternative to the Western Front.[52]

Adding to Lloyd George's confusion was a report prepared by an informal member of his war cabinet. While South Africa's defence minister, Lieutenant-General Jan Smuts, had no official status, he enjoyed considerable stature—far out of proportion, certainly, to his actual ability—and in late April 1917, Lloyd George sent him to France to assess the situation. Smuts returned with a recommendation to pursue the very strategy that Haig had previously outlined to the cabinet, that is, an offensive "to recover the northern coast of Belgium and drive the enemy from Zeebrugge and Ostend." As Smuts declared in his report to cabinet on 1 May:

> I have no confidence that we can break through the enemy line on any large scale.... But my visit has only strengthened my impression that a decision on this front can only be reached by a process of remorselessly wearing down the enemy.

In other words: "if we could not break the enemy's front we might break his heart."[53]

This was, of course, precisely what Sir Douglas Haig had in mind. But there was, in Haig's view, added urgency to resume offensive operations on the Western Front. The French, deflated by the disappointing outcome of Nivelle's spring campaign, had lost the will to fight. Haig was appalled to learn, via Lloyd George, "that it was the intention of the French Government...to stop...and do nothing till 1918 when the Americans would be able to help." It was a policy favoured by Pétain, the new French commander-in-chief, but

Haig felt that it "would be the height of folly," because "the enemy will be given time to recover from the blows he received on the Somme, at Verdun, Arras and now on the Aisne."[54]

To finalize Allied strategy in the second half of 1917, an Anglo-French conference was convened in Paris on 4 May. At a dinner party the night before, Haig saw for himself the prime minister's drastically different temperament. Lloyd George "is here, he says, to press whatever plan Robertson and I decide on," Haig wrote in his diary. "Rather a changed attitude for him to adopt since the Calais conference!"[55]

The Paris conference began with a private meeting of military men: Haig, Robertson, Pétain, and a lame-duck Nivelle. According to Robertson, "we arrived at the unanimous opinion that it is essential to continue offensive operations on the Western Front." But Robertson contended that these attacks would be different from earlier efforts.

> It is no longer a question of aiming at breaking through the enemy's front and aiming at distant objectives. It is now a question of wearing down and exhausting the enemy's resistance, and if and when this is achieved to exploit it to the fullest extent possible.... We are all of opinion that our object can be obtained by relentlessly attacking with limited objectives, while making the fullest use of our artillery. By this means we hope to gain our ends with the minimum loss possible.[56]

That afternoon, the British and French governments accepted this policy. Lloyd George, in particular, continued to be a pleasant surprise to Haig, who happily observed that the prime minister "stated that he had no pretensions to be a strategist, that he left that to his military advisers, that I, as C. in C. of the British Forces in France had full power to attack where and when I thought best. He (Mr. L.G.) did not wish to know the plan, or where or when any attack would take place." Upon returning to GHQ next day, Haig wrote approvingly to his wife:

> I was very pleased with the way Lloyd George tackled the military problem at the conference in Paris yesterday. In fact, I have quite forgiven him his misdeeds up to date in return for the very generous words he said yesterday about the British forces in France, and the way in which he went for the French Government and insisted upon *vigorous action*. He did well.

Haig gathered from this that he had been given carte blanche approval to proceed with his campaign in Flanders. He could not have been more mistaken.[57]

Lloyd George had, in fact, qualified his support for the policy adopted at the Paris conference. While he agreed that "the enemy must not be left in peace for one moment," and that "we must go on hitting and hitting with all our strength until the Germans ended, as they always do, by cracking," he added that the BEF could not do it alone. The French, he said, must attack too, "otherwise the Germans would bring their best men and guns and all their ammunition against the British army, and then later against the French." The point was stressed several days later, when Robertson reminded Haig that Lloyd George had acquiesced to a renewed offensive on the Western Front "on express condition that the French also play their full part...because Cabinet would never agree to our incurring heavy losses with comparatively small gains, which would obviously be the result unless the French co-operate wholeheartedly."[58]

Haig did not disagree. As he commented at the time, "There is always the difficulty, however (which one has always had in agreements with the French), to know to what extent we can depend on the French to carry out their attacks. In this case, if the French do not act vigorously, the enemy will be free to transfer his reserves to oppose our attacks in the north." Clearly, Haig—whose mistrust of the French is most apparent in this passage—shared Lloyd George's reluctance to take on the German army single-handedly.[59]

Accordingly, he sought assurances on this point. On 18 May, three days after Pétain was confirmed as commander-in-chief in Nivelle's stead, he and Haig met at Amiens. They got on quite well, as Haig remarked in his diary: "I found him businesslike, knowledgable and brief of speech. The latter is, I find, a rare quality in Frenchmen!" Pétain, he continued, "gave me full assurance that the French Army would fight and would support the British in every possible way," promising two attacks, one in June—which was not carried out until 23 October—and another in July, which was postponed until 20 August. Further, Pétain approved of Haig's offensive in Flanders, writing a few days later to say "that I am in full agreement with you." As a sign of good faith, Pétain placed at Haig's disposal the six divisions of the French First Army, under General Paul Anthoine.[60]

But all was not well within the French forces. Mutinies had broken out in the wake of the frustrating failure of the spring campaign: French soldiers were weary of being used as cannon and machine-gun fodder, with little to show for their sacrifices. The first breach of discipline occurred on 20 April, then quickly spread. By the middle of May, wrote Pétain, "These unhappy incidents multiplied to a point where *the safety and cohesion of the whole army were in jeopardy.*" The mutinies "reached their peak on 2nd June, when seventeen outbreaks were reported. The situation remained serious up to the 10th June, with an average of seven incidents a day. During the rest of the month the daily average was one. In July the total fell to seven incidents altogether, in August to four, and in September to one." Although there was no question of French determination and ability to fight if attacked, and there were literally dozens of examples during these anxious weeks, the troops flatly refused to take part in any more futile attacks on impregnable German positions.[61]

It soon became apparent that the French would be able to offer little assistance in Haig's offensive. On 2 June, Pétain sent a staff officer to warn the field-marshal of the "bad state of discipline"—to use Haig's words—in the French forces, and five days later Pétain himself visited Haig to describe the situation. "He told me," Haig wrote, "that two French divisions had refused to go and relieve two divisions in the front line, because the men had not had leave. Some were tired and were shot.... The situation caused Pétain grave concern." Haig's intelligence chief, General Charteris, had already concluded, as he remarked on 25 May, "that we cannot expect any great help from the French this year," and Haig agreed. On 10 July he met French President Poincaré, who, according to Haig's diary, "assured me that the French Army would 'continue to press the enemy to the utmost extent possible.' But owing to the bad 'moral' of the French Army, this does not mean very much really." The French, said Haig, "are a broken reed."[62]

This seems to have neither surprised nor overly concerned Haig. This is because, from the outset of the war, he had had little confidence in the French army, which he considered to be vastly overrated, or in its leaders, who were, he complained, "either unduly elated or groundlessly depressed." Haig had long believed that there was only one force in the Allied camp capable of defeating the Germans, and that was his own. "There is no doubt to my mind," he had written in January 1916, "but that the war must be won by the Forces of the British Empire." It was an observation that was subsequently proven correct, and by the summer of 1917 nothing had changed his mind: "The British troops are the only troops in the field at the moment on whose capacity to carry through successful attacks we can rely." And Haig intended to wield this potent weapon in Flanders.[63]

Another factor had by now emerged that lent apparent urgency to his cherished campaign. On 1 February 1917 the Germans had resorted to unrestricted submarine warfare. It was a calculated risk; it might—and, in April, did—bring the United States into the war against them, but the Germans gambled that their submarines could strangle Britain before the Americans could muster their strength. They were inadvertently aided by the Royal Navy, which for several months and a variety of reasons refused to employ convoys for merchant ships, though the convoy system had been spectacularly successful since the start of the war in the safe transporting of the overseas troops. The navy's error had tragic results: in the first half of 1917, British shipping losses were nearly twice the total for all of 1916, and only one-third of the sunken ships could be replaced. Colonel Repington, the military correspondent for *The Times,* wondered, as did many others, "whether our armies could win the war before our navies lost it."[64]

It was widely, but incorrectly, believed that many if not all of these deadly enemy submarines were operating from Belgian bases: a successful offensive in Flanders would, therefore, deprive the Germans of these bases. On 28 April, Wully Robertson wrote Haig:

> The situation at sea is very serious indeed. It has never been so bad as at present, and [First Sea Lord Sir John] Jellicoe almost daily announces it to be hopeless. There may soon be a shortage of food in this country, and this has to be taken into consideration in regard to all theatres of war. For us to stop fighting now would seem to be a confession of failure and would allow the enemy to do as he likes.[65]

Haig took the hint. He replied that "I think the time has nearly come for me to take up our 'alternative plan' in earnest...." Two days later, he informed his staff "that I am preparing for the Ypres operations." Buoyed by the Paris conference on 4 May, and heartened by Lloyd George's unexpected but welcome show of support and confidence, Haig proceeded with his plans. On the seventh he met with his five army commanders at Doullens, where he announced that "the objective of the French and British will now be to wear down and exhaust the enemy's resistance by systematically attacking him by surprise. When this end has been achieved the main blow will be struck by the British forces operating from the Ypres front, with the eventual object of clearing the Belgian coast and connecting with the Dutch frontier."[66]

Haig envisaged four surprise attacks in the wearing-down process. The French would carry out the pair promised by Pétain, while the BEF delivered the other two: a diversionary attack in the vicinity of Lens, a coal-mining centre in northern France, and a much larger operation at Messines Ridge, scheduled for 7 June, which would serve as a preliminary to Haig's main effort in Flanders the following month.

With preparations well under way, the campaign in Flanders, so long under consideration, would soon be a certainty. Or would it? A cynic might have suggested that things were going rather too smoothly, and he would have been right. Sir Douglas Haig was about to discover that the road to Passchendaele was long and rocky, indeed.

3 / "Correct Principles"

Slowly but surely, Prime Minister Lloyd George had come full circle. When he took office in December 1916, he was determined to end the slaughter on the Western Front. Within weeks, he had reversed himself, falling under Nivelle's spell. Now, in May 1917, he was once more a staunch advocate of the side-shows that he believed were preferable to the futility of the Western Front.

However, the change was not readily apparent, due to the disparity in Lloyd George's public and private pronouncements. As late as 10 May, when the House of Commons held a secret session to discuss war policy, the prime minister had, in the words of an observer, "very ably" defended the agreed-upon strategy on the Western Front. He did so in the face of an impassioned attack by Winston Churchill, who demanded no further offensive action "before the American power begins to be felt." Privately, Lloyd George agreed with him—he credited Churchill with making "an excellent speech" and in July appointed him minister of munitions—and was again flirting with an old idea, that of throwing British support behind an Italian offensive against Austria-Hungary. And, he thought, with good reason. Through an intermediary, he had received in mid-April "an autograph letter from the Austrian Emperor making peace overtures." This letter had been the subject of secret talks among British, French, and Italian leaders; to Lloyd George's disgust, his allies rejected the possibility of a separate peace with Austria-Hungary. Still, the peace feeler seemed to indicate that the Austrians were war-weary and might be knocked out by a timely offensive in Italy.[1]

By late May he had made up his mind. After the bitter disappointment of the Nivelle campaign, Lloyd George wanted no part of further bloodbaths on the Western Front. There was, by now, a related consideration: despite the introduction of conscription the previous year, recruiting remained a problem in Britain throughout 1917, and the prime minister was understandably sensitive to the issue. He conveyed his concerns to Sir William Robertson, who subsequently warned Haig on 26 May that "from the point of view of man-power... the overlook is not good by any means." The prime minister, related Robertson, had stated that "the time had now arrived when we must face the fact that we could not expect to get any large numbers of men in the future, but only 'scraps.' He said this was so because of the large demands for men for shipbuilding and food production, and owing to labour unrest."[2]

Haig was distressed by Robertson's warning. The implication was clear: Lloyd George was looking for a way to avoid fighting on the Western Front, an attitude the field-marshal was unable to understand.

> There seems little doubt...that victory on the Western Front means victory everywhere and a lasting peace. And I have further no doubt that the British Army in France is capable of doing it, given adequate *drafts and guns*.... For the last two years most of us soldiers have realised that Great Britain must take the necessary steps to win the war by herself, because our French Allies had already shown that they lacked both the moral qualities and the means for gaining the victory. It is thus sad to see the British Government failing at the XIIth hour.[4]

Haig honestly believed that the war was being won. The situation seemed so obvious, the solution so apparent. In a 5 June memorandum to his army commanders he went so far as to suggest "that the power of endurance of the German people is being strained to such a degree as to make it possible that the breaking point may be reached this year"—a reference to reported food riots in Germany. "If, during the next few weeks, failure to stop the steady, determined, never-wearying advance of our Armies is added to the realization of the failure of the submarine campaign the possibility of the collapse of Germany before next winter will become appreciably greater." Haig pursued the argument in a memorandum to Robertson a week later:

> I feel justified in stating that continued pressure with as little delay as possible certainly promises at least very valuable results; whereas the relaxation of pressure now would strengthen belief that the Allies are becoming totally exhausted and that Germany can outlast them.

He went on to claim "that if our resources are concentrated in France to the fullest possible extent the British Armies are capable of and can be relied on to effect great results this summer—results which will make final victory more assured and which may even bring it within reach this year." Haig had fallen into the Nivelle trap of unrealistic expectations, in which anything less than complete success could, and would, be regarded as a failure.[5]

Preparations for the offensive continued. On 7 June, Sir Herbert Plumer's Second Army carried out the preliminary operation by attacking Messines Ridge. Sixty-year-old "Daddy" Plumer—with his perfectly round, cherubic face highlighted by ruddy cheeks and white hair and moustache—was not only a favourite of the troops, but also Haig had great confidence in him, calling him "a thorough gentleman."[6] Plumer justified that confidence by winning what was arguably the most impressive and clear-cut British victory of the entire war. For two years, long, deep tunnels had been dug under the ridge; just before the attack, nineteen of these mines, containing more than a million tons of explosive, were ignited, obliterating the German defences and most of the defenders. By taking the ridge, or what was left of it, the British had secured the right flank of the main operation to the immediate north, if it went ahead as planned.

But there was considerable doubt that the Flanders campaign would be carried out. On 8 June, the day after Messines, Lloyd George had formed a war policy committee, composed of General Smuts, Lord Curzon, Lord Milner, Andrew Bonar Law, and himself, with Sir Maurice Hankey as secretary. An alarmed Robertson wrote Haig: "There is trouble in the land just now. The War Cabinet, under the influence of L.G., have started, quite amongst themselves plus Smuts, to review the whole policy and strategy of the war, and to 'get at facts.' They are interviewing different people singly, and sending out to Departments various specific questions to be answered." Warning Haig that he would be called before the committee later in June, Robertson explained that

> the L.G. idea is to settle the war from Italy, and to-day the railway people have been asked for figures regarding the rapid transfer of 12 Divisions and 300 heavy guns to Italy! They will never go while I am C.I.G.S. but all that will come later. What I wish to impress on you is this:—Don't argue that you can finish the war this year, or that the German is already beaten. Argue that your plan is the best plan—as it is—that no other would even be *safe* let alone decisive, and then leave them to reject your advice and mine. They dare not do that.[7]

However, even Robertson was wavering. During a visit to GHQ on 9 June, a mortified Haig wrote in his diary that Robertson had warned of "the difficult situation in which the country would be if I carried out large and costly attacks without full co-operation by the French. When Autumn came round, Britain would then be without an Army!" The CIGS also suggested that Lloyd George's proposed Italian offensive had merit. "I told him," wrote Haig, "that I thought the German was now nearly at his last resources, and that there was only *one sound* plan to follow," namely, to send to France every available man, gun, and aircraft. Haig's lecture seemed to work. Next morning the commander-in-chief noted that Robertson "was less pessimistic and seemed to realise that the German Army was in reduced circumstances." Nevertheless, Haig for the first time, but not the last, had reason to doubt Robertson's reliability in the ongoing battle with Lloyd George and his cronies.[8]

Haig was sufficiently concerned that he tried to rally political support for his cause. He dispatched a letter to Lord Derby, the secretary of state for war:

> I do beg of you to do your utmost to prevent our Government delaying to take action until the American Army is in the field. We heard in 1916 the same arguments used regarding the advantages in waiting till Russia should be ready this year! There is no time like the present. Do your utmost to turn the present very favourable military situation in France to account. That is to say send us every available man (as drafts) as soon as possible, as many aeroplanes as possible and ditto guns! Now is the time for showing the greatest energy and activity—all talk should cease. We cannot tell how our Allies will stand another winter.[9]

Fearing that his message was not getting across, Haig submitted another long memorandum to Robertson on 17 June. It would, he said, "assist the War Cabinet in considering the various possible courses of action open this summer" by explaining "my views as to the strategical advantages which would be gained by successful operations to secure the Belgian coast."

> Comparing this operation with anything that we might do in other theatres its advantages are overwhelming.
>
> It directly and seriously threatens our main enemy, on whom the whole Coalition against us depends.
>
> It is within the easiest possible reach of our base by sea and rail and can be developed infinitely more rapidly, and maintained infinitely more easily, than any other operation open to us.
>
> It admits of the closest possible combination of our naval and military strength.
>
> It covers all the points which we dare not uncover, and therefore admits of the utmost concentration of force; whereas, for the same reason, any force employed in another theatre of war can never be more than a detachment, with all the disadvantages of detachments....
>
> Amid the uncertainties of war one thing is certain, viz., that it is only by whole-hearted concentration at the right time and place that victory ever has been or ever will be won.

> In my opinion the time and place to choose are now beyond dispute. We have gone a long way already towards success. Victory may be nearer than is generally realized if we act correctly now. But we may fall seriously short of it if at this juncture we fail to follow correct principles.

This was Sir Douglas Haig at his most persuasive; it was also Haig at his most outrageously optimistic. Yet, even Prime Minister Lloyd George would admit that this memo "provided a very powerful statement in favour of the plans he wished to carry out."[10]

The showdown came on 19 June, in London, when Haig and Robertson confronted Lloyd George's newly formed war policy committee. A bitter affair, it was also decidedly anticlimactic, lasting six acrimonious days without reaching a conclusion. Haig, who turned fifty-six on the nineteenth, outlined in detail his plans for the Flanders campaign, using a large map, and Lloyd George later recalled that he "made dramatic use of both his hands to demonstrate how he proposed to sweep up the enemy—first the right hand brushing along the surface irresistibly, and then came the left, his outer finger ultimately touching the German frontier with the nail across." As historian John Terraine points out, "Lloyd George never forgave that finger-nail."[11]

The prime minister would make several misleading—indeed, downright dishonest—claims. Complaining that this was the first that he had heard of plans for a British campaign in Flanders, which can only be described as an outright lie, he charged that the war policy committee was "misled on several critical points" by Haig and Robertson. He contended that the soldiers "withheld or minimised" the French mutinies, and "concealed" the opposition of leading French generals, angrily concluding: "If the whole truth as it was known at the time, to the military staffs, had been exposed before the members of the War Committee, the Flanders offensive would have been turned down." But Lloyd George—who, in any event, had no right to expect candour from the generals he so wilfully and skilfully abused—was being far from forthright. The London conference which he had convened in mid-January committed his government to support an offensive in Flanders if the Nivelle scheme failed; Haig had also expressly outlined his intentions in London on 14 March. It will also be recalled that General Smuts, a member of this very committee, later prepared a report endorsing the Flanders campaign. And Lloyd George most certainly did not have to rely on Haig and Robertson for information about the mutinies. On 6 June, Sir Frederick Maurice, the director of military operations at the War Office, had informed the war cabinet "that there was serious trouble, practically amounting to mutiny, in a number of French regiments," and two days later General Sir Henry Wilson, the liaison officer at Grand Quartier Général (GQG)—the French equivalent of GHQ—had told the war policy committee that he had "grave doubts as to whether we could count on the continued resistance of the French army and nation." And so far as the views of French generals were concerned, the only opinion that counted was that of Henri Pétain, the new commander-in-chief, who had approved of Haig's proposed offensive.[12]

His honesty, or lack of it, notwithstanding, Lloyd George was at his passionate and eloquent best at these hearings. More than anything, he feared another Somme: "Brilliant preliminary successes followed by weeks of desperate and sanguinary struggles, leading to nothing except perhaps the driving of the enemy back a few miles—beyond that nothing to show except a ghastly casualty list." Continuing to advocate the side-shows, the prime minister argued that efforts to knock Turkey and Austria-Hungary out of the war "would be the beginning of the disintegration and consequent destruction of the Central Powers." There was, he said, another obvious advantage to fighting the Germans elsewhere, such as Italy: "if we fought them in France we should be doing it at the expense of our own troops, whereas in Italy we can use the enormous reserves of Italians." And, finally, he reminded his cabinet colleagues that the soldiers had a credibility problem, pointing out "that during nearly three years of war I had never known an offensive to be undertaken without sure predictions of success." He was "sceptical" of the Flanders operation, and worried that it would result in "a hopeless and costly struggle bringing us no nearer victory."[13]

Both Haig and Robertson were annoyed and angered by the prime minister's performance. Lloyd George, Haig complained in his diary, "seemed to believe the decisive moment of the war would be 1918. Until then we ought to husband our forces and do little or nothing...," which Haig rightly considered a serious if not fatal mistake. On another occasion he observed that "Lloyd George made a long oration, minimising the successes gained, and exaggerating the strength of the enemy. His object was to induce Robertson and myself to agree to an expedition being sent to support the Italians. It was a regular lawyer's effort to make black appear white! He referred with a sneer to my optimistic views." Robertson was even more displeased, comparing the proceedings to a kangaroo court.

> Instead of being received as a military chief, the accuracy of whose views, so far as they were military, were not in dispute, I

was made to feel like a witness for the defence under cross-examination, the Prime Minister appearing in the dual capacity of counsel for the prosecution and judge.

Of course, the two soldiers laboured under a severe disadvantage. Uncomfortable at the best of times in the presence of politicians, neither Haig nor Robertson could come close to matching Lloyd George's glib, impassioned oratory—few men of that era could do so—and their cause was not aided by their peculiar inability to articulate. Robertson, it seems, was further handicapped by the great effort it required to keep his temper under control.[14]

Ironically, the most controversial comment was not made by a politician or soldier, but by a sailor. The first sea lord, Sir John Jellicoe, who had long been depressed by the Royal Navy's apparent inability to deal with Germany's growing fleet of U-boats, bluntly declared "that unless we cleared the Germans out of Zeebrugge this year, we could not go on with the war through lack of shipping." Jellicoe's "startling and reckless declaration," as Lloyd George called it, was challenged by the prime minister, but to no avail. Even Haig described it as "a bombshell." The admiral had struck a sensitive nerve, knowing that the government shared his concern about the submarine threat; it was, in Sir Maurice Hankey's words, "the main preoccupation of the War Cabinet during the first half of 1917." Thus, a sailor had given the soldiers one more powerful argument—perhaps, ultimately, a decisive one—in their efforts to justify an attack in Flanders.* Tragically, the navy had overestimated the importance of the Belgian ports; it was later found that the German submarines based in Ostend-Zeebrugge "probably did not exceed more than ten in number."[16]**

The war policy committee was left in a quandary. Torn between Lloyd George's eloquence and the determined professionalism of Haig and Robertson, the committee could not come to a conclusion. Most, if not all, the members shared the prime minister's uncertainty about the necessity of the Flanders campaign—cabinet papers reveal their concern for casualties and doubts about the degree of French participation—but they were also unwilling to reject it and hand the

---

* Jellicoe, whose defeatism would eventually cost him his job, knew that he was in hot water as a result of his testimony. "I fancy there is a scheme afoot to get rid of me," he wrote in late June. "The way they are doing it is to say that I am too pessimistic."[15] However, Jellicoe was not sacked until December 1917.

** Though it has since been shown that the U-boat fleet based in Belgium was insignificant, it is interesting to note that the German army commanders on the Western Front, Paul von Hindenburg and Erich Ludendorff, both refer in their memoirs to the importance of defending these submarine bases.

soldiers a vote of nonconfidence. The committee, concluding its hearings on 25 June, gave Haig permission to continue his battle preparations, pending a final decision.

However, it would be weeks before that happened. In late June, Robertson reported to Haig that the "Prime Minister is more than ever keen on the Italian project! Several of the other members of the War Cabinet are equally keen on some other equally foolish strategical project. Alexandretta [on the Turkish coast]—the Balkans, for instance. Yet I suppose that these same Ministers will be held up in years to come as far-sighted statesmen and the saviours of their country." By 18 July, his preliminary bombardment in Flanders already under way, Haig was still waiting for word from London. All he received was a sympathetic letter from the CIGS:

> You will remember that when you left here the Cabinet had not definitely approved of your plans, but said that you were to go on with your preparations. The War Policy Committee of the Cabinet, whom you met, have been continuing their discussions ever since... but up to the present no official approval of your plans has been given.... Apparently the Prime Minister is the only one who is sticking out against them, and who continues to be in favour of the Italian venture. I have twice reminded him that time is running short, and that your preparations will soon be completed.[17]

It was not until 20 July that the war cabinet gave Haig the green light. Even at that, it came as the result of "a rough and tumble meeting," as Robertson termed it. "The fact is that the Prime Minister is still very averse from your offensive," the CIGS explained in a letter to Haig, "and talks as though he is hoping to switch off to Italy within a day or two after you begin." That is precisely what the cabinet intended, as Sir Maurice Hankey wrote in his diary: "the final decision was to allow Haig to begin his offensive, but not to allow it to degenerate into a drawn out, indecisive battle of the 'Somme' type. If this happened, it was to be stopped and the plan for an attack on the Italian Front would be tried."[18]

Neither Lloyd George nor Haig was happy. The prime minister later wrote of his losing battle with the soldiers:

> I had no expert military counsel which I could weigh against theirs.... Profound though my own apprehensions of failure were, I was a layman and in matters of military strategy did not possess the knowledge and training that would justify me in

overriding soldiers of such standing and experience. Accordingly, the soldiers had their way.

But Lloyd George made one last attempt to derail Haig's plans. At a hastily called conference in Paris on 25 July, less than a week before the start of the Flanders offensive, the prime minister tried to win support for a scheme to send substantial aid to Italy. But "Robertson dug in his toes and refused to budge," fumed Lloyd George. "He doggedly held the Cabinet on its assent [for the Flanders operations].... We had therefore either to proceed with the Ostend operation or to dismiss both Robertson and Haig and appoint Generals who were not so committed. The Cabinet were not prepared for so sensational a change."[19]

Haig, too, was dissatisfied. "I have formed the impression," he complained to Robertson, "that the plan of operations, though approved, has neither the full confidence nor the whole-hearted support of the War Cabinet...if the impression is not justified I respectfully ask for assurance to that effect." He also railed against the prime minister's predilection for Italy. "The chance of anything positive being achieved in Italy is—to anyone acquainted with the A.B.C. of war—infinitesimal...," he raged. "Every man and gun that we send to Italy reduces our power in one respect or another. I consider it so dangerous and so unsound to adopt such a course that, in my opinion, any responsible soldier who consents to issue an order for it must expect to be adjudged by history to have failed in his duty to his country."[20]

Several more days passed. Then, on 25 July, a telegram from Robertson reached GHQ:

> War Cabinet authorizes me to inform you that having approved your plans being executed you may depend on their whole-hearted support and that if and when they decide again to reconsider the situation they will obtain your views before arriving at any decision as to cessation of operations.

Haig was hardly reassured. "How different to the whole-hearted, almost unthinking support given by our Government to the Frenchman (Nivelle) last January," he bitterly remarked. Nevertheless, Haig had had his way. Having staked his reputation on the Flanders offensive, he felt confident that his beloved BEF would now prove to the politicians that the professional soldiers knew what they were doing. Of that, Haig had no doubt whatever.[21]

Part Two: **Flanders**

4/Wipers

There is one remarkable trait about the geography of Flanders. The land is extraordinarily level. Hills are but little lumps in the landscape, ridges mere ripples. Such features are always militarily important, but here their value is exaggerated by the generally flat terrain. One notable exception to the flatness, however, is a system of ridges rising around Passchendaele and running generally southward to Wytschaete and Messines, swinging westward into France. The main ridge is much like the trunk of a tree, sprouting many shorter and smaller ridges that protrude like branches. This high ground dominated the Ypres salient, where Sir Douglas Haig intended to launch his offensive.

The Ypres salient had long been the scene of fierce fighting. This bulge in the Allied line was considerably smaller than it had been in 1914, when it was created during the so-called "race to the sea" which occurred after the German invasion of France and Belgium had been halted—the flank along the coast was the only one that offered either side an opportunity for manoeuvre. Neither side won the race, however, and the Western Front subsequently settled into stagnant trench warfare.

The Germans had made the first bid to break the deadlock. In October 1914 they attacked the newly formed salient around Ypres—tongue-tied British Tommies nicknamed it "Wipers"—in western Belgium. The salient, battered and shrunken, survived the furious onslaught, but just barely. This struggle, which would go down in history as the First Battle of Ypres, deeply impressed Haig, who at the time commanded the BEF's I Corps. The heavily outnumbered British were forced to employ clerks and cooks in the firing line in the face of the relentless German attacks. At one stage Haig was told by two of his brigadiers "that if the enemy makes a push at any point, they doubt our men being able to hold on."[1] But the decisive attack failed to materialize. The British had thus been saved by the enemy's inability—German losses had been so staggering that they called this battle *Kindermord*, "slaughter of the innocents"—to press his advantage at the critical moment. The lesson was not lost on Haig.

The Ypres salient remained a thorn in the side of the Germans. In April 1915 they used poison gas in another attempt to snuff it out; French colonials fled in panic, but Canadians, in their baptism by fire, saved the day. Once again, the salient had been much reduced in size, but it held on. Desultory fighting continued in the neighbourhood for another two years, as the Germans made half-hearted efforts to capture Ypres, the most notable attempt coming in June 1916 at the Battle of Mount Sorrel, which involved another splendid performance by the Canadians. As a result of these repeated failures, the Germans had to content themselves with holding most of the high ground in the vicinity, which gave them full observation over the salient. This advantage, combined with their ability to shell it on three sides, made life miserable, and costly, for the defenders.

Still, the importance of Ypres and the surrounding salient was largely symbolic. Located in the small corner of Belgium left unconquered in the opening weeks of the war, Ypres stood as a symbol of Allied determination: withdrawal was out of the question. The temptation to do so must have been great, though; a canal ran across the base of the salient and it made military sense to withdraw behind it, for the position would have been more easily defensible. But such a move was never seriously considered. In war, symbols count for much.

However, one look at a map reveals the significance of Flanders as a whole. On either side, there was precious little room for manoeuvre. The British had their backs to the sea. The Channel ports, so vital to the BEF's line of communications with England, were but a short distance away; a defeat on the Flanders front would have been catastrophic. The German position was only slightly better. A mere thirty-three miles from the British lines at Ypres lay the Dutch border—Holland, it will be recalled, remained neutral; within this constricted space, German railway lines were very vulnerable. Twelve miles northeast of Ypres was the key rail centre of Roulers, which one historian describes as one of "the most tempting strategic objectives on the Western Front." A shallow advance by the British would bring the Roulers-Thourout railway under fire; an advance of twenty miles—admittedly unheard-of by 1917 standards—would enable the British to bombard Bruges and would, according to the British official history, "bring about not only the evacuation of Zeebrugge and of the whole Belgian coast, but probably that of all western Belgium, a first-class military, naval, economic and moral disaster to the enemy."[2]

This is what Sir Douglas Haig had in mind. As he argued in a 17 June memorandum, the advantages offered by a Flanders campaign were overwhelming.

> Even a partial success in the operation for which I am preparing will give very useful results, apart from the effect on the German army and nation of another defeat.

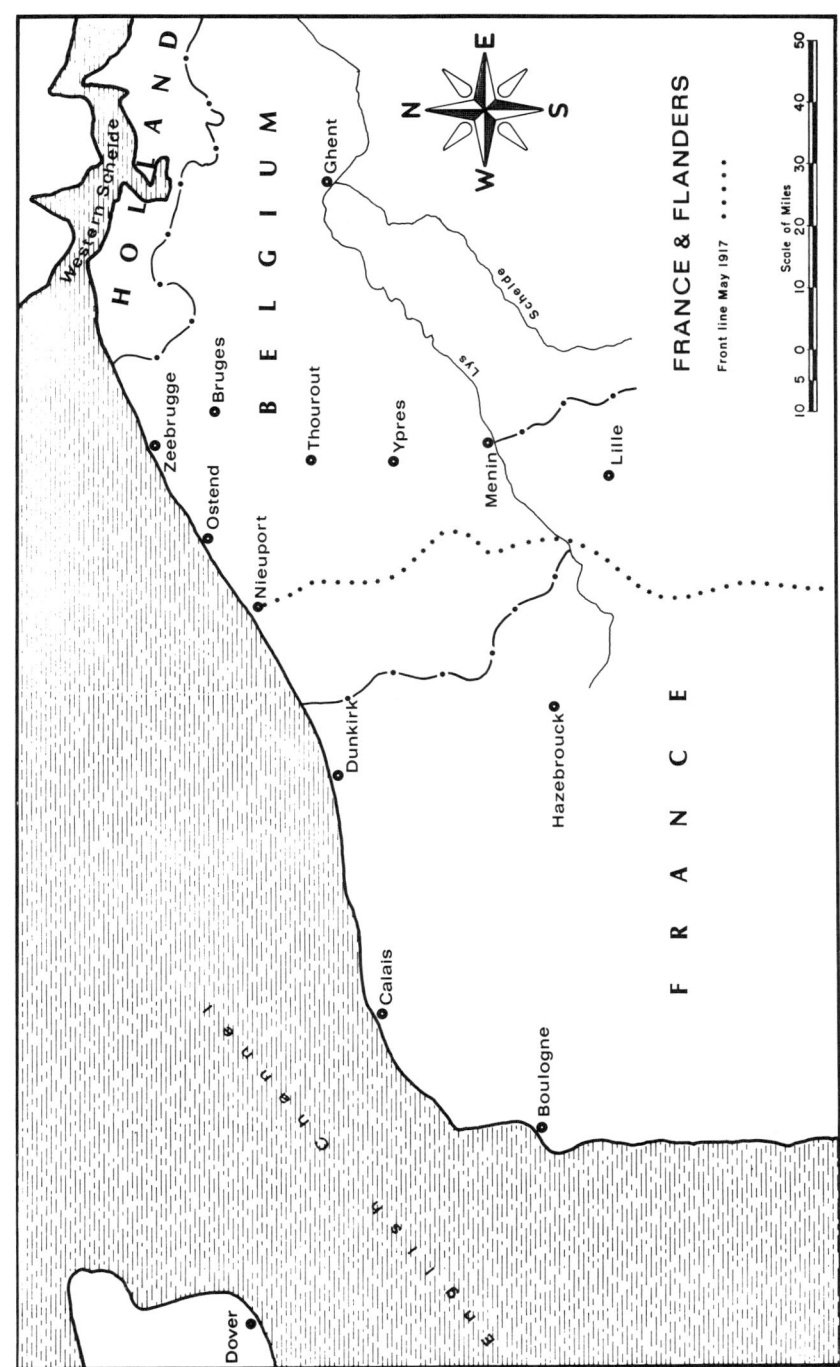

> A very limited advance will enable our guns to make OSTEND useless to the German navy, and will, at the same time, render DUNKIRK—one of our most useful ports—immune from long-range hostile gunfire.
>
> The enemy's communications with the coast are not numerous, and run through such a narrow space between our lines and the Dutch frontier that an advance sufficient to bring the ROULERS-THOUROUT railway within effective range of our guns would restrict his railway communications with the coast to those passing through GHENT and BRUGES.
>
> A short further advance, bringing us within effective heavy-gun range of BRUGES, would most probably induce the evacuation of ZEEBRUGGE and the whole coastline.
>
> The consequences of extending our front to the Dutch frontier would be so considerable that they might prove decisive. Following on the successes we have already gained such a failure to stop our advance would leave little room for German hope of successfully opposing our further advance, even if temporary exhaustion imposed a halt on us for a time.
>
> Realizing this, the enemy would find himself faced by a most serious situation. His main lines of retreat run through the bottlenecks north and south of the ARDENNES, and any reasonable possibility of our being able to continue the advance on GHENT and BRUSSELS would probably suffice to determine the enemy to undertake a retreat, if not to accept our [peace] terms at once, in view of the dangers and difficulties of retreat under such conditions....[3]

Haig's offensive was designed to exploit the enemy's vulnerability. The field-marshal outlined his plan as follows:

> Underlying the general intention of wearing out the enemy is the strategical idea of securing the Belgian coast and connecting our front with the Dutch frontier.
>
> The nature and size of the several steps which we take towards the objective must depend on our *effectives* and the replacement of *guns*.
>
> Roughly these steps are:
>
> (*a*) Capture the bridgehead formed by the Passchendaele-Staden-Clercken ridge.
>
> (*b*) Push on towards Roulers-Thourout, so as to take the German coast defences in the rear.

(*c*) Land by surprise on the Ostend front in conjunction with an attack from Nieuport.

If our effectives or guns are not adequate, and progress is delayed, it may be necessary to call a halt after (*a*) is gained.[4]

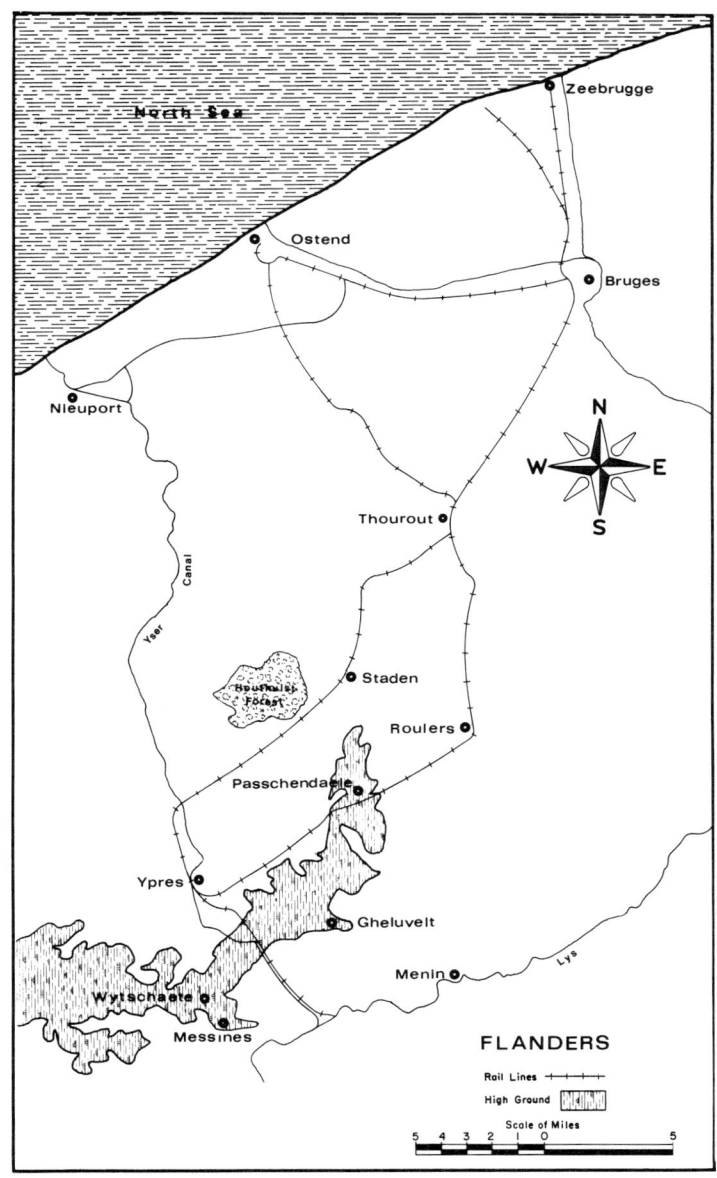

It is important to stress that all of these goals were merely "underlying" Haig's primary objective, that is, the German army. The capture of Passchendaele Ridge, Roulers and Thourout, and the Belgian coastline would be a bonus, in Haig's view. "The guiding principles on which my general scheme of action is based," he wrote, "are those which have proved successful from time immemorial— viz. that the first step must always be to wear down the enemy's power of resistance until he is so weakened that he will be unable to withstand a decisive blow; then to deliver the decisive blow; and, finally, to reap the fruits of victory." Haig was convinced that "even if a full measure of success is not gained we shall be attacking the enemy on a front where he cannot refuse to fight, and where, therefore, our purpose of wearing him down can be given effect to, while even a partial success will considerably improve our defensive positions in the Ypres salient and thus reduce the heavy wastage which must otherwise be expected to occur there next winter as in the past."[5]

Yet, Haig allowed himself to be carried away by his eternal optimism. "The general situation," he suggested in a 5 July memo to his army commanders, "is favourable to the attainment of considerable results in the offensive operations we are about to undertake." He admitted that the first objective, Passchendaele Ridge, would be "likely to entail very hard fighting lasting perhaps for weeks," after which he foresaw "opportunities for the employment of Cavalry in masses" on the flat plain beyond, leading to the capture of the Belgian ports. Even John Terraine, Haig's chief apologist, concedes that this paper "is probably the most wildly optimistic to which he ever put his signature."[6]

Herein lie the seeds of trouble, for Haig had endowed his project with a schizophrenic personality. It was to be both a wearing-down battle and a decisive breakthrough; the question was, when did one end and the other begin? The incongruity becomes apparent when the evolution of the plans for the Flanders offensive is traced. When detailed planning had begun in early 1916, Haig had assigned to it two army commanders, Sir Henry Rawlinson and Sir Herbert Plumer, both of whom were proponents of the step by step, deliberate advance, each limited push supported by massive concentrations of artillery. Rawlinson had applied these methods, with indifferent results, at the Somme later in 1916, and Haig was unhappy when, after resurrecting the Flanders campaign at year's end, he learned that Plumer had decided to employ the same principles. Haig's chief of staff, Lieutenant-General Sir Launcelot Kiggell, icily wrote Plumer in early January 1917 that the commander-in-chief had rejected "a sustained and deliberate offensive such as has been carried out recently on the Somme front. In these circumstances the enemy will have time to bring up fresh reinforcements and construct new lines of defence. The object of these operations is to inflict a decisive defeat on the enemy and to free the Belgian coast." A GHQ directive issued on 8 January was even more definite: "the whole essence is to attack with rapidity and push right through quickly." At one point, in February 1917, Haig even toyed briefly with the idea of using "tanks in a surprise attack...without artillery preparation"—a revelation, surely, to his many critics who, succumbing to the myth of his lack of imagination, accuse him of being unable to grasp the proper use of this powerful but primitive new weapon.*⁷

It would seem that Haig was unduly influenced by the bold thinking of the ill-fated French commander-in-chief, Nivelle. And this influence lingered, even after the disappointing attacks in the spring of 1917 made it apparent that the Germans were far from ready to collapse, that the Allies would have to engage in more "wearing down," to use Haig's favourite phrase, before delivering the coup de grâce.

And so he made a fateful decision. Dissatisfied with the plodding ways of Rawlinson and Plumer, Haig sought a more energetic man with whom to entrust his main offensive. Leaving Plumer in charge of the preliminary attack on Messines Ridge, Haig shunted Rawlinson aside and brought in Sir Hubert Gough and his Fifth Army. At forty-seven, Gough was the youngest of the BEF's five army commanders, "a balding but boyish chap...invariably courteous, witty and personable." He was, like Haig, a cavalryman by training, with a reputation for dash and determination, with the confidence to match—"We can beat the Germans when and where we like," he once declared.⁸

It was, nevertheless, a strange choice, and one that has been questioned. Historian John Terraine contends that the decision to entrust the offensive to Gough was "Haig's gravest and most fatal error." Even contemporaries were puzzled. Colonel Repington of *The Times* remarked in his diary on 5 July, following a discussion with the CIGS, Sir William Robertson:

* The proposal was eventually scrapped when tank experts deemed the ground unsuitable for tanks en masse—it was too heavily wooded—and when it became apparent that there would not be enough tanks anyway. In fact, there was a chronic shortage of tanks during the Great War and only twice were there enough to mount mass attacks, at Cambrai in November 1917 and at Amiens in August 1918. This critical shortage is usually overlooked by Haig's detractors.

> I did not think that the choice of Gough for this particular operation was good, much though I admired his gifts. R. was inclined to agree, and wished that Plumer, who knew every stone in the north, had been placed in charge.

Gough himself would admit that it was "a mistake not to entrust the operation to the General [Plumer] who had been on that front for more than two years, instead of bringing me over on to a bit of ground with which I had practically no acquaintance."[9]

In drawing up the plans for the Fifth Army's attack in Flanders, Sir Hubert believed that he was adhering to the wishes of his commander-in-chief. Many years later, he wrote:

> I have a very clear and distinct recollection of Haig's personal explanations to me, and his instructions, when I was appointed to undertake this operation. He quite clearly told me that the plan was to capture Passchendaele Ridge, and to advance as rapidly as possible on Roulers. I was then to advance on Ostend. This was very definitely viewing the battle as an attempt to break through, and moreover Haig never altered this opinion till the attack was launched, so far as I know.[10]

More serious, and less defensible, was the manner in which Gough went about carrying out his orders. The Fifth Army, according to Haig's instructions to Gough in mid-May, was to strike northeastward from Ypres. Its objective would be "the Passchendaele-Staden Ridge and the railway Roulers-Thourout.... The right of your attack should move on the high ground through Gheluvelt, Becelaere, Broodseinde, and Moorslede. As your advance progresses this high ground will be taken over from you by the Second Army, which will then be charged with safeguarding your right flank and rear against attack from the south. Your left flank should be directed to the south of Houthulst Forest." General Paul Anthoine's French First Army would operate on Gough's left.[11]

However, Gough arbitrarily altered his army's objectives. On 6 and 7 June he conferred with his corps commanders, and he later recalled:

> The details of the operations which lay before us were considered, and a slight change in the plan was made; it was proposed to pivot on the left flank with the French, while the right flank advanced along the Passchendaele Ridge. This would eventually bring our general direction northwards to clear the Houthulst Forest, and Roulers would thus cease to be an objective of the Fifth Army.[12]

This was hardly "a slight change," as Gough calls it. After all, Roulers was supposed to be one of the main objectives of the campaign, and Gough knew it.

Haig was understandably upset. At a 28 June meeting with Gough, he wrote, "I urged the importance of the right flank.... The main battle will be fought for the ridge so we must make our plans accordingly.... I impressed on Gough the vital importance of the ridge in question, and that the advance north should be limited until our right flank has really been secured on this ridge."[13] But Haig was less persuasive than his recollection suggests; typically, there was a wide gap between what Haig thought he had said and what others believed he had said. In this case, Haig's point was lost on Gough; the latter's plan prevailed. The Flanders offensive would thus be launched in what the commander-in-chief considered to be the wrong direction!

Nothing so dramatically calls into question Gough's competence. His own explanation, written in 1944, is far from satisfactory. Gough complained then that he had insufficient resources, that GHQ had "failed to mass anything like sufficient forces to carry out so ambitious a task—20 to 30 divisions were necessary [Gough had sixteen]—and the front of attack was too narrow and directed at the wrong place. It should have been directed farther south—with its left, say, on Zonnebeke and its right on Messines."[14] In fact, Gough's front was too broad and ignored the cardinal military rule of concentration of force at the decisive point; instead of delivering a powerful punch, the Fifth Army would be administering a severe slap. Gough's own recollection confirms that Haig had assigned Roulers as a primary objective for the Fifth Army, yet Gough had taken it upon himself to change it. Not only that, he had shifted the focus of the attack much further north than Haig had in mind, and Gough admits that it should have been made more to the south. One can only wonder whether Gough and his staff really knew what they were doing.

Who was right, Haig or Gough? It was not that Gough failed to appreciate the importance of the high ground on his right flank; he merely had a different appreciation. Whereas Haig saw it as the focal point of the main battle, because it blocked his advance toward Roulers, Gough preferred to include it in an attack on a broad front, denying the enemy the opportunity of concentrating his own resources on the ridge. Ultimately, Haig was correct, though it is a moot point in the final analysis. Given the horrific weather conditions that prevailed in August 1917, it seems likely that no plan, however brilliantly conceived, could have gained any measure of success.

The real importance of this episode, besides raising questions about Gough, is that it reveals a flaw in Haig's leadership qualities. He was reluctant to interfere with his subordinates, having implicit trust in their ability to execute his wishes. As a result, he was in command but not necessarily in *control*—an important distinction—and this was neither the first nor the last time he exhibited this trait. Haig's desire to give his lieutenants as much leeway as possible was admirable when the man concerned was skilled and efficient, but these were prerequisites that Sir Hubert Gough did not meet. Haig overrated him, and must bear the full responsibility for doing so. Also, the commander-in-chief must be held responsible for the breakdown in communication with Gough; once again, he was betrayed by his notorious inability to express himself verbally.

Amid this lamentable confusion, the preparations for the offensive continued. For an undertaking of this magnitude, they were truly awesome, and represent an administrative triumph of the first order. They included

> the intensive training of the troops selected for the attack, arrangements for their unobtrusive concentration and accommodation at the moment of attack, the accumulation of vast dumps of ammunition for the guns and howitzers, the massing of batteries, the preparation of elaborate communications by road and rail in order to maintain the stream of munitions and supplies for a prolonged battle; the provision of aerodromes and the concentration therein of the aircraft required to maintain aerial supremacy; water supply, drafts of men to replace casualties, dressing-stations, sanitation and a thousand other details.[15]

Little wonder that Haig was disturbed at the delay in the war cabinet's approval of his plans. Amateurs like Lloyd George failed to realize that military ventures on this scale could not be turned on and off like tap-water.

The British, unfortunately, forfeited all possibility of surprise. "No offensive—including Nivelle's—on the Western Front was ever so clearly heralded or so confidently awaited," commented one historian. With the Germans holding the high ground about the salient, they could hardly help but notice the massive build-up that was taking place. Moreover, security was distressingly lax—not only was the offensive openly discussed in pubs across England, it was even reported in German newspapers. As early as 9 June, the German Fourth Army, which was responsible for the Ypres sector, predicted that a British attack was "certain." The Germans prepared accordingly, moving up men and guns, and by the eve of the offensive Crown Prince Rupprecht of Bavaria, who commanded Germany's northern group of armies, could confidently write: "My mind is quite at rest about the attack, as we have never disposed such strong reserves, so well trained for their part, as on the front [to be] attacked."[16]

To make matters worse, the offensive was twice postponed. Originally it had been scheduled to begin on 25 July. But on the twelfth, Sir Hubert Gough asked for, and received, a three-day delay. With the attack now slated for 28 July, the French army commander, Anthoine, came to Haig seeking another three-day postponement, in order to complete his artillery program. Haig reluctantly agreed, but he was not pleased. "What a nuisance these French are!" he told his dairy.[17] The Flanders campaign would be launched on 31 July.

It was preceded by one of the most devastating bombardments in history. Between 17 and 30 July, the British blasted the German defences with 4.3 million shells of various calibres, at a cost to the exchequer of £22,211,389 14s. 4d., or more than $100 million in Canadian funds of the day. In addition, the artillery fired an average of two million shells per week for the balance of the campaign.[18]

The impact of this expenditure of high explosive was staggering. According to the enemy's official account, "the German infantry suffered severely.... The losses in men [estimated at 30,000 between 20 and 30 July] and equipment were enormous." General Hermann von Kuhl, Rupprecht's chief of staff, later wrote: "Some of the front line divisions had to be relieved before the storm broke, for their strength had been consumed. The trenches and [barbed-wire] entanglements were destroyed and dug-outs smashed." The final barrage, in the early morning hours of 31 July, was simply stupendous. Von Kuhl called it "a storm of fire the like of which had never been experienced before. The whole Flanders earth moved and appeared to be in flames. It was not drum fire any longer, it was as if Hell itself had opened. What were the horrors of Verdun and the Somme in comparison with this giant expenditure of power?"[19]

So violent was the shelling on the thirty-first that it awakened Sir Douglas Haig at his advanced headquarters, in a railway car parked on a specially constructed siding at Godeswaersvalde, during the night. "The whole ground was shaking with the terrible bombardment," he told his diary.[20]

As zero hour neared, nervous anxiety gripped GHQ. "It is impossible to forecast the result," wrote Brigadier-General Charteris, Haig's usually optimistic intelligence chief, on 30 July.

The only thing that is certain, is the most unfortunate of all things, a big casualty list.... My one fear is the weather. We have had most carefully prepared statistics of previous years—there are records of eighty years to refer to—and I do not think that we can hope for more than a fortnight, or at the best, three weeks of really fine weather.... To-day it has been raining the whole time, a bad outlook for to-morrow.[21]

It would, indeed, be bad. Very bad.

5/Rain, Mud, and Blood

The Fifth Army launched its attack at 3:50 A.M. on 31 July 1917. The ground was wet from the previous day's rainfall, but it did not adversely affect the advance of the heavily laden troops who found, to their astonishment, that in several places the German front line had ceased to exist. "There was not a bit of wire, hardly a trench left, that hadn't been blown to smithereens by our barrage...," one soldier recalled. "On the ground all around us it was simply carnage. Bits of bodies and knocked-out guns lying all over the place...."[1]

"This was a fine day's work," a happy Haig wrote, while Gough called it "decidedly successful," a description justified by the capture of 5,600 prisoners and numerous trench mortars and machine-guns. But nowhere did the British come close to achieving their first day's objectives drawn on maps at GHQ; the average gain was a modest 3,000 yards along a fifteen-mile front. More ominous was the enemy's heavy retaliatory artillery fire—a grim indication that while the British bombardment had battered the German defences to a pulp, most of the German guns to the rear had escaped virtually unscathed.[2]

There was a more subtle effect resulting from the millions of artillery shells fired by the British. The countryside is not only remarkably flat, but also the water-table is very high and the drainage system very delicate. Much of that system was destroyed in the initial bombardment, although this would not be a factor unless and until it rained.

It rained heavily on the afternoon of 31 July. At a conference of corps commanders that night, Gough called the downpour "a perfect bloody curse." The rainfall continued for several more days. "A terrible day of rain," Haig remarked in his diary on 1 August. "The ground is like a bog in this low-lying country." By 4 August conditions had deteriorated to such an extent that Haig reluctantly put a temporary halt to his offensive, though his orders merely confirmed reality: the BEF was already bogged down. The same day, his intelligence chief, Charteris, commented:

> All my fears about the weather have been realized. It has killed this attack.... I went up to the front line this morning. Every brook is swollen and the ground is a quagmire. If it were not that all the records of previous years had given us fair warning, it would seem as if Providence had declared against us.[3]

Charteris's persistent claims about the weather records have given rise to one of the oddest aspects of Passchendaele. "Careful investigation of the records of more than eighty years showed that in Flanders the weather broke each August with the regularity of the Indian monsoon," he later wrote, adding that this information was "pressed on Haig by his staff, and particularly by the Intelligence Service." Lieutenant-Colonel E. Gold, the officer commanding GHQ's meteorological section, many years afterward disputed the intelligence chief's contention, saying that it was "too ridiculous to need formal refutation." On the contrary, Gold insisted, the precipitation was far from predictable. "The rainfall directly affecting the first month of the offensive was more than double the average; *it was over five times the amount for the same period in 1915 and in 1916.*" What is beyond dispute, however, is the fact that the rain fell remorselessly, and stopped the BEF in its tracks.[4]

The battlefield conditions were terrible. "The low-lying clayey soil, torn by shells and sodden by rain, turned to a succession of vast muddy pools," Haig later wrote.

> The valleys of the choked and overflowing streams were speedily transformed into long stretches of bog, impassable except by a few well-defined tracks, which became marks for the enemy's artillery. To leave these tracks was to risk death by drowning.... In these conditions operations became impossible, and the resumption of our offensive was necessarily postponed until a period of fine weather should allow the ground to recover.

Haig's distress was evident in a letter to his wife on 7 August. "It has stopped raining here, but is still very cloudy and misty in the mornings," he lamented. "This is rather disappointing especially as the weather is brilliantly fine in Paris I hear."[5]

It was doubly frustrating because the field-marshal believed that he was on the brink of a great victory. "Everything points to a distinct deterioration of the enemy's morale," he told his diary. "We hear of their men refusing to stay in the front trenches and, guns no longer being accurate through wear, German infantry are losing faith in their own artillery." He suggested the same thing in a letter home: "It is highly satisfactory to see that the morale of the German troops is steadily getting worse. In fact quite a change has occurred since Messines."[6]

One of the lingering controversies concerning this campaign relates to the use of tanks. First introduced in September 1916 at the Somme, tanks had become a familiar sight on British battlefields.

The standard model in use at this time was the Mark IV, twenty-six feet long, eight feet high, and weighing thirty tons or more, depending on the armament: the "male" tank was equipped with two 6-pounder guns and four machine-guns while the "female" carried six machine-guns. Manned by a crew of seven, the Mark IV was mechanically unreliable and had a very limited range. And it was slow: a 105-horsepower, six-cylinder Daimler engine meant that the Mark IV was "somewhat under-powered," capable of a mere 3.7 miles per hour—on a pocked and battered battlefield, it struggled to manage even half that speed. Clearly, the tank was not yet a weapon that could win wars.[7]

The employment of tanks in Flanders angered and embittered the officers and men of the newly formed Tank Corps. "If a careful search had been made from the English Channel to Switzerland, no more unsuitable spot could have been discovered," claimed Brigadier-General C.D. Baker-Carr, a tank brigade commander. According to Colonel Ernest Swinton, the man most responsible for creation of the tank, "nothing can be said in defence of the fatuous employment of machines, weighing over thirty tons, in the liquid mud of what degenerated into a swamp battle...." As early as 3 August, the Tank Corps had appealed to GHQ to withdraw the tanks. A memorandum issued that day claimed: "From a tank point of view, the Third Battle of Ypres may be considered dead. To go on using tanks in the present conditions will not only lead to good machines and better personnel being thrown away, but also to a loss of morale...."[8]

These criticisms are rather one-sided. True, the tanks were operating at a disadvantage. But their worth in overcoming enemy strongpoints and uncut barbed wire cannot be exaggerated: to deny the infantry the support of these invaluable weapons, even when tactically misused, would have been irresponsible. The losses were regrettable—of 117 tanks engaged, seventy-seven broke down or were ditched, and more than half of them could not be salvaged—but the fact remains that the mechanical monsters were most helpful in those instances where they could find traction. As a consequence, the tanks remained in action in Flanders until 9 October, when they were finally withdrawn.

The Fifth Army tried three times in August to revive the offensive. Gough's brave but weary troops struggled forward on 10 August, again on the sixteenth, and once more on the twenty-second. The fighting added to the British military annals several infamous and heartbreaking names: Glencorse Wood, Inverness Copse, Polygon Wood, Nonne Boschen. The weather remained a steadfast enemy of the British. Incredibly, each time they attacked during August 1917, it rained—"deluged" would be a better word. One disillusioned observer declared, "It is very odd how each of the attacks we have delivered...this summer has been accompanied by an exceptional storm. I had never really believed in a personal devil until this summer." The condition of the battlefield went from bad to worse. "The shape of the ground was by this time frightful," Sir Hubert Gough wrote.

> The labour of bringing up supplies and ammunition, of moving or firing the guns, which had often sunk up to their axles, was a fearful strain on the officers and men, even during the daily task of maintaining the battle front. When it came to the advance of infantry for an attack, across the water-logged shell-holes, movement was so slow and so fatiguing that only the shortest advances could be contemplated.

Gough's conclusion was amply justified: "No battle in history was ever fought under such conditions as that of Passchendaele."[9]

The weather did more than slow the British advance. It led to an exaggerated view of the casualties being suffered. The BEF's August gains were minuscule, to be sure, but its losses, contrary to popular belief, were not unduly heavy. By month's end, British casualties numbered 68,010, hardly extraordinary by Great War standards, and considerably less than those incurred during the first month of the Somme offensive a year earlier. What was unusual, however, was the large number of dead, both British and German, left unburied on the battlefield. The heavy rain seriously impeded the normally efficient British burial squads, and even hardened veterans were shocked at the spectacle of so many corpses strewn about, a grotesque sight that left the mistaken impression that casualties were much heavier than they really were—and myths die hard.

There was another factor with which the British had to contend. The Germans had adopted a new scheme of defence, abandoning the familiar trenches in favour of something more suitable and effective in these wet and muddy conditions, as Gough later related:

> The defence now took the form of small machine-gun posts in the most defensible localities and in the driest places, supporting each other. The Germans during the course of the previous two years had also built small but very powerful concrete shelters [called "pillboxes"]. These were covered with mud and scattered throughout the desert of wet shell-holes which stretched in every

direction. They were impossible to locate from a distance, and in any case were safe against anything but the very heaviest shells. The farms, most of them surrounded by very broad wet ditches, or moats, had also been heavily concreted within their shattered walls; every one of these was a fort in itself.[10]

The cumulative effect of these factors—the slow advance, the seemingly catastrophic casualties, an unseen enemy—was most debilitating. Gamely, the troops tried and tried again to reach their objectives: as their frustration mounted, morale sagged in direct proportion. Typical of these feelings is a comment by a survivor, Lieutenant J.W. Naylor of the Royal Artillery:

> I came to hate the salient. Absolutely loathed it.... It wore you down. The weather, the lack of rations, everything seemed to be against you. There didn't seem to be anything left. You were wet through for days on end. We never thought we'd get out alive. You couldn't see the cloud with the silver lining. There wasn't one.... I just felt, "What the hell's the use of going on? I don't care a damn who wins this war." Well, the morale can't get much lower than that. It was a nightmare.[11]

Others echoed those sentiments. Second-Lieutenant H.L. Birks of the Tank Corps remembered that "you got the strangest feeling" when entering the salient. "You'd almost abandon hope. And as soon as you got further out you got this awful smell of death." Major George Wade of the South Staffordshire Regiment recalled "that there were bodies every few yards. Some lying face downwards in the mud; others showing by the expressions fixed on their faces the sort of effort they had made to get back on the track. Sometimes you could actually see blood seeping up from underneath." The mud and its hidden horrors were etched indelibly in the minds of many, including Private Charlie Miles of the 10th Royal Fusiliers:

> The moment you set off you felt that dreaded suction. It was forever pulling you down, and you could hear the sound of your feet coming out in a kind of sucking "plop" that seemed much louder at night when you were on your own. In a way, it was worse when the mud didn't suck you down; when it yielded under your feet you knew that it was a body you were treading on. It was terrifying. You'd tread on one on the stomach, perhaps, and it would grunt all the air out of its body. It made your hair stand on end.

The widespread devastation added to the troops' misery. "There was no sign of civilisation," recalled Lieutenant Paddy King of the East Lancashire Regiment. "No cottages, no buildings, no trees. It was utter desolation. There was nothing at all except huge craters, half the size of a room. They were full of water and the corpses were floating in them. Some with no heads. Some with no legs." Lieutenant Jim Annan of the 1/9th Royal Scots Regiment spoke for many when he said that he "couldn't understand why, in the name of God, anyone had ordered an attack like that over terrain like that. It was impossible."[12]

The strain soon showed among senior officers as well. An angry Major-General G.M. Harper of the 51st (Highland) Division growled to war correspondent Philip Gibbs, "We tell the public that an enemy division has been 'shattered.' That is true. But so is mine." Gibbs talked with brigadiers in two Irish divisions, the 36th (Ulster) and the 16th (Nationalist), which had been roughly handled by the Germans on 16 August; the officers denounced what they called the "murder" of their men, while others were critical of what they claimed was "atrocious staff-work" at Fifth Army headquarters.[13]

The widespread lack of confidence in Sir Hubert Gough, specifically, and in his staff, generally, was alarming. Gibbs wrote of meeting a group of officers departing for another front. "You must be glad to leave Flanders," he said, to which one officer bluntly replied: "God be thanked we are leaving the Fifth Army area!"[14]

Gibbs was deeply disturbed. "For the first time," he wrote, "the British army lost its spirit of optimism, and there was a sense of deadly depression among many officers and men with whom I came in touch. They saw no ending of the war, and nothing except continuous slaughter, such as that in Flanders." In what Gibbs called "that Slough of Despond," the BEF teetered dangerously near the brink of demoralization. Only the discipline and dogged determination for which the British soldier is rightly renowned kept the army from slipping over the edge.[15]

It was, ironically, General Gough who was trying hardest to end his army's suffering. He told Field-Marshal Haig that "tactical success was not possible, or would be too costly, under such conditions, and advised that the attack should now be abandoned." Years later, Gough would charge that Haig lacked what he called "a proper sense of proportion" in pursuing the Flanders offensive.[16]

But Haig had no intention of quitting just yet. "In my opinion the war can only be won here in Flanders," he insisted, contending that "there is only one possible plan to win the war and that is to go on attacking in Flanders until we have driven the German Armies out of it." Never was Haig more determined than he was in August 1917. "We are now fighting what may well be the decisive battle of the war," he told an army commanders' conference on the twenty-first. "It is essential that we should be in a position to *continue the battle well into November.* By this means, and by this means only, can we ensure final victory by wearing out the enemy's resistance."[17]

Haig seems to have been blissfully unaware that in his single-minded effort to wear out the Germans, he was also wearing down the British army. Insulated from reality by an overprotective staff, and handicapped by his inability to communicate with the common soldiers, such a possibility could not have occurred to him, so great was his blind faith in the superiority of his army to that of the Germans. Certainly, he was as optimistic as ever. "The time is fast approaching," he declared, "when the enemy will be unable to maintain her armies." And he had no doubts about the outcome of the clash of empires now taking place in Flanders. "Personally I feel we have every reason to be optimistic, and, if the war were to end tomorrow, Great Britain would find herself not merely the greatest Power in Europe but in the world."[18]

One man who did not share Haig's high hopes was Prime Minister David Lloyd George. The stage was set for still more political interference in the military conduct of the war.

6 / "A Battle of Attrition"

The Flanders offensive had no sooner bogged down in early August than Lloyd George prepared to call the whole thing off. "I have said, and am still saying, that we must hit the enemy elsewhere," he told Sir George Riddell on 6 August. "We must formulate new plans. Our soldiers have no imagination."[1]

The prime minister wasted no time. He convened, on 8 and 9 August, an inter-Allied conference in London to resurrect that old chestnut: aid for Italy. "It was of the usual character and resulted in the usual waste of time," Sir William Robertson wrote Haig afterward. Robertson once again waylaid Lloyd George's proposal, arguing "that no reinforcement of the Italian Front could be made before next Spring and could not be *considered* until after the present operations on the Western Front have been completed and we see the results of them."[2]

Haig was delighted. He promptly wrote Robertson to press for more men and guns, arguing that since Flanders was "the decisive point, the only *sound* policy is for the Govt. to support me *wholeheartedly* and concentrate all possible resources here. And do it *now* while there is time, instead of continuing to discuss other enterprises.... Moreover, I have been in the field now for 3 years and know what I am writing about. The Foreigners have certainly misled our Govt. Yet, from what you say, I see the Prime Minister himself prefers the advice which they tender to your and my opinion."[3]

As Robertson would soon find, Haig's plea for more manpower and material would become a familiar refrain. On 16 August, when the CIGS arrived at GHQ for a brief visit, Haig told him that "what I want is *tangible* support. It is ridiculous to talk about supporting me 'wholeheartedly' when men, guns, rails, etc. are going in quantities to Egypt for the Palestine expedition; guns to the Italians, to Mesopotamia and to Russia." A few days later, Haig again appealed to Robertson: "You must force the Govt. to give me the means to keep going."[4]

This was easier said than done. In fact, the CIGS was already making himself most unpopular with the prime minister, who later complained:

> As the futile massacres of August piled up the ghastly hecatombs of slaughter on the Ypres Front without achieving any appreciable result, I repeatedly approached Sir William Robertson to remind

him of the condition attached to the Cabinet's assent of the operation. It was to be abandoned as soon as it became evident that its aims were unattainable this year and our attention was to be concentrated on an Italian offensive. He was immovable.... According to him everything pointed to the growing exhaustion of the German Army. Why give in when we might be near a real triumph for our arms?[5]

But Lloyd George's nagging was taking its toll. "The powers that be," a concerned Robertson wrote Haig, "are beginning to get a little uneasy in regard to the situation. The casualties are mounting up, and Ministers... will persist in asking whether *I* think a loss of, say, 300,000 men will lead to really great results, because if not we ought to be content with something less than we are now doing...."[6]

Robertson resented the prime minister's meddling in military matters. He also despised Lloyd George's close associates. "The other members of the War Cabinet seem afraid of him," the CIGS confided in Haig. "Milner is a tired, dyspeptic old man. Curzon is a gas-bag. Bonar Law equals Bonar Law. Smuts has good instinct but lacks knowledge. On the whole he is best, but they help one very little." Haig shared Robertson's frustration. "How unfortunate the country seems to be to have such an unreliable man at the head of affairs in this crisis."[7]

However, Lloyd George was bent on thwarting the designs of his generals. The only thing that held him back was the fear of precipitating a crisis that could cost him the prime-ministership. In mid-August, for example, Sir Maurice Hankey remarked, "The P.M. is obviously puzzled... how far the Government is justified in interfering with a military operation." Another opening soon presented itself. On 17 August the Italians, under their commander-in-chief, Luigi Cadorna, had launched the Eleventh Battle of the Isonzo in another brave but fruitless attempt to break through powerful Austrian positions in the Alps. Initial reports, however, seemed to suggest success, which had a considerable impact on 10 Downing Street. On 26 August, Hankey "found Lloyd George in a ferment of excitement about Cadorna's victory" and raving about "the great opportunity opened up, particularly in view of the failure of the Flanders offensive, consequent on the continuous rain."[8]

Lloyd George moved quickly. Two days later, on 28 August, he convened his war cabinet to review Haig's campaign. Although he was unable to convince his colleagues to order a halt to further Flanders attacks, he did win an important concession: an inter-Allied conference would be held in London on 4 September. At that time, Lloyd George renewed his proposal to send aid to Italy, in the form of heavy artillery which the Italian army lacked. Haig and Robertson, predictably, opposed the measure, but they were undermined by the French military representative, General Ferdinand Foch, who favoured support for the Italian front, wrote Haig, "because the *political* effect of a success there would be greater, in his opinion, than one in Flanders." Haig reluctantly acquiesced, announcing that "I was prepared to liberate 100 guns (about) from French First Army provided General Pétain could replace them in time for the attack as planned." When Pétain agreed to Haig's condition, the guns were promptly dispatched to Italy.[9]

The prime minister was overjoyed. "My colleagues and I are much gratified," he wrote Haig, "at the manner in which you have met them in regard to Italy. Please accept our best thanks for the promptitude with which you have carried out our wishes in a matter which was of great importance to the interallied policy."[10] However, his happiness was short-lived. The French guns had no sooner been dispatched than the Italians, tired of battering their heads against a brick wall in the Alps, abruptly ended their offensive and dug in for the winter.

Lloyd George could scarcely conceal his anguish. "This Italian volte-face has given him a rude shock," observed Lord Derby, the secretary for war, in a letter to Haig, "and in that way has done good in showing how absolutely we must rely on ourselves and not on our Allies." Haig, at his next meeting with the prime minister, commented that Lloyd George was "most friendly. Very much down on the Italians; there is now no intention of sending a British force there!" But the prime minister was a man of mercurial moods, as Sir Maurice Hankey discovered in mid-September: "I found him rather despondent at the failure of the year's campaigning, and disgusted at the narrowness of the General Staff, and the inability of his colleagues to see eye to eye with him and their fear of overruling the General Staff." The prime minister later summed up his dilemma this way:

> Passchendaele could not have been stopped without dismissing Sir Douglas Haig.... But I could not have done it without the assent of the Cabinet. I sounded the Ministers of the Cabinet individually on the subject and I also spoke to some of the Dominion representatives. They—or most of them—were under the spell of the synthetic victories distilled at G.H.Q.[11]

At least one of his ministers shared his concern about the Flanders offensive. In a letter to Lloyd George on 18 September, Andrew Bonar Law admitted having "lost absolutely all hope of anything coming of Haig's offensive" and warned that "the time must soon come when we will have to decide whether or not this offensive is to be allowed to go on." Lloyd George, certainly, did not want it to go on, telling Hankey that he preferred "to abandon all activity on the Western Front and to concentrate our efforts against Turkey."[12]

The prime minister quickly produced a plethora of ideas, all of which Wully Robertson resisted to the best of his ability. "I have had to knock out a scheme for operating in the Aden hinterland involving the employment of not less than a division," the CIGS advised Haig on 24 September. "I have also had to destroy one for landing ten divisions at Alexandretta, all of which would have come from you. Further, I have had to fight against sending more divisions to Mesopotamia. Generally, all round, I have been quite successful, although the expenditure of energy which ought to have been otherwise employed has been a little greater than usual."[13]

Haig, meanwhile, was preparing to resume his offensive in Flanders. He maintained that the most effective strategy for the British was "that we should go on striking as hard as possible with the object of clearing the Belgian coast. We should be prepared to make and win this campaign."[14]

Eminent historians, taking their cue from Lloyd George's vitriolic memoirs, have condemned the commander-in-chief for continuing his campaign. "To persist after the close of August in this tactically impossible battle," commented J.F.C. Fuller, "was an inexcusable piece of pigheadedness on the part of Haig...."[15] But such criticism does not stand up to close scrutiny. Unaware of the morale problems and having unbounded confidence in the BEF, Haig had no reason to stop at this point. He believed, with justification, that it had been the weather, far more than any obstacles imposed by the Germans, that had slowed his advance. The bad weather, he knew, could not last forever, and he rightly looked forward to more substantial progress when the ground firmed up.

But he recognized that changes had to be made. He was finally ready to admit that Sir Hubert Gough had been a mistake. Haig had been thoroughly frustrated by Gough's unwillingness to devote his full attention to the high ground on his army's right flank. On 2 August, Haig had met Gough and, as he told his diary, "I showed him on my relief map the importance of the Broodseinde-Passchendaele ridge, and gave it as my opinion that his main effort must be devoted to capturing that. Not until it was in his possession could he hope to advance his centre." But Gough persisted in making his attacks on a broad front, with the emphasis to the north. Haig repeated his concerns in a meeting with Gough on the fifteenth. "I told Gough that, looking at the development of his advance, I did not wish a direct attack made on the Forêt D'Houthoulst [sic]. It would be very costly, and would be playing the enemy's game to embark on a large battle in a forest." Haig's dissatisfaction was evident the next night, with the failure of the day's attack by Fifth Army.

> The cause of the failure to advance on the right centre of the attack of the Fifth Army is due, I think, to commanders being in too great a hurry! Three more days should have been allowed in which (if fine and observation good) the artillery would have dominated the enemy's artillery and destroyed his concrete defences.[16]

Haig was profoundly disappointed with Gough. Later, he privately admitted that "some orders he issued and things he did were stupid," complaining that "the Fifth Army staff work is not so satisfactory as last year." On 25 August, Haig acted. He placed Sir Herbert Plumer in overall command of the campaign, in effect reversing his and Gough's roles: Plumer's Second Army would now make the main effort, against the ridge that Haig considered so important, with Gough and the Fifth Army protecting its flank.[17]

This time, there would be no mistaking the main objective. Haig made sure of that at a conference of senior officers on 1 September. According to General Charteris, Haig's intelligence chief, it was the British intention now to "concentrate everything on the capture of Passchendaele Ridge, which D.H. has designated of overwhelming tactical and strategical importance." Plumer would employ a policy of strictly limited and deliberate advances, as outlined in tactical notes issued in early August by GHQ to army, corps, and divisional headquarters:

> We must exhaust the enemy as much as possible *and ourselves as little as possible* in the early stages of the fight. Later, when he is so exhausted and disorganized that he cannot hit back effectively, we can push our advance to its utmost limits and call on our men to the utmost limits of their endurance; at that stage all the ground we desire to gain can be taken with comparative ease.
> In short, in the earlier stages of the offensive our further objective must be not only within the power of our artillery, but within the power of our infantry (having regard to the state of the

and not play second fiddle to the French, etc., etc., and all this when shortly before he must have quietly acquiesced at the Conference in Painlevé's demands! R. comes badly out of this, in my opinion....[22]

The Haig-Robertson partnership had been dealt a fatal blow. Haig doubtless remembered Robertson's momentary loss of heart in June, prior to their joint appearance before the war policy committee in London. Now there was the Boulogne affair and Robertson's inexplicable lack of candour. Whatever the reasons for his reticence, Robertson must have realized he had made a serious error, as he wrote Haig several days later: "I gather...that you are perhaps a little disappointed with me in the way I have stood up for correct principles, but you must let me do my job in my own way. I have never yet given in on important matters and never shall. In any case, whatever happens, you and I must stand solid together."[23] But the damage had been done, as Robertson would discover a few short months hence.

In the meantime, Plumer's Second Army launched its next attack on 4 October. It was a complete success. Spearheaded by tough Australian troops, the British captured the village of Broodseinde and the surrounding heights. The advance cost 20,000 casualties, but Plumer called it "the greatest victory since the Marne [in 1914]."[24] He now cast his eyes on the primary objective, the high ground around Passchendaele, which was at last within striking distance.

It is interesting to contrast the outcome of 4 October's operations on the respective high commands. The Germans called it a "black day." Their losses had been, according to the German official history, "extraordinarily severe.... The Army High Command came to the conclusion that there was no means by which the positions could be held against the overpowering enemy superiority in artillery and infantry. Loss of ground in these heavy attacks was unavoidable. Up to now the High Command had tried to cover the heavy losses suffered in these giant battles but it would not be possible to do this for very long...." A change in tactics was needed; the Germans would now be "less concerned with a determined retention of the marked fighting zones than in a more elastic defence—where necessary, a limited yielding at the main points of pressure and counter-attacks against the flanks of an attack." There can be no mistaking German policy at this point; the enemy was simply hoping to buy time until the advent of winter mercifully forced an end to the bludgeoning being inflicted by the British.[25]

So desperate were the Germans that they planned a pre-emptive attack of their own. Tentatively scheduled for 5 October, it was to have been delivered about Gheluvelt, against the Second Army's right flank. While admitting that they did not expect to make a significant advance, the Germans hoped that such a blow "would constrict the British, would compel them to regroup and would bring their offensive to a halt. It would be of great significance if we could win just eight days until the onset of winter."[26] But the British, attacking on the fourth, beat them to the punch. Unable to muster the necessary resources, including fresh troops, the German attack was cancelled.

Haig, on the other hand, was justifiably pleased, calling 4 October "a very important success." At long last, his plans were paying dividends. The Germans, he believed, were close to collapse—at the very least they were, as shown above, reeling under the repeated British blows—and he felt the the fruits of victory would soon be his. Like a boxer looking for the knockout punch, he moved in for the kill. Given continued fair weather, great things were still possible, as he outlined in his diary on the fifth:

> My view is *first,* capture the Passchendaele-Stadenburg ridge; *second,* clear Forêt d'Houthoulst [*sic*] by advancing to Staden on the east side of it, so as to turn it; *third,* Second Army to take Moorslede ridge and Roulers, Fifth Army Hooglede and Thourout. The French to take Cortemarck, Zarren and Hill N.E. The Belgians to cover flank.[27]

The offensive in Flanders was, finally, unfolding as Haig had envisaged it. But it was about to enter its most controversial phase.

7/More Mud and Blood

It rained on 4 October, a fine, light shower that settled the dust. During the night it developed into a downpour, drenching everything in sight. The rain continued to fall, day after day, and the battlefield once more dissolved into "one vast tormented bog," in the words of an observer; so grim were things that the artillery's guns "sank in the mud till they became useless and ultimately disappeared beneath the surface" in several instances.[1]

Haig conferred with his army commanders, Plumer and Gough, on 5 October. GHQ's intelligence chief, General Charteris, commented on the lack of enthusiasm for continuing the campaign. "We are far enough on now to stop for the winter," he wrote after the meeting, "and there is much to be said for that. Unless we get fine weather for all this month, there is now no chance of clearing the coast.... Most of those at the conference, though willing to go on, would welcome a stop." However, Haig was determined to carry on. In view of the adverse weather, he decided to advance the dates of the Second Army's next two operations, to 9 and 12 October, hoping that they could be mounted before the ground became impassable. Haig told Plumer "that there should be no postponement unless absolutely necessary."[2]

Why did Haig persist? "The year was far spent," he later explained. "The weather had been consistently unpropitious, and the state of the ground, in consequence of rain and shelling combined, made movement inconceivably difficult." At the same time, he observed that "there was no reason to anticipate an abnormally wet October. The enemy had suffered severely, as was evidenced by the number of prisoners in our hands, by the number of his dead on the battlefield, by the costly failure of his counter-attacks, and by the symptoms of confusion and discouragement in his ranks." Weighing all of these factors, Haig concluded: "I decided to continue the offensive further." It was a predictable decision; Haig would not quit after the repeated failures in August, and was not about to quit after three successive and impressive victories in late September-early October.[3]

Prime Minister Lloyd George was convinced that Haig "had completely lost his balance by this point," that he "alone retained his faith in the merits and ultimate triumph of his project." And for this the prime minister blamed Charteris, the intelligence chief at GHQ. Lloyd George believed that Haig's unbounded optimism was largely due to "Charteris' extravagant reports as to German losses, German morale, broken German divisions, German shortage of ammunition, and generally, to the gradual fading away of German might...." There is, for once, some truth in Lloyd George's comments.[4]

Brigadier-General John Charteris was a loyal and devoted servant of Haig's. He had been on the latter's staff in the peacetime army and had accompanied him to the Continent in 1914, being named an intelligence officer despite his lack of specific training. Charteris, who wryly remarked that "Military Intelligence...is a contradiction in terms," learned his trade quickly. As his confidence grew, so too did his belief in his own reports and forecasts. Like Haig, he was by nature an optimist and was admittedly influenced by Wully Robertson's declaration that "a pessimist is more useless than a coward in war."[5]

It is possible that Charteris tried too hard to please his master, that he fed the commander-in-chief information that Haig wanted and expected to receive. And, by the same token, he ignored negative news and views, as illustrated by an incident early in the Flanders offensive. The Tank Corps was protesting the use of its precious and few tanks, and a staff officer, Major J.F.C. Fuller—the same Fuller who, years later, denounced Haig's "pigheadedness" in pursuing the offensive—sent Charteris a map showing the flooded ground on which the tanks would have to operate. Charteris was not merely uninterested, he was rather annoyed with Fuller and bluntly told him, "Pray, do not send any more of these ridiculous maps." He then confided in a fellow staff officer: "I'm certainly not going to show *this* to the Commander-in-Chief. It would only depress him."[6]

Yet, Haig was not blameless. "In war," he once said, "we tend to believe what we wish for," and this was true in Haig's case. He sometimes read too much into Charteris's forecasts, causing his intelligence chief no little discomfort. There are two notable examples, in June and August 1917. In June, an alarmed Charteris observed that in Haig's presentation to the war policy committee in London, "D.H. gave the definite opinion that if the fighting was kept up at its present intensity for six months Germany would be at the end of her available man-power. This is going rather further than the paper I wrote for D.H. on the 11th of June." In August, Charteris complained that "D.H. has not only accepted in *toto* my report on fighting up to the 16th, but has gone much farther. He has reported to W.O. [War Office] that 'the time is fast approaching when Germany will be unable to maintain her armies at their present numerical strength [and that] a large portion of their defending troops are reported both by our own men and by prisoners to have run away'."[7]

Haig was man enough to accept his responsibility. Aware of the criticism directed at Charteris, he wrote: "The responsibility for the judgment formed on the evidence obtained... rests on me and not on him; and if the War Cabinet are not satisfied with the views put forward by me it is I, and not Charteris, who must answer for those views."[8]

But there is no doubt that Haig was influenced, consciously or otherwise, by Charteris. The commander-in-chief's innate optimism was fuelled by the glowing reports from his intelligence chief. The Charteris factor was most evident in early October 1917, when Haig was convinced that he had the German army on the ropes. At a conference on 2 October, Haig noted in his diary that "Charteris emphasised the deterioration of the German Divisions in numbers, morale and all-round efficiency." Following another conference two days later, Haig again observed that "Charteris, who was present, thought that from the number of German regiments represented amongst the prisoners, all Divisions had been seriously engaged and that there were few more available reserves."[9]

How accurate were these views? The Germans were nowhere near the breaking point, as Haig believed—or wished—but the German army had been rocked to its very foundation by the Flanders offensive. The enemy's de facto commander-in-chief, Erich Ludendorff, later confessed that this "was a period of tremendous anxiety." He was personally under "a terrible strain," and German casualties "had been so high as to cause grave misgivings, and had exceeded all expectations." His troops "no longer displayed that firmness which I... had hoped for." The British tactics, too, were causing concern. "The depth of penetration," Ludendorff admiringly admitted, "was limited so as to secure immunity from our counter-attacks, and the latter was then broken up by the massed fire of artillery." The British offensive, in Ludendorff's opinion, "proved the superiority of the attack over the defense...."[10]

And so Sir Douglas Haig prepared to continue his campaign. But before he could so, he had to endure another confrontation with Prime Minister Lloyd George. The prime minister, during his visit to GHQ in late September, had asked for Haig's opinion of the overall war situation, particularly in view of Russia's imminent demise as an ally. Haig's lengthy memorandum was presented to a meeting of the war cabinet on 8 October. In it, he repeated all the familiar arguments, insisting that the

> indispensable condition of decisive success on the Western Front is that the War Cabinet should have a firm faith in its possibility and

resolve finally and unreservedly to concentrate our resources in seeking it, and to do so at once. To gain decisive success... we have need of every man, gun and aeroplane that can be provided.... We cannot afford to assist [our allies] directly, and it is not in their own interests that the efforts of the only really effective offensive army [i.e., the BEF] which will exist in the Alliance next year should throw away what is a good prospect and practically the only prospect of a real victory by disseminating its forces. Victory against a strong and determined foe has never been won by such a course and never can be.[11]

Sir William Robertson considered Haig's memo to be "splendid," but the prime minister begged to differ. Calling it an "inebriated document," Lloyd George sourly observed that "it seemed to me to be more concerned with convincing the Cabinet of the importance of prosecuting the Passchendaele offensive and of guaranteeing to the Commander-in-Chief an unfailing supply of men to fill up casualties than it was with the problem which I had submitted to him." But Lloyd George was unable to convince his cabinet colleagues that the Flanders campaign should be halted, much to his anguished disappointment: "We are losing the flower of our army, and to what purpose?" he raged. "What have we achieved?"[12]

To someone reading the daily war maps published in *The Times* of London, it must have seemed as if nothing was being achieved in Flanders. But wars are not won by moving calipers on a map.

Nevertheless, Haig's offensive was headed for its nadir. The rain in Flanders fell mainly in torrents. (The Germans were, naturally, delighted. Crown Prince Rupprecht described the rain as "our most effective ally.") The evening before the Second Army's scheduled attack, a concerned Haig went to Plumer's headquarters. "It was raining and looked like a wet night," Sir Douglas related in his diary. "[Plumer] stated that 2nd Anzac Corps (which is chiefly concerned in to-morrow's attack) had specially asked that there should be *no postponement*.... I ordered them to carry on."[13]

The assault on 9 October was a failure. Due to the hurried preparations and poor weather, there was little co-ordination between the artillery and the infantry. The mud was, unbelievably, worse than ever: one British battalion, the 2/8th Lancashire Fusiliers, exhausted itself moving up to the front lines, spending more than eleven hours struggling to cover a distance that normally would have required barely an hour's march. By the end of the day, the Second Army had little to show for the 20,000 casualties it had suffered. It was "the saddest day of the war," according to General Charteris, at GHQ.

> We did fairly well but only fairly well. It was not the enemy but mud that prevented us doing better. But there is now no chance of complete success here this year. We *must* still fight on for a few more weeks, but there is no purpose in it now, so far as Flanders is concerned.

Late that night he discussed the situation with Haig who, he noted, "was still trying to find some grounds for hope that we might still win through here this year, but there is none."[14]

However, Haig was not ready to give up just yet. He insisted that "we ought to have only one thought now in our minds, namely, *to attack*," explaining his reasoning this way: "Though the condition of the ground continued to deteriorate, the weather after this was unsettled rather than persistently wet, and progress had not yet become impossible. I accordingly decided to press on while circumstances still permitted...."[15]

His mood was buoyed by the attitude of the Australians and New Zealanders who would spearhead the Second Army's next thrust. Haig commented in his diary on 10 October:

> The 3rd Australian Division and New Zealand Division [which comprised Sir Alexander Godley's II Anzac Corps] go into the line again tonight. Gough told me they are determined to take Passchendaele in the next attack and will put the Australian flag on it! The advance will be then over 2,000 yards. But the enemy is now much weakened in morale and lacks the desire to fight.[16]

Had confidence alone been enough, the Australians and New Zealanders would have taken Passchendaele on 12 October. A patrol of the 38th Australian Battalion actually reached the ruined little village on the ridge; Passchendaele was empty, but the Australians had no support and quietly withdrew. Elsewhere, II Anzac Corps was stopped in its tracks. The torrential rain made movement in the mud almost impossible and, even worse, the infantry had virtually no artillery support. The barrage was so feeble that, according to one battalion history, "We made no attempt to conform to it. There was really nothing to conform to."[17] Particularly deadly was a massive barbed-wire entanglement that was left intact at Bellevue Spur, which blocked the approach to Passchendaele; hung up on the uncut wire, the Anzacs were mowed down by the German machine-guns on the heights.

These back-to-back failures had a devastating impact on the Anzacs. Morale was crushed, just as it had been in the rest of the BEF during the reverses in August. "Our men are being put into the hottest fighting and are being sacrificed in hair-brained ventures...," fumed Major-General John Monash, commanding the 3rd Australian Division. (In fairness, it should be pointed out that Monash had earlier been in favour of these "hair-brained ventures" and endorsed the hurried preparations that had contributed to defeat.) His troops were overcome by sheer exhaustion, which was intensified by feelings of futility. Confessed one young lieutenant: "I feel about eighty years old now." An Australian war correspondent was shocked at the sight of his countrymen returning from the front lines. "They were white and drawn and detached, and put one foot slowly in front of another, as I had not seen men do since the Somme winter... but these men looked whiter."[18]

It would have been small consolation to know that the Germans were in equally bad shape. Crown Prince Rupprecht commented on 11 October:

> Our troops, on the chief fighting front in Flanders, are in a fair degree of confusion. The disentangling of formations is in progress.... Most troublesome is the fact that our fighting force becomes all the time of poorer quality, and that every means [of defence] that we thought out is ineffective as a counter to the overwhelming superiority of the enemy's artillery. As it is a matter, for us, of fighting to gain time, nothing else remains except by repeated withdrawal to force the enemy to a fresh time-consuming advance of his artillery.[19]

Sir Douglas Haig was far from discouraged, and intended to continue the offensive. Deeming it "desirable to maintain the pressure on the Flanders front for a few weeks longer," he informed Plumer and Gough of his decision on 13 October. However, he insisted that further attacks on Passchendaele Ridge "should only be launched when there is a fair prospect of fine weather. *When the ground is dry* no opposition which the enemy has put up has been able to stop our men." In other words, it was the weather, and not the German army, which was Haig's main obstacle.* Having fought here in the first few months of the war, Haig had reason to believe that the weather would get better. "The rain has upset our arrangements a great deal," he wrote Lady Haig, "but I still hope that the weather

---

* It was a conviction shared by many. Lieutenant-General Sir William Birdwood, commanding I Anzac Corps, later wrote: "I still feel that if only the weather had held, Haig might well have achieved an epic victory."[20]

may take up before long and the ground become as dry as it was in 1914 at the end of October."[21]

Haig did himself no favours by conjuring up a post-war excuse for continuing the campaign. In a 1927 letter to General Charteris, Haig claimed that "the possibility of the French Army breaking up in 1917 *compelled me to go on attacking.*" In another letter to his former director of military operations, Sir John Davidson, he wrote:

> The problem for us was how to prevent the Germans from attacking the French who were incapable of offering an effective resistance. The mere suggestion of a pause in our attacks in the north at once brought Pétain in his train to see me and beg me to put into another effort against Passchendaele without delay. Knowing as I did what the *rotten* state of the French Army was in 1917 (for Pétain told me more than once of his awful anxieties), I felt thankful when the winter came and the French Army was still in the field.

This is nonsense. As Haig's personal correspondence reveals, he believed—correctly—that the French army had recovered from its internal troubles by late September; on the twenty-ninth of that month, he was advised "that the morale of the French troops is now excellent." Indeed, he raged at Pétain, privately, for repeatedly postponing a promised attack. When it was finally carried out, on 23 October, at Malmaison, it was a complete success, "*a definite turning-point*," in Pétain's opinion. And while complete recovery would not come until the emergence of the elderly, feisty Georges Clemenceau as premier the following month, the French had proven, in dozens of defensive actions since the spring, that they were hardly "incapable of offering effective resistance," as Haig claimed.[22]

In fact, Haig had valid military, and personal, reasons for continuing his offensive. From a military point of view, his options were limited. To simply stop and dig in—the latter being, at any rate, physically impossible in the mud—would have been as irresponsible as it was unacceptable; it would have left his soldiers right under the enemy's guns, in positions that were arguably worse, and certainly no better, than they were before the offensive was launched in July. To withdraw to more secure positions would have thrown away the tremendous sacrifices of the past two and a half months, not to mention the consequent impact on morale, both in the BEF and at home; that would have been equally irresponsible and unacceptable. Unable to stand, unable to pull back, Haig was faced with the only practicable course of action: to carry on.

There were other factors to take into account. Haig had every intention of renewing this campaign in April 1918, and possession of Passchendaele Ridge would give him a suitable springboard for further campaigning in Flanders.[23] In addition, Haig had authorized General Sir Julian Byng's Third Army to mount a history-making mass tank attack near Cambrai, in northern France, in November. It was therefore desirable to keep the Germans distracted as long as possible in Belgium.

And, finally, there was an important personal consideration: his job was on the line. Passchendaele had by now become a symbol of the fighting in Flanders, the focal point of the entire offensive. Failure to capture Passchendaele undoubtedly would have cost Haig his job; even his many political supporters could not have saved him—and probably would not have tried—from Lloyd George's wrath. As we have seen, Haig had good reason to fear for his future.* To date, Haig had little to show for his campaign, aside from a few square miles of muddy shell-holes and intelligence estimates of the damage inflicted on the German army—estimates which Lloyd George openly mocked and flatly refused to believe. The conclusion is inescapable: if Sir Douglas Haig was to continue as commander-in-chief of the BEF, he had to have Passchendaele.

The prospects were decidedly bleak. By most measures, his Flanders offensive had been a disappointment. The decisive victory he had anticipated had not materialized. The fighting he had expected to last a few weeks had now dragged on for the better part of three months. Far to the rear, Haig's cavalry continued to collect saddle sores, waiting in vain to exploit the promised breakthrough. Since 31 July the BEF had pushed a paltry six miles, at the cost of perhaps 200,000 casualties. Almost every division available to Haig had been committed to the Passchendaele battle at one time or another; fresh troops were a rare commodity in October 1917.

However, Haig did have a trump card, and he proposed now to play it. This was Sir Arthur Currie's Canadian Army Corps. The victors of Vimy Ridge would be summoned to save Haig's battle, not to mention his reputation and, quite possibly, his career.

On 13 October 1917, Haig decided that the Canadians should begin moving to Flanders "at once." The same day, General Currie received instructions to "submit plans for the capture of PASSCHEN-DAELE as soon as possible."[24]

---

* It is true that on several occasions during 1917, and again the following year, Haig expressed a willingness to be replaced if the government decided that it was in the Empire's best interest. But Haig's bid for martyrdom was not convincing. He said so privately, in letters to his wife, the King, and political friends like Lord Derby; significantly, he never mentioned it to the prime minister.

Part Three: The Canadians

8/Professional Amateurs

Lieutenant-General Sir Arthur Currie was not pleased at the prospect of going to Passchendaele. Currie, like many Canadian soldiers, had grim memories of the Ypres salient, and freely admitted that his "experience[s] in the salient in 1915 and in 1916 were such that I never wanted to see the place again." The orders to take the Canadian Corps to Flanders came as "a most bitter disappointment" to him.[1]

Sir Arthur was a remarkable man. Certainly, he did not look like the great soldier he had become. A very tall man, at six-foot-four, he was also somewhat overweight, tipping the scales at 250 pounds. His pear-shaped physique made it difficult to obtain uniforms that fit properly.

But appearances were deceiving. Currie's boyish smile, dry sense of humour, and inherent shyness endeared him to his staff. Blessed with abundant common sense and a prodigious memory, he knew how to delegate authority and stand by the decisions of his subordinates, who were encouraged to come up with original ideas. Currie "always considered that any success that has come to me came largely from the fact that I endeavoured to surround myself with capable and efficient people." However, having made up his mind, he would stubbornly pursue what he considered to be the proper course. As a rule, Currie was calm and cool, even in a crisis, a reflection of his self-confidence and deep religious conviction. On those infrequent occasions when he lost his temper, he displayed "a tremendous command of profanity... when he cut loose he could go for about a minute without repetition." He was that rare animal, a born leader, and eminently suited for senior military command.[2]

Currie was not, however, a professional soldier. Ontario-born (5 December 1875) and -raised, he had moved to Canada's west coast in his late teens. Making his home in Victoria, British Columbia, he had become a schoolteacher, an insurance salesman, and, most recently, a real estate speculator, an occupation that made him one of Victoria's leading citizens—and saddled him with numerous debts when the west coast real estate boom went bust in early 1914. At the same time, Currie had made a name for himself in the militia, which in turn-of-the-century Canada was as much a social institution as a military force. In 1897, he had enlisted as a lowly gunner in the 5th Regiment, Canadian Garrison Artillery; by 1909, he was the lieutenant-colonel commanding the regiment. "With him in command," it was later

89

written, "the 5th was known as the best gunnery corps in the Dominion."³ In late 1913, Currie accepted the challenge of raising and training an infantry unit, the 50th Regiment, Gordon Highlanders of Canada.

When the war broke out in August 1914, the highly regarded Currie was given command of an infantry brigade, and he accompanied Canada's division-sized first contingent overseas in October. His brigade distinguished itself at Second Ypres in April 1915, when it stood firm in the face of poison gas. When the two-division Canadian Corps was created in September that year, Currie was promoted to major-general and placed in command of the First Canadian Division. At thirty-nine, he was not only one of the youngest men to hold that rank in the Great War, he was the first non-regular officer to rise above brigadier-general in the BEF, in which the Canadians served. The First Division had performed brilliantly under Currie, at Mount Sorrel and the Somme in 1916 and at Vimy Ridge, Arleux, and Fresnoy in the spring of 1917. Sir Henry Horne, commanding the First Army, called Currie's division "the pride and wonder of the British Army."⁴

In June 1917, Currie had been knighted and named commander of the Canadian Corps, now four divisions strong. It was a notable departure from previous practice: his two predecessors had both been British career officers, Sir Edwin Alderson and Sir Julian Byng. Byng, who later served as governor-general of Canada, considered Currie to be "one of the remarkable successes of the war.... His character inspired one when one got to know him well and I know no one in his position whose friendship I valued more."⁵ When Byng had been promoted to command the Third Army, he had recommended that Currie succeed him. Now, at forty-one, Sir Arthur was the only non-regular officer commanding a corps in the BEF.

One of Currie's most impressive and important achievements had come during the winter of 1916–17, while he was still a divisional commander. Analyzing the fighting he had witnessed on the Western Front, Currie had drawn up what proved to be a blueprint for tactical success. In a paper presented during a lecture at Canadian Corps headquarters in January 1917, Currie synthesized the best of British and French concepts, liberally spiced with many of his own beliefs based on personal experience. His formula for victory was predicated on powerful and accurate artillery support, including elaborate counter-battery techniques to neutralize the enemy's guns; it also stressed platoon tactics, to give the infantry flexibility and manoeuvrability on the battlefield. Painstaking preparations, including intimate knowledge of the enemy and his positions as well as rehearsals by the attacking troops, were, in Currie's view, indispensable. His theories were vindicated by Vimy Ridge and by the subsequent minor operations at Arleux and Fresnoy, enabling him to comment:

> The great lesson to be learned from these operations is this: if the lessons of the War have been thoroughly mastered; if the Artillery preparation and support is good; if our Intelligence is properly appreciated; there is no position that cannot be wrested from the enemy by well-disciplined, well-trained and well-led troops attacking on a sound plan.[6]

It was a startling statement coming from a Great War general, but very true so far as the Canadians were concerned.

Under Sir Arthur Currie, the Canadian Corps emerged as the outstanding formation on the Western Front. No force—British, Australian, French, American, or German—could match its marvellous, unblemished record, a series of successes without a single setback, by the end of the war. With only a tiny peacetime army to draw on, Canada's soldiers were mostly amateurs, whose skills, esprit de corps, and organization enabled them to perform like professionals. The Corps numbered just over 100,000, every man a volunteer; Canada did not adopt conscription until December 1917. Half its strength was made up of infantry, organized in four divisions. Patterned on the British model, with minor refinements, each division comprised more than 18,000 men and was a self-contained fighting unit: three infantry brigades, each of four battalions of 1,000 men apiece, plus artillery, engineers, and intelligence, medical, and supply services. The Canadian Corps differed from the standard corps in the British army in one important aspect. It was Canada's army. While a British corps was a flexible formation, with divisions added or deleted according to its assigned operation, the Canadian Corps—with rare exceptions—fought with the same four divisions under its command. Besides benefitting from this familiarity, the Corps nurtured a national spirit unprecedented in Canadian history, sentiments that the British often found difficult to comprehend.

The divisional commanders under Currie were excellent officers who, today, are almost unknown: Archie Macdonell, Harry Burstall, Louis Lipsett, and David Watson. All but Watson were regulars; all but Lipsett were Canadian-born.

Archibald Cameron Macdonell, at fifty-three years of age, was the elder statesman of the group. Born in Windsor, Ontario, the silver-haired Macdonell looked every inch a soldier, standing ramrod straight, his cap perched on his head at a jaunty angle. A veteran of the Boer War, he had commanded a cavalry regiment, Lord Strathcona's Horse, when the Great War began. Macdonell enjoyed a well-deserved reputation as a fighter; he was twice wounded in action in 1916. Currie, who became a close friend, affectionately called him "Old Mac" and fought political pressure to ensure that Macdonell succeeded him in command of the First Division in the summer of 1917.

Henry E. Burstall, the officer commanding the Second Division, was, like Macdonell, a veteran of Canada's tiny pre-war permanent force. An artilleryman by training, the native of Quebec City was a rarity: a Canadian who had graduated from the Staff College, Camberley. At forty-seven, the amiable-looking Burstall had commanded his division for nearly a year and remained in command until the end of the war.

Forty-three-year-old Lipsett was British-born, a native of Wales. A career soldier, he had been seconded to the Canadian army for training purposes prior to the war; he had instructed Currie at a staff officers' course in early 1914, and subsequently served under him overseas, first as a battalion commander and then as a brigadier, before being entrusted with the Third Division in mid-1916. A daring leader, he was often found in the front lines, a habit that led to his death less than a month before the war ended. He was the senior, as well as the youngest, divisional commander in the Canadian Corps; only Macdonell rivalled him in ability.

The lone militia officer in this select group was Watson. A newspaperman, he was the managing director of the *Chronicle* in his hometown of Quebec City, where he also commanded a local militia unit, the 8th Royal Rifles. The forty-six-year-old Watson had taken command of the Fourth Division when it was formed in 1916; he was its only commander during the war.

With the help of these able officers, Currie had fought his first battle commanding the Canadian Corps in August 1917. The previous month, Sir Douglas Haig, desiring to distract the Germans from the forthcoming Flanders offensive, instructed Sir Henry Horne's First Army to mount a diversionary attack near Lens, an important coal-mining centre in northern France. Horne handed the assignment to the Canadians and their rookie commander.

Currie was only too pleased to accept, but he soon found himself at odds with certain British officers. He first clashed with General Horne, who proposed that the Canadian Corps strike at a rail line south of Lens. But Currie, after personally surveying the terrain, came up with what he felt was a better idea. Arguing that Horne's plan "would not have the effect of holding the enemy, that it offered no serious threat to his position and that he would soon see that it did not amount to much," Currie pointed to Hill 70, a commanding height north of Lens, maintaining "that if we were to fight at all we ought to fight for something worth having."[7] Horne was not convinced and referred the matter to Haig, who promptly endorsed Currie's proposal: Hill 70 would be the Canadian objective.

A second clash came a short time later. Currie, knowing that the Germans would not easily give up Hill 70, prepared a massive artillery killing-ground to greet the inevitable enemy counter-attacks. On 23 July, when Haig visited Canadian Corps headquarters, Currie outlined his plans and concluded with a request for a few more guns, "to make certain of a clean job." This brought a protest from Haig's artillery chief, Sir Noel Birch, who, sensitive to the possible disruption of his own bombardment then under way in Flanders, argued that the Canadians already had more than enough guns. Haig cut him short with a sharp order: "See that General Currie gets the extra guns he wants."[8]

As these incidents indicate, Haig and Currie were on good terms. Haig, who made it a practice to know his divisional and corps commanders, had been rather a regular visitor at First Canadian Division headquarters in 1916 and early 1917, and had often complimented Currie. Haig seemed to enjoy these visits immensely; once, referring to Currie's considerable girth, he had even joked, "Give me fat counsellors." When political considerations threatened to complicate Currie's appointment to the Corps command, Haig had flatly declared that Currie "was the only Canadian officer whom (he) would place in command of the Canadians," the alternative being another British officer.[9]

Currie, by the same token, admired the field-marshal. He commented after the war:

> I met him many times and although he never had much to say, he always impressed one greatly. Leaving to one side his manner, his bearing, his appearance—all of which fitted so well with his high rank—one felt that here you were dealing with a thoroughly honest, decent, manly man.

But Currie was by no means intimidated by Haig either. His chauffeur, Sergeant-Major Lewis Reece, recalled the time that Haig outlined his plan on a map and then asked for Currie's opinion.

"Well, sir," he replied with typical frankness, "I don't think it is worth a God damn." The shocked expressions on the faces of Haig's aides told Reece that the commander-in-chief was not often addressed in such a manner.[10]

It was not until 15 August that the Canadians attacked Hill 70— heavy rain in early August delayed the operation—but it was an "entire and complete success," according to Currie.

> During the course of the next eight days the Boche launched against our newly won positions no less than 35 counterattacks. We identified no less than 69 German Battalions although we were employing not more than 24. Not only did we succeed in holding the Boche opposite us but he became so alarmed that he withdrew from the battle line of Ypres two divisions and put them in the line against us at Hill 70.

Canadian intelligence later estimated "that the casualties suffered by the enemy in the fight at Hill 70 were more than 30,000. Our gunners," said Currie, "have always maintained that they never had such shooting throughout the great war at the enemy's personnel as they had at the battle of Hill 70. Our own casualties were less than 8,000." Currie's artillery killing-ground had been a devastating success.[11]*

Even the Germans confirmed that the Canadians had done well. While not deceived that the Hill 70 action was anything more than a diversion—the German high command correctly believed that the British lacked the resources for two major offensives and pinpointed Flanders as the BEF's main effort—they had to admit that the

---

* Currie, remarkably, orchestrated this fine operation while under considerable duress. Not the least of his problems was a sprained knee, suffered while playing badminton, which hobbled him for much of August. Field-Marshal Haig, visiting the Corps late that month, noted the Canadian commander's obvious discomfort as a result of this injury.

Potentially more serious, and certainly more embarrassing, was a skeleton that fell out of Currie's closet around this time. Three years earlier, Currie had defrauded his militia unit, the 50th Regiment, Gordon Highlanders of Canada, of $8,300. The funds were destined to pay for regimental uniforms, but Currie, in a display of panic most uncharacteristic of him, used them to avoid personal bankruptcy during the West Coast real estate bust in early 1914. Before departing Victoria for overseas service, he arranged to have two close associates replace the missing money if it was called for. Then, in early 1915, Currie was told by Sam Hughes, the minister of militia and defence, not to worry about the matter. That suited Currie, because he had a number of other real estate-related debts to repay while serving his country. However, Hughes was forced to resign in late 1916, and thus was no longer in a position to protect Currie from potential scandal. The affair was finally brought to the attention of Hughes's successor, Sir Edward Kemp, in

Canadian Corps had caused them concern. "The fighting at Lens cost us, once again, the expenditure of considerable numbers of troops who had to be replaced," wrote the German general, Hermann von Kuhl. "The whole previously worked out plan for relieving the fought-out troops in Flanders had been wrecked."[12]

Sir Douglas Haig was most impressed. He later told Currie that he considered Hill 70 to be "one of the finest minor operations of the war." On 27 August, Haig inspected the First and Second Divisions, which had spearheaded the Canadian fight, and wrote afterward:

> These two Canadian divisions have "knocked out" 7 German divisions, viz.: the 7th, 220th, 4th Guard, 1st Guard Reserve (these are four of the very best divisions in the German Army), 11th Reserve, 36th Reserve (these are not so good) and 8th Division (also very good).... The experience and training of the past year have done wonders for the Canadians. Their morale is now very high, and though they have been opposed by the flower of the German Army (Guards, etc.) they feel that they can beat the Germans every time.

Obviously, these were troops who could be counted on in the most difficult circumstances.[13]

The Canadians were soon preoccupied with what was, ostensibly, their next operation. Plans were prepared for the capture of Sallaumines Hill, southeast of Lens; despite the disturbing loss of Hill 70, the Germans stubbornly refused to relinquish the city. But, as Currie later wrote, the Sallaumines project "was known, only to myself, to be camouflage." The Corps, he had learned, was to be

> June 1917. Mortified, Kemp tossed the hot potato to Sir George Perley, the London-based minister responsible for the Overseas Military Forces of Canada. Perley, appalled, was inclined to pay off the debt himself, but eventually referred it back to Ottawa. There, on 7 August 1917, the cabinet of Prime Minister Sir Robert Borden decided to cover it by having the militia department repay the funds and collect them from Currie after the war. That measure proved to be unnecessary. Some highly placed person—most likely either Perley or Eugène Fiset, Kemp's deputy—quietly informed Currie of these goings-on. He acted quickly and calmly. On leave in early September, after Hill 70, he borrowed most of the money from two of his subordinates, Major-General Watson and Brigadier-General Victor Odlum, wiring his former regiment the sum of $10,883.34. Currie repaid Watson and Odlum in instalments by June 1919.
>
> Despite the misguided efforts of certain scandal-mongering historians to exaggerate the importance of this isolated incident and discredit Currie, it must be pointed out that at no time did it jeopardize his position as Corps commander. The reason is simple: he was demonstrably the only qualified Canadian, and the government of Prime Minister Borden was unwilling to accept the alternative, namely, to place a British officer in command of the Corps.

entrusted with a top-secret mission: the first attack by tanks en masse, to be made in November by Sir Julian Byng's Third Army. Byng had long been enthusiastic about the potential of tanks, as Currie recalled: "General Byng had often discussed with me the utilization of tanks in a surprise attack, and I paid many visits to him during the summer months to see trial attacks by tanks, and to further discuss the matter with him." Nothing would have made Currie happier than to be associated with such an ambitious and imaginative scheme.[14]

Passchendaele disrupted these plans. On 3 October, Currie was warned that the Corps might be sent north, to take part in the offensive in Flanders. Common sense being one of his outstanding characteristics, Currie could make no sense of Passchendaele, and he was furious. "Passchendaele!" he raged in front of his staff. "What's the good of it? Let the Germans have it—keep it—rot in it! Rot in the mud! There's a mistake somewhere. It must be a mistake! It isn't worth a drop of blood."[15] Later in the day, General Horne, First Army's commander, confirmed the bad news, adding that if the Canadians did go to Flanders, they were to be assigned to Sir Hubert Gough's Fifth Army.

Currie drew the line right there. He bluntly told Horne "that the Canadian Corps would not fight under General Gough," explaining "that I had talked to many Divisional Commanders who had fought in the Ypres battle beginning on July 31, 1917, and that I learned that they were greatly dissatisfied with the way in which the battle had been conducted. But my lack of confidence in Gough arose from our experiences with him on the Somme in 1916"—after which Currie had sworn never again to serve in an army commanded by Gough. Horne was appalled at Currie's forthright and frank utterance. "My God, Currie," he replied, "that is a terrible thing to say." Currie later admitted that he had gone too far, that "had I been a British Corps commander I know I would have been sent home for making such a statement." However, Horne agreed to discuss the matter with Haig.[16]

As usual, Currie got his way. Haig bowed to the Canadian's wishes, noting in his diary that if its services were required "the Canadian Corps should be sent to General Plumer and not to Gough because the Canadians do not work well with the latter. The idea seems prevalent that he drove them too much in the Somme fighting last year."[17]*

* Ironically, Gough had a much more flattering opinion of Currie, describing the Canadian Corps commander as "tall, big, calm and self-reliant."[18]

There was, Currie knew, only one way the Canadians could be spared a share in the Flanders fighting. If the attacks of 9 and 12 October were successful, there might be no need to call the Canadian Corps to Passchendaele. But, of course, Currie's hopes were dashed when both assaults failed so utterly and miserably, and when he received his orders on 13 October he had no choice but to obey them.

He did, however, make one final bid to spare his men the horrors of Passchendaele. Summoned to Second Army headquarters on the thirteenth, Currie decided to appeal to General Plumer, for whom he had high regard, later commenting "that my experiences with General Plumer were always of the happiest." Currie estimated—with stunning accuracy, it would turn out—that "our casualties would be at least 16,000, 250 per battalion for 48 battalions is 12,000, 3,000 for roads and 1000 or more for other services." He asked Plumer "if a success would justify the sacrifice." Plumer was sympathetic, but there was nothing he could do. He could only shrug and say, "My orders are clear."[19]

Haig must have learned of this exchange, because he promptly paid a personal visit to Currie. Major-General Archie Macdonell, the officer commanding the First Canadian Division, recalled that the commander-in-chief arrived at Corps headquarters during a divisional commanders' conference. Currie went outside to greet him, and Macdonell watched them from a window.

> It was... apparent to me that Haig was putting a proposition to Currie, he was not for. Haig was very earnest and very animated and after a halt during which he had failed to convince Currie, would take him by the arm and walk up a[nd] down with him in a very animated wa[y] and evidently full of argument. Finally they stopped right below my window. I saw that Currie was beginning to nod his head in acquiescence. Then they turned... and came into the room where we were.[20]

Haig then delivered a brief and eloquent—for him, at least—speech to the assembled Canadian officers.

> Gentlemen! *It has become apparent that Passchendaele must be taken*, and I have come here to ask the Canadian Corps to do it. General Curry [*sic*] is strongly opposed to doing so. But I have succeeded in overcoming his scruples. Some day I hope to be able to tell you why this must be done, but in the mean time I ask you to take my word for it.... I may say *General Currie has demanded an unprecedented*

amount of artillery to protect his Canadians and I have been forced to acquiesce.

It was a masterful performance, and Haig clinched his case by flashing what Macdonell called "one of those wondrous smiles of his."[21]

And so General Currie and his Canadian Corps began to prepare for the move to Flanders fields.

9/Preparations

Currie responded to the challenge with characteristic energy. Although he was not at all happy that the Canadians had been told to take Passchendaele, he was determined to make the best of an obviously bad situation. As the Canadian official history notes, "There is ample evidence of Currie's skilled and forceful generalship and the efficiency of his well organized staff in the smoothness and despatch with which the preparations for the Canadian assault were carried to completion."[1]

One of Currie's first moves was to assign intelligence officers to the various headquarters with which the Canadian Corps would be associated: Second Army, II Anzac Corps, which was responsible for the sector the Canadians would be taking over, and its front-line divisions, the New Zealand and 3rd Australian. These intelligence officers, wrote Percy Radcliffe, Currie's brigadier-general, general staff (BGGS)—the chief of staff at the corps level—were to acquire "early and thorough information as regards to details of German defences and dispositions, and especially for the purpose of arranging the daily programme of bombardment...."[2]

This exercise was a sparkling success. Currie later wrote that the Canadian "Corps and Divisions were so thoroughly in touch with the situation that, on the day on which they became responsible for the line, the actual handing over was merely a matter of form...."[3]

But this was just the start. As early as 17 October, parties of observers from designated infantry battalions established advanced headquarters east of Ypres, whence they carefully reconnoitred the battlefront. In addition, joint infantry and artillery observation posts were established, charged with assessing the impact of each day's artillery work and determining future requirements. Currie would comment of this arrangement:

> I wish to lay stress on the above methods because I am convinced that this reconnaissance and close liaison between the artillery, the infantry units, and the staff is vital to the success of any operation. Before committing our Infantry to the assault of a position we must be quite sure that every detail of the enemy's defences, especially wire, is known and adequately dealt with, and the infantry must be satisfied that this has been done.[4]

To co-ordinate the information that was being compiled, Currie decided to hold "a conference every evening at 9 p.m." This would enable him "to keep in touch with the daily progress of preparations," and senior officers were instructed to "be prepared to report the exact situation as regards artillery, ammunition, roads, light railways, tramways, etc. and furnish maps showing the situation up to date, so that a report can be made to Second Army Headquarters early each morning."[5]

The earliest reports were alarming, to say the least. Currie had dispatched reliable staff officers to Flanders, with instructions to bring back their initial impressions. Lieutenant-Colonel Edmund Ironside, a British officer serving on the staff of the Fourth Canadian Division and a future field-marshal, told Currie that the situation was "truly awful," that "the mud was quite indescribable." Ironside believed that the ridge could be taken, but only "with great loss," and concluded his report with "a plea for the impossibility and futility of the operations as regards results."[6]*

Equally distressing was the report of the two top artillery officers in the Canadian Corps, Brigadier-General Edward Morrison and Lieutenant-Colonel Andrew McNaughton. McNaughton, the Corps counter-battery officer, later recalled what he told Currie:

> I remember reporting that if I were the German counter-battery officer, and I had one brigade, I would see to it that that artillery never fired a single round. The [Allied] guns were all strung out in a line and the batteries mixed up in the most heterogeneous fashion. Orders were being given to fire ammunition that was not being fired. There were cases where light railway teams, bringing the ammunition up, came under bombardment well back and dumped the shells off the cars. It would be reported in returns as expended, when it was actually thrown in the mud. Morale had gone and the effectiveness of the artillery was played out....[8]

Currie soon saw for himself the conditions in the salient. Moving into the area ahead of his Corps, Currie opened his headquarters in the ruined village of Poperinghe on Monday, 15 October. That night the Germans saluted his return to Ypres by shelling and bombing Poperinghe. Two days later, Currie toured the front lines for the first time. The scene, he admitted, exceeded his worst expectations. "Battlefield looks bad," he told his diary. "No salvage has been done and very few of the dead buried...."[9]

There were some who seemed surprised to see a man of his rank

---

* Interestingly, in post-war lectures at the Staff College, Camberley, Ironside ridiculed such reporting as "hardly cricket," likening it to spying on fellow formations.[7]

so far forward. One of these was a Canadian war correspondent, Fred McKenzie, who wrote of meeting the mud-spattered Currie one morning near Ypres. "He had been up to the front, seeing things for himself," remarked the admiring McKenzie. "The place that morning was very unhealthy. Fritz was searching the roads behind, and bursts of his shrapnel were making little white clouds in the sky.... Now... this is a place where the commander of an army corps should not be [but] Currie goes up to see things for himself. I am quite certain that he never even noticed that morning the shelling that was going on."[10]

It was clear to Currie that, in conditions such as these, the infantry would be operating at a severe disadvantage. To minimize the problems, particularly that of rifles being jammed by mud, Corps headquarters issued specific orders, based on the British experience:

> The Corps Commander wishes special attention paid to the protection of rifles from mud in the forthcoming operations.
>
> It is essential that all Units should be fully provided with muzzle protectors and breech covers. With regard to the latter, it has been found useful to tack one side of the breech cover to the rifle to prevent the cover being lost. This must be carefully done so as not to damage the rifle.[11]

Thanks to this precaution, there were remarkably few instances of mud clogging the firing mechanisms of the Canadians' rifles. It was typical of Currie's attention to even the smallest detail.

On Thursday, 18 October, General Currie formally took command of this sector. It was an unusual arrangement: no Canadians would enter the front lines for another four days. In the meantime, the New Zealand and 3rd Australian divisions temporarily came under control of the Canadian Corps. Currie moved into new quarters on the eighteenth, shifting to the nondescript, shell-shocked hamlet of Ten Elms, north of Poperinghe. According to Fred McKenzie, Currie took over "a little hut divided into two. One section of the hut was his sleeping and living room. The other was heaped with papers. Close to the door there was just room for one or two people to stand. To the side there was a relief map of the district where we were fighting. Here Currie sat for a large part of each day interviewing commanders, settling problems and arranging the plans that soon were to bring us victory." Modest as these quarters were, they were characteristic of Currie. Although an officer of his rank was entitled to the safety and comfort of a château far from the front lines, Currie always spurned such accommodation whenever the Corps was in action, preferring to share—to a certain extent, at least—the discomfort and danger his men were facing. Consequently, his headquarters at Ten Elms were shelled several times in the course of the Passchendaele battle, once causing Currie to comment in his diary: "Too close to be comfortable." In any case, comfort was of little concern to Currie: aside from occasional catnaps, he rarely slept while the Canadians were fighting. That he was able to stay alert and attentive, despite the lack of sleep, speaks highly of his personal endurance and energy.[12]

He did, indeed, seem to be tireless. In addition to the seemingly endless details with which he had to concern himself, he insisted on meeting many of his battalions en route to Flanders, drawing them aside for roadside chats. Many years afterwards, Private Pat Burns of the 46th (South Saskatchewan) Battalion vividly recalled his unit's encounter with the Corps commander:

> I never seen a battalion look so smart in all my life. Buttons polished, rifles cleaned, all equipment in order—a perfect, perfect, perfect battalion if there ever was one. When Currie came on we all had to fix bayonets and "present arms." He spoke to us man-to-man. Currie was a wonderful leader.

He made no attempt to downplay what was in store for them. The 20th (Central Ontario) Battalion's history commented that Currie's speech was "characteristically brief and to the point," which the soldiers appreciated. Currie explained that "Passchendaele Ridge had to be captured, for reasons he was unable to divulge, and for that task the Canadians had been chosen. He pictured, wisely without minimizing them, the nature and trying conditions of operations in the Salient."[13]

As if the Canadians did not have enough difficulties before them, Currie discovered one that was particularly annoying. The attitude of some high-ranking British officers was lethargic, almost defeatist; many of them did not believe that the Canadians could succeed where the cream of the BEF had failed. Indeed, there was very real resentment of the Canadians, as one staff officer, Captain Bernard Montgomery, candidly admitted in a letter home in early November. "The Canadians are a queer crowd; they seem to think they are the best troops in France and that we get them to do our most difficult jobs," Montgomery wrote. "I reminded them that the Ypres Battle began on 31st July and the only part they have taken is during the last ten days." Montgomery went on to say that he was "disappointed" in the Canadians. "At plain straightforward fighting they are magnificent, but they are narrow minded and lack soldierly instincts." Captain Montgomery, who rose to the rank of field-marshal during World War II, never forgot or overcame his resentment of these cocky colonials.[14]

Accordingly, Currie found numerous man-made obstacles placed in his path. The most serious, and aggravating, of these concerned the additional artillery Haig had promised to provide. The Canadians were to take over 360 British and Australian field guns in this sector, but on arrival only slightly more than 200 could be found. The rest had been destroyed in action, sunk in the mud, or been hauled away for repairs. Currie went to see Sir Herbert Plumer to request replacements from the Second Army for the missing guns. To his disgust, Plumer's artillery commander, Major-General C.R. Buckle, disputed the Canadian claims. "I was told," related a chagrined Currie, "that if I had taken over 360 guns I should have taken over the indents for those which were missing." At that, Currie lost his temper. "Goddammit, I can't fight the battle with indents!" he raged.[15]

Soon afterwards, Sir Douglas Haig attended a conference at Canadian Corps headquarters at Ten Elms. Currie was uncharacteristically late, testing Haig's patience, for the field-marshal detested unpunctual people. When Currie finally did appear, he was covered in mud and seemed to General Macdonell to be ill or tired. Haig evidently had the same impression, for he asked, "Everything all right, Currie?"

"No, Sir," the Canadian replied. "I was promised so many guns to cover our front and they are not there."

"Careful, Currie—careful!" cautioned the commander-in-chief. "If you make a positive statement you will be required to substantiate it and you could not do that unless you had counted the guns yourself."

Currie's reply was measured and deliberate. "I have just returned from counting the guns."

"Some one will smoke for this," Haig muttered and, turning to his artillery chief, Sir Noel Birch, said, "Investigate. Someone will be dealt with."[16]

Whether heads rolled is not known. What is known—and is more important, anyway—is that Currie got his guns.

The Canadian Corps already boasted an impressive artillery arsenal. Each of its four divisions was provided with two brigades of field artillery, each brigade composed of three six-gun batteries of 18-pounders and one six-gun battery of 4.5-inch howitzers, plus one heavy trench-mortar battery (four 9.45-inch mortars) and two medium trench-mortar batteries (each with six 6-inch mortars). The 18-pounder field gun was the workhorse of the British artillery in the Great War; it could fire an 18.5-pound shell up to 9,000 yards, at a rate of twenty per minute. The howitzers were "capable of delivering plunging fire on targets behind crests and in other locations that offered protection from the field guns, with their higher muzzle velocities and flatter trajectories." In addition, the Corps had at its disposal a fifth divisional artillery—belonging to the Fifth Canadian Division, which had been formed in early 1917 but, aside from its artillery component, never left England, being broken up to provide reinforcements for the rest of the Corps in early 1918—as well as three brigades of heavy artillery: forty-eight Vickers 6-inch howitzers; twelve 60-pounder breech-loading Armstrongs; twelve 8-inch howitzers; and twelve 9.2-inch howitzers which, at thirteen tons were the biggest guns in the Canadian Corps, capable of firing a 290-pound shell.[17]

The Canadians could, under normal circumstances, bring to bear 320 guns. Haig nearly doubled that figure, allotting to the Canadians forty-seven heavy or siege batteries and eleven field brigades, two of them from New Zealand, the balance British. Thus the Canadians would be employing a total of 587 guns at Passchendaele:

270 18-pounders	4 12-inch howitzers
90 4.5-inch howitzers	1 15-inch howitzer
106 6-inch howitzers	48 60-pounders
32 8-inch howitzers	8 6-inch guns
26 9.2-inch howitzers	2 9.2-inch guns

Between 17 October and 16 November, the Canadian Corps artillery fired a total of 1,453,056 shells, or 40,908 tons of high explosive, nearly twenty times the amount fired by both sides in the Boer War at the turn of the century.[18]

Yet, Passchendaele was to be the most trying experience of the whole war for the Canadian gunners. Of the 587 guns available, only a daily average of 406 were in action. The support they were able to give the infantry ranged from devastatingly accurate to utterly ineffective, more often the latter. A Corps report later concluded that "at least 25% of the artillery power available was lost owing to the scarcity of roads and railways." These conditions "cramped the whole deployment of the artillery and did not allow of its proper distribution, batteries were necessarily crowded rendering them more liable to casualties and neutralization, the replacement of damaged guns became a lengthy and difficult proceeding, and the general efficiency of the personnel was greatly reduced by the difficulties of manhandling equipment."[19]

Manhandling the guns was exhausting, backbreaking work. Mired in "mud knee-deep in many parts," the gunners relied on brains as much as brawn to get the job done. "Guns were moved over tracks made by laying down segments of 'mule track,' planks, corrugated iron or any other available material...," reads a Corps report. "When the guns were badly bogged, it was necessary in some cases to dismount the piece and skid it over the mud, the carriage being hauled separately." Infantrymen were often detailed to provide added muscle, as Private Gordon Brown of the 46th (South Saskatchewan) Battalion ruefully recalled:

> We had ropes tied onto the wheels and they had these big wooden cleats fastened on to stop them from sinking. I'd venture to say there was two hundred and fifty, maybe three hundred men on one gun trying to pull it up. We might get a hundred yards or so.

It was a job that had to be done, and so it was. As one participant later commented, "inch by inch and curse by curse, all [the] guns were moved."[20]

The gunners were left weary, both physically and mentally. Unlike the infantry, who were moved in and out of the firing lines and thus endured short stretches of intense hardship offset by longer periods of rest, the artillery spent the whole time—four full weeks and, in some cases, even longer—in constant action. Sergeant-Major Donald Patterson of the 39th Battery, Canadian Field Artillery (CFA), wrote: "I did not get more than a few hours sleep at any time, and I was half asleep all the time."[21] This was common, and an important factor in the artillery's sub-par performance at Passchendaele.

It was frustrating for these men who were trying so hard and, through no fault of their own, achieving so little. Their feelings of exasperation are evidenced by a brief, bewildered entry in the Second Divisional Artillery log at one point in the battle: "72nd [Battalion] say no protective barrage going on. We are all firing."[22]

Adding to their frustration was the fact that this action was not typical of Western Front engagements. Normally, the artillery would detect and destroy the enemy's defences prior to each attack; at Passchendaele the characteristic mazes of trench systems and strongpoints were absent, the enemy relying instead on a checkerboard pattern of pillboxes and fortified shell-holes and farms. There were few trenches and little barbed wire. The massive field of wire at Bellevue Spur, where the Anzacs had come to grief on 12 October, was one of the first targets for the Canadians: "its destruction did not offer any great difficulties." Then the gunners turned their attention to the pillboxes, pounding them in prolonged bombardments by heavy-calibre guns. But this practice was eventually discontinued when it was found that "it increased the difficulties of attacking these defences by rendering the ground surrounding them even more impassable." Practice barrages, a typical feature of trench warfare that enabled the Canadians to perfect their firing patterns, were also discontinued after the infantry bitterly complained about the violent responses from the German artillery. Consequently, the gunners had to content themselves with less elaborate daily bombardments that were "mainly directed against the hostile personnel, with the object of demoralizing the defenders, and inducing them to keep under cover for as long a period as possible whenever a barrage was in pr[o]gress."[23]

Canadian counter-battery work, too, left much to be desired. This was ironic; the Canadians had been leaders in developing and employing techniques to neutralize the enemy's artillery. Indeed, theirs had been one of the first corps in the BEF to appoint a counter-battery officer in early 1917—this was the brilliant Andy McNaughton, a scientist in peacetime and one of the war's outstanding gunners—and at Vimy Ridge and Hill 70 the Canadians had played havoc with the German guns. But at Passchendaele, several factors combined to virtually negate the Canadian counter-battery efforts until the late stages of the fighting. The most significant of these was German aerial superiority during the month the Canadians were in the Ypres salient, and the consequent inability of 21 Squadron of the Royal Flying Corps to produce adequate reconnaissance data concerning the enemy's rear positions.

The Canadian gunners had a miserable time. Philip Debney of the 32nd Battery, CFA, later recalled that during this battle "we moved about six times, and we never found a piece of ground for a gun platform where we didn't have to fill a shell hole." This made for more work, as another gunner related:

> It was a man-killer. You'd laid wooden plank platforms under [the gun], but it was impossible to build a firm foundation in that muck, so you fired your gun and she'd recoil and jump about four inches to one side, and you'd fire another one, and by the time

you fired half a dozen she would be practically off the platform. So there was nothing to do but haul it forward in the mud and bolster up your platform on that side and put her back again, and half a dozen more shots, she'd be off the other side.[24]

They were under constant heavy fire. Inviting targets that they were, the gunners were forced to endure the hazardous conditions. Sergeant Gordon Howard of the 18th Battery, CFA, recalled the morning his position came under German shell fire, and a heavy shell exploded between two of the guns.

> The crater was so wide that both guns slipped into the crater. The mud deluged down on the remaining guns and ammunition making it unfit to use until cleaned, so we were all out of action. The mud rained down on me and I was plastered from head to foot; you could hardly see my buttons. No one was hurt. The shell went in so deep that the mud saved us.

The losses in men and guns were, nevertheless, extraordinary. For example, the 10th Battery, CFA, suffered a staggering 200 per cent casualties during the battle. Another field battery, the 15th, lost no fewer than thirteen guns in a single six-day stretch. Corps headquarters found it useful to establish a reserve pool of guns consisting of ninety 18-pounders and twenty-four 4.5-inch howitzers. "This facilitated replacement of field guns, which were knocked out at the average rate of 11 a day by hostile artillery."[25]

The lack of roads hampered not just the artillery but all phases of the Canadian operation. There were only three roads capable of carrying lorries into the salient, and two others suitable for pack animals only. General Currie, who believed that roads were "an essential to victory," once again ran afoul of unco-operative British officers in his search for solutions.

> We thought that plank roads, somewhat after the lines of the old corduroy roads of Ontario, would serve a useful purpose. We suggested it and were pooh-poohed at first, yet finally we were given permission to go ahead. Then there were no planks available, and none could be brought up. We next suggested that we be given a saw-mill, and permission to cut down trees in the forest near where we were preparing to fight. In due time we got this saw-mill, set it up, and made our own planks and our own roads.[26]

This innovation proved so successful that similar plank roads were constructed along the entire BEF front in Belgium and France.

Still, it was no easy task, as shown by one road built from Spree Farm by engineers of the First Division. The division's three engineer companies, plus a pioneer battalion,* and aided by a daily average of 450 all ranks infantry—drawn from battalions not taking part in the scheduled attacks on the ridge—worked around the clock, in four six-hour shifts. It "was constructed by ditching the sides and digging numerous dikes, and constructing a formation in the centre with sandbags and the poor quality of planks...." Up to 3 November, the road progressed at the rate of 375 yards per day, but that slowed considerably, to less than fifty a day, after it crossed the Honnebeek, a stream west of Gravenstafel, and came in plain view of the enemy's guns, which caused extensive disruptions: "working parties were continually dispersed, so that time was lost while they were taking cover during the shelling, and being collected after the shelling had slackened."[27]

It was, like all else at Passchendaele, as exhausting as it was dangerous. It was sometimes sickening, too, as one engineering unit reported: "the ground was covered with bodies, making grading very unpleasant." The diary of Private P.H. Longstaffe of the 107th Pioneer Battalion reveals the mind-numbing nature of the road work:

> *21 October.* Up at 2.30 a.m. Very dark. Breakfast. Started at 3.15. Long walk past transports and ammunition column. Arrive at Dump at 4.30. Work on plank road. Huge guns all round. Mud awful. Dead men and horses all round. Thousands of men working. Rush job on road through swamp. Ammunition, mules and horses passing in continuous stream. Fritz shelling both sides.
>
> *22 October.* Up at 2.30. Drizzle of rain. Fritz overhead. Dressed and ate in darkness in shell-hole and lost tea. Same work as 21 Oct. Arrive 4.15. Terrific bombardment opens up. Hundreds of guns all around us flashing and banging away. Impressive sight. Guns being hurried up. Exciting scenes as mules and horses flounder in mud. Wrecked tanks and pillboxes all round. Worked on road, sandbags and carrying planks. Shells dropping quite close. Up to our knees in mud. Shell on road, three killed, five injured. Horrible sights. Quit at 11am.[28]

---

* Pioneers were infantrymen whose primary task was to assist the engineers in various construction projects. Unskilled labour, the pioneers worked under the close supervision of the engineers. Dissatisfied with this arrangement, General Currie reorganized the pioneers and retrained them as engineers in early 1918. It was so successful that the rest of the BEF followed suit.

Important, too, was the laying of duckboards, or "bath mats," as the Canadians often called them. These were "sections of platform six feet long made of two pieces of scantling with nailed cross pieces at intervals,"[29] portable sidewalks laid over the sea of mud that enabled single-file movement between the front lines and the immediate rear. Dozens of these frail paths snaked their way over the battlefield, facilitating the movement of men and supplies. They also drew their share of enemy shell fire, which ripped great gaps in the walkways. Not all the gaps were due to German shells, though. Light-fingered Canadians were sometimes responsible; at least one battalion commander urged that the bath mats be made of heavier material, to discourage their theft by troops trying to shore up their flimsy front-line accommodations.

The Canadian Corps by itself was unable to provide all the necessary manpower and expertise to complete these invaluable projects. However, it was able to draw on the resources of the BEF, and British engineers and pioneers were assigned to assist their Canadian counterparts. From 17 October, "there was a daily average of ten field companies [of engineers], seven tunnelling companies and four army troops companies, assisted by two infantry and seven pioneer battalions [including four Canadian]"[30] at work in the Corps sector. The Canadians alone suffered more than 1,500 casualties; their sacrifice was vital in the victory that was eventually won.

Equally essential was the provision of supplies. Water was a daily requirement—more than a few veterans noted the irony of being surrounded by water on the battlefield, none of it fit for human consumption—and while the infantry carried up their own food and ammunition, the artillery had to be resupplied continuously. The Canadian Army Service Corps lived up to its informal motto at Passchendaele: "The impossible we do immediately; the miraculous takes a little longer." The lorry drivers who risked life and limb to deliver supplies to the forward dumps more than merited this tribute from a grateful gunner:

> They drove without lights, feeling their way as best they could in the darkness, never knowing where the road had been broken by a great shell hole, strewn by debris, or blocked by fallen trees. They were so utterly exhausted that sometimes they fell asleep while driving; and yet, shaken and exhausted as they were, they never failed to respond to the demands made upon them.[31]

But the trucks could go forward only as far as the plank roads. Beyond, the supplies had to be entrusted to pack animals, mules and horses. This was, for example, the sole method of meeting the never-ending demand for artillery ammunition. It was miserable work, leading these animals over muddy tracks and fragile bath mats, as Gunner Frank Hazlewood of the 23rd Howitzer Battery, CFA, attested in a letter home:

> We are packing our ammunition up these days. Each man has two horses or mules, eight rounds per horse. It takes about five or six hours return trip to the guns and back to the horse lines. So you can bet we are ready for breakfast when we return, splashed generally from head to foot with mud. We sure must be some queer looking specimens.[32]

Stumbling about in the dark, under shell fire, negotiating uncertain territory, led to inevitable mishaps. Sergeant T.T. Shields of Princess Patricia's Canadian Light Infantry (PPCLI) recalled seeing a mule train that had become bogged down. "The mules were up to their bellies in mud," he would remember. "They couldn't get out. The drivers couldn't get them out. They couldn't get another step, and the mules brayed there in the darkness, you know, helpless. I have actually seen artillery drivers standing there crying, crying in their helplessness." Ed Youngman of the 19th (Central Ontario) Battalion witnessed a similar episode involving a mule hopelessly mired in the mud:

> the poor thing kept sinking down and down, inch by inch, and we were frantic. And finally the transport officer of the 18th Battalion decided there was only one thing to do, and when [the mule's] head was just above the mud the officer pulled his revolver out of his holster, and I will never forget the look in that poor brute's great brown eyes when he looked at the officer, and the officer shot him and then cried like a kid.[33]

The attachment between the men and these faithful animals was very real, and it worked both ways. One of the legends of Passchendaele concerns Lieutenant Howard Sutherland of the 87th (Canadian Grenadier Guards) Battalion, who commanded a mule-train. On one trip a shell-burst blew him off the plank road and into a deep, water-filled crater. Sutherland struggled unsuccessfully to climb out of the slimy, icy water. Exhausted, he was apparently doomed to drown here, when "one of his faithful mules clamped its teeth on his coat collar and drew him back." Sutherland survived Passchendaele to be awarded the Military Cross; like many who toiled ceaselessly on these pack trains, he had to be hospitalized for exhaustion.[34]

The mud was everyone's enemy. It played havoc with communications which, in any and every military operation, are a critical factor in success or failure. Ever innovative, the Canadians now looked to modern technology to solve some of their problems. "For some time," observed the late historian, John Swettenham, "the Canadians had been experimenting with continuous wave wireless sets to improve battle communications and for the attack on Passchendaele this method was tried under combat conditions for the first time by the Canadian Corps." But these wireless sets were too bulky to be employed outside the Corps and division headquarters. Elsewhere in the battle zone, more traditional means had to be used. The telephone had by this point emerged as the main method of communication on the Western Front, with the cable buried far below the ground to protect against shell-bursts. At Passchendaele, however, the utilization of telephones quickly "became impossible." The cable could not be properly buried in the mud, and when laid on the surface it was blown to pieces as fast as it could be put down. Signal lamps proved to be an effective alternative, though they tended to draw fire and cause heavy casualties among the signallers. The Canadians also employed pigeons and dogs, but with the latter "there was a tendency to make pets of them, which militated against their usefulness." All too often, unfortunately, human messengers, runners, were the only way of transmitting information back and forth; the heroism of these men was exceeded only by their casualty rate.[35]

Inevitably, there were breakdowns in communications. The results could be tragic, particularly when the artillery was involved. Short-shooting—the Canadian guns inadvertently shelling their own men—was a constant problem at Passchendaele. The damage could be minimized if the offending battery was warned fast enough. More often, however, the short-shooting went on for a considerable time; as a result, recalled one rueful gunner, "some of our troops were killed with our own fire, and we couldn't do anything about it."[36]

Medical difficulties, too, were compounded in conditions such as these. It was seen from the start that it would take herculean efforts just to remove the wounded from the battlefield, "a matter of extreme difficulty," according to Colonel A.E. Ross, the deputy director of medical services in the Canadian Corps:

> The evacuation from the forward area can only be conducted during the day. At night stretcher parties lose themselves, as there are no land marks. Added to this, the deep soft mud, the number of shell holes, and the absence of roads, render the work

of carrying stretchers extremely arduous. During the present fighting, it required six men to a stretcher, six hours, to carry from the regimental aid posts to the nearest point where wheeled transport was available. These men were completely worn out.[37]

General Currie responded to this alarming report with typical alacrity, ordering redoubled efforts to lay down bath mats and build plank roads. As well, he ordered his out-of-battle battalions to allot extra men for stretcher-bearing duty.

Evacuation was, of course, merely the first step in the lifesaving procedure. The Canadians were fortunate in the high level of skill of their Corps medical services, which was unexcelled on the Western Front. Indeed, during the Great War, Canadian medics managed to save the lives of nine out of ten men who were wounded. Their efficiency was never tested more severely than at Passchendaele.

Canadian medical expertise reflected the high standards that prevailed within the British army at this time. The BEF had evolved, through much trial and error, an effective system for processing the injured. Closest to the front was the regimental aid post, where the lightly wounded in each battalion could be treated and the remainder directed toward the rear; next was the advanced dressing station, where more serious cases could be handled, with travelling teams of doctors even performing certain surgical procedures under fire; farther back was the casualty clearing station, which had by now "become the principal seat of life-saving surgery"; farthest from the front were the base hospitals, in France and Britain, where the most sophisticated treatment, and rehabilitation, took place. The medical profession as a whole had made impressive strides to this stage of the war, within certain limitations, as historian John Keegan has written:

> anaesthetics, antiseptics, dressings and instruments were freely available (and every soldier carried, sewn to his uniform, a packet containing a sterile "first field dressing"). Blood ... was fairly freely transfusable from 1917 onwards.... But much surgery had perforce to be radical, decisions for amputation being far commoner than they would be in the Second World War.... And, in cases of gross, abdominal, chest and head wounds, where infection was present from the outset, surgery offered no remedy. None would be found until antibiotics became available towards the end of 1943.[38]

The vast majority of wounds in the Great War were caused either by artillery shells or by rifle and machine-gun bullets. Unpleasant as a bullet wound might be, a bursting shell could cause much more damage.

> Shell wounds were the most to be feared, because of the multiple effects shell explosion could produce in the human body. At its worst it could disintegrate a human being, so that nothing recognizable—sometimes apparently nothing at all—remained of him.... Less spectacular, but sometimes as deadly, shell blast could create over-pressures or vacuums in the body's organs, rupturing the lungs and producing haemorrhages in the brain and spinal cord.... Much the most common wounding by shell fire, however, was by splinter or shrapnel ball. Such projectiles...often travelled in clusters, which would inflict several large or many small wounds on the same person. The splinters were irregular in shape, so producing a very rough wound with a great deal of tissue damage, and they frequently carried fragments of clothing or other foreign matter into the body, which made infection inevitable. Very large shell splinters could...amputate limbs, decapitate, bisect or otherwise grossly mutilate the human frame.[39]

It is estimated that two-thirds of all wounds in the Great War were inflicted by shell fire.

Under optimum conditions, such terrible injuries would test the talents of the most skilful surgeon. But it goes without saying that conditions in Flanders were far from ideal. As Sir Andrew Macphail has written, "never was a filthier war waged" than in this corner of Belgium. For centuries, farmers had fertilized the land with all forms of excreta, human included, leaving the soil "deeply infected. With the disturbance of the ground by trenches, graves, and shells, the infection was general and virulent." A particularly unpleasant form of infection was gas gangrene. The name refers not to poison gas, but to a gas bacillus in the soil which breaks up decaying animal and vegetable matter and fertilizes plants.

> When a group of these gas-producing bacteria in the soil are blown on a piece of shell deep into the human body they find themselves in clover. The fragment of the tissues which have been torn and crushed and mangled out of all vitality by the shells furnish dead animal matter for them to grow on. They are deeply enough buried to be freed from the thing they hate most—the oxygen of the air; and the warmth of the body "forces" them like a hothouse.

The wound swells and turns a ghastly greenish colour; the body becomes bloated and distorted; death comes in twenty-four to forty-eight hours. By 1917, however, an anti-toxin had been developed to deal with this problem. And when, as often happened, it was not available in sufficient quantities, skilful surgery could be effective—but, as noted above, there were limits to what surgery could accomplish.[40]

Gas warfare, too, had been considerably refined by this point. Poison gas, first introduced by the Germans at Second Ypres in April 1915, was now in common use by both sides. Gas masks limited its effectiveness, but it still claimed its share of victims. By late 1917, the Germans were using primarily two types, one to complement the other, both delivered by artillery shells; the gas clouds used earlier in the war had been rendered obsolete. First, they would saturate an area with sneezing gas, diphenyl chlorarsine, which made respirators uncomfortable and caused many men to remove them. Then mustard gas, dichlorethyl sulphide, would be delivered, blistering and blinding its victims. Interestingly, the aim of gas warfare was not necessarily to kill; it was sufficient to render one's opponent hors de combat.

The effect of mustard gas could be insidious. Walter Bapty, the medical officer of the 102nd (Central Ontario) Battalion, made the mistake of sitting in mud where several gas shells had earlier exploded. Soon after, he was horrified to find that "the area over my right hip and buttock looked half cooked; red, blistered and weeping." Bapty was given an alkaline bath at a field hospital, declared a casualty, and sent to England to recover. Similarly, Private James Johnson of the 5th Canadian Mounted Rifles moved into a sector in which the ground was tinged "a yellowish green." Before long, Private Johnson was stricken:

> Blisters had started to form on my legs and back. One blister on my thigh was about eight inches long and four in width.... Later I was ordered on a stretcher and told not to move until I had a thorough examination.... Early in the afternoon I along with many others were carried out to the plank road where all the stretchers were lined up in a row to await ambulances. There were hundreds of us in line.[41]

In the face of this daunting array of obstacles, both man-made and natural, the Canadians prepared to assault Passchendaele Ridge. At least there was no chance that they would succumb to over-confidence.

10/Ready and Waiting

At Canadian Corps headquarters, planning for the attack was well under way. By 16 October, just three days after receiving his orders, General Currie had completed his preliminary plans, which he described in a letter to the Second Army's Sir Herbert Plumer.

> The operation will be carried out in three stages, the objective of each stage being...the RED, BLUE and GREEN lines.... It is proposed to employ the 3rd and 4th Canadian Divisions for the capture of the RED and BLUE lines (4th on the Right—3rd on the Left), keeping the 1st and 2nd Canadian Divisions for the capture of the GREEN line and any subsequent operations it may be decided to undertake. It is considered that a pause of three days will be necessary between the 1st and 2nd stages, and a pause of 4 or 5 days between the 2nd and 3rd stages.

Next day, Currie revised his schedule slightly in another letter to Plumer. "I would prefer to wait seven days between the 2nd and 3rd stages of the operation." Plumer approved.[1]

By 19 October, Currie had tentatively set dates for these operations: 28 and 31 October and 6 November. A fourth phase, if required, could be carried out on 10 November.

That such planning could be carried out so quickly and efficiently speaks highly not only of Currie but of the entire staff at Corps headquarters. Staff officers require a high degree of training. They are also an indispensable part of twentieth-century warfare; it would be impossible to function without them, such are the complexities of maintaining a fighting force on a modern battlefield. Canada began the war with only *seven* trained staff officers and, as a result, early Canadian formations were heavily stocked, out of necessity, with British staff officers, right down to the brigade level. By the fall of 1917, the majority of these had been replaced by Canadians who had learned their trade "on the job," so to speak. However, it is important to note that the two top staff officers at Corps headquarters were British, Brigadier-General Percy Radcliffe and Brigadier-General George Farmar. Radcliffe was so highly regarded that he later moved to the War Office in London. Farmar, on the other hand, remained with the Canadians till the end of the war; so valuable was he that Currie flatly refused to allow him to transfer to a British headquarters, saying, "When I want to get rid of you, George, I will tell you."[2]

A clash with Sir Hubert Gough forced Currie to slightly alter his arrangements. Currie had been pleased that the Canadian Corps had been assigned to Plumer's Second Army rather than Gough's Fifth because it meant that they would be, in his words, "spared being forced to comply with Gough's hasty judgments and the decisions of his incompetent staff." But, at a 19 October conference at Ten Elms, when Currie outlined his intentions to Plumer, Gough, and selected staff officers, the Fifth Army's commander objected. Having scheduled a minor attack for the twenty-second, Gough asked that Currie's operations be moved forward to enable the Canadians to co-operate. Currie, who had already seen enough of local conditions to be "amply confirmed...in my opinion that we should not fight under Gough"—the sector the Corps occupied had earlier been in the Fifth Army's jurisdiction—was in no mood to dicker. Warning Plumer that it would be impossible to properly prepare an attack so quickly, Currie bluntly stated: "In my opinion if the corps attacks on the 22nd it will fail to get its objectives."[3]

The was good enough for Plumer. "If Currie [will] not fight on the 22nd," said Sir Herbert, adjusting his monocle, "then the 2nd Army [will] not fight."[4]

Gough was indignant. "Who the devil is running the Second Army?" he fumed and, turning on his heels, "he flounced out of the room," in Currie's words.[5]

After Gough's angry departure, Plumer wondered whether a compromise might be worked out. Currie readily agreed and subsequently changed the dates of his initial attacks to 26 and 30 October, leaving the remainder of his plan intact. But it was not the last of his difficulties with either Gough or the Fifth Army.

Currie had plenty of company at Ten Elms as he oversaw preparations for the Canadian operations. Sir Douglas Haig, accompanied by Plumer, visited Corps headquarters "almost every day," according to Currie. Haig, he recalled, "deeply regrett[ed] the terrible conditions of mud and weather and the consequent suffering." More than once, Currie questioned the need to take Passchendaele Ridge, but Haig would merely reply: "Some day I will tell you why, but Passchendaele must be taken."[6]

The big Canadian was reluctant to be too persistent, however, because he was aware of the pressures facing the field-marshal. "I always sympathized with Haig," he later wrote, "because I knew of his troubles with the British Cabinet." Currie noted that there "those in authority in England"—"whom we may call the politicians," he commented derisively, for he, too, had little regard for elected officials—"who wanted to fight the war in many places other than the

Western Front.... I knew that none regretted the casualties more than he and when he was urged to go on and win victories, but to do it without casualties, he was almost in despair. When you are fighting stubborn, well-trained soldiers like the Germans, entrenched in splendidly fortified positions, who for a long time had greater resources in artillery and other weapons, it is impossible to win battles without casualties." It is ironic that Currie, who shared Haig's conviction that the Western Front was the decisive theatre of the war, would eventually be designated the commander-in-chief's successor.[7]

Haig's reticence notwithstanding, Currie did wring one concession from him. At Currie's request, he agreed to allow the Canadian Corps to leave the Ypres salient after its assignment was completed. Currie, who had no desire to spend a costly winter there, remarked to a staff officer, "Canada is prepared to lose her sons in a big offensive but won't stand for their lives to be frittered away."[8]

On 23 October, ten days after receiving his orders to proceed to Passchendaele and just five days after taking command of this sector, Currie presented his finalized plans to Haig at a conference at Corps headquarters.* Haig was so pleased that he stayed to lunch with the Canadians. "It seems he never before had lunched at a Corps Headquarters," Currie later commented. "It was regarded by my staff as a special compliment." Haig, apparently, allowed himself to be carried away again by his eternal optimism, as a British staff officer, Major Alan Brooke—another future field-marshal, one of three who served with the Canadian Corps in the course of the Great War—observed with some surprise: "I could hardly believe that my ears were not deceiving me! He spoke in the rosiest of terms of our chances of breaking through. I had been all over the ground and to my mind such an eventuality was quite impossible."[9]

There were a lot of Canadian soldiers who would have agreed with Brooke. The previous day, 22 October, Canadian troops had begun relieving the Australians and New Zealanders in the front lines. Their reception was hardly heart-warming. Private Don McKerchar of the 46th (South Saskatchewan) Battalion remembered riding in a lorry into Ypres and meeting a group of Australian soldiers waiting to take the truck back out. One Australian turned to a chum and said in a loud voice: "My God, look what they've sent up to take the ridge."[10]

The Anzacs probably felt they had good reason to be cynical. They were rightly regarded as first-class troops; if they had been

---

* See Appendix 2.

unable to take Passchendaele, who could possibly do it? Nothing they could say could have prepared the Canadians for what they were about to experience. Indeed, no words were necessary: the looks on their faces said more than enough. Corporal Will Bird of the 42nd (Royal Highlanders of Canada) Battalion would forever remember seeing "the remnants of a relieved battalion... men who looked like grisly discards of the battlefield, long unburied, who had risen and were in search of graves." A 46th Battalion private, Vic Syrett, echoed those sentiments: "The Australians we relieved were very white and walked and looked like zombies."[11]

The journey to the front was equally unforgettable. Typical is the recollection of Stewart Scott of the 78th (Winnipeg Grenadiers) Battalion:

> Through the dead city of Ypres in the dark of night with the flares from the forward areas forming this backdrop, so you got a shimmering outline of this Cloth Hall, for instance, and these partially destroyed buildings with scampering troops. You hurried through because the exit was a place called Hell Fire Corner, and it was well named, and that led out onto the Menin Road through the Menin Gate.
>
> The accuracy of the shelling was appalling. And it was much worse, of course, when you got on the road to Menin. It was just Dante's *Inferno*, with dead carcasses, and dead men, men who had just died ten minutes before, and who was going to stop to clear the dead when you might be joining them yourself if you didn't just keep going? You scampered along trying to keep the fellow in front of you in view, because he might take a right wheel or a left wheel, and if you missed him—God knows where you'd land up.
>
> And then, having gone up the Menin Road for goodness-knows-how-far, we turned left. The guide said, "We turn here. Come this way, sir." So, we'd turn left and we get on to about a fifth-class road that was slippery as the devil and probably an inch or two of slime over the top of it, and you went along there I-don't-know-how-far until you turned right again, and this time you travelled on these duckboards. They were just laid on the ground and, of course, there were many intervals where the duckboards had ceased to be because a shell had got them, so you would step off in the mud to the next duckboard, and you might go to your ankles, you might go to your shins, and if you weren't careful... you could step off into three or four feet of water....
>
> You eventually get to the front line and your guide said, "This is it...."

> "Well, where is the trench?"
> "Well, you are looking at it."
> Just kind of a ditch.[12]

Private Arthur Turner of the 50th (Calgary) Battalion remembered the words of his commanding officer just before setting out. "It is not going to be a picnic," Lieutenant-Colonel Lionel Page had warned them, and he knew what he was talking about, as Private Turner soon discovered.

> There were no trench mats to walk on at that time, [we] just had to find our way around the shell holes. Each step we took we had to reach down and pull the other leg up out of the mud. Besides our regular equipment, and ammunition, each man was given an extra 30 rounds of ammunition, a shovel, and an extra day's ration to carry, we were weighted down like pack mules, and all the time shells were exploding around us.

Inevitably, one of Turner's buddies fell into a muddy shell hole. "He got up plastered from head to foot...looking the picture of misery. I know he needed sympathy. But all I could do was laugh."[13]

Others told similar stories. Major George Kilpatrick of the 42nd (Royal Highlanders of Canada) Battalion wrote home:

> I cannot describe the road we had to travel. It was indeed a via dolorosa. The mud was so deep and tenacious that it was labor to walk at all and we were laden down with supplies. I had a pack, a sand bag full and a great bundle of splints. The way ascended the whole time—when we finally arrived, a sorrier looking bunch you never saw, mud to the waist and dripping with perspiration.

Lieutenant A.L. Barry of the 26th (New Brunswick) Battalion recalled seeing an ironic sign posted at the roadside near Ypres: DRIVE SLOWLY, DUST DRAWS SHELL-FIRE. At the time, the battalion was slopping through ankle-deep mud.[14]

Initial impressions were uniformly negative. To Corporal Bird of the 42nd Battalion, one of the most striking features was the distinctive aroma, "a sour smell of disinfectants, stale gas, sodden clothing, and a faint, sickly odor of decay—the breath of the Salient." Related a member of the 31st (Alberta) Battalion, death was omnipresent. "You would pass somewhere and the water would move a little and you would see men's heads bobbing up and down, drowned in sloughs—whether or not they were wounded or killed first, we didn't know, of course, and they had been there for some little time." More than a few had a premonition of evil. One such was Private Ernie

Harris of the 46th. "I never felt it before, but something has just struck me," he told anyone who would listen. "This is my last trip in the line. I don't know whether I'll get wounded or whether I'll get killed, but this is going to be my last trip." And so it would be, not only for Harris, but for thousands of young Canadians.[15]

The sector assigned the Canadians lay a mile southwest of Passchendaele village. Their front was about 3,000 yards long, with the right-hand boundary marked by the Ypres-Roulers railway. "Front" is a misleading term: this sector was actually split in two by the Ravebeek, a normally inconsequential stream now swollen to impassable bog half a mile wide. The first few days following 18 October, the date that General Currie took command here, gave hope that the weather might not be a factor in the coming operations. Conditions were, for a time, rather pleasant, as Captain Harold McGill of the 5th Canadian Field Ambulance noted in his diary:

18 October: "Fine day. S.W. wind."
19 October: "Bright sunny morning, S.W. wind."
20 October: "Bright clear morning. S.E. wind."
21 October: "Bright morning. S. wind. Hard frost."[16]

The improvement was most welcome, but it had a minimal impact on the battlefield, which, as Lyn Macdonald has written, "was now so battered, so flooded, that the weak sunshine was as effective in drying the ground as a lighted match held over a bathtub full of water."[17]

It was, in any case, too good to last, and it did not last, as Captain McGill's diary reveals:

22 October: "High South W. wind. Rain.... Fine afternoon."
22 October: "High S. wind. Heavy rain... all day. Cold."
24 October: "Bright clear morning. S.W. wind. Cool.... Sky is clouding up.... Raining. Everybody is dripping. Very heavy rain with S.W. gales."
25 October: "Still raining."
26 October: "Raining heavily."[18]

Even before the renewed rainfall, the battlefield was a shocking sight. The utter desolation was astonishing, even to grizzled veterans of this terrible war. "The ground is one mass of water filled shell holes stretching away to the east," reads the diary of Lieutenant L.V. Shier of the 20th (Central Ontario) Battalion, "where there are several ridges which we have already taken. Here and there a few broken off tree stumps show where a wood once stood." The description is repeated again and again in the records and recollections of the survivors. "The condition of the ground baffles description," wrote Major Kilpatrick of the 42nd Battalion. "It is far worse than Vimy and I thought that the last word in desolation. Rain has fallen and overflowed shell holes till acres are a grey mire." Lieutenant-Colonel Agar Adamson of Princess Patricia's Canadian Light Infantry (PPCLI) told his wife:

> The condition of the ground beggars description. Just one mass of shell holes all full of water. The strongest and youngest men cannot navigate without falling down. The people we relieve tell me in the attack, a great many of their men were drowned in shell holes for want of strength to pull themselves out when dog tired.

Major George Pearkes of the 5th Canadian Mounted Rifles (CMR) would never forget "the appalling state of the ground. Everywhere there were deep shell holes filled with water." Indeed, it seemed incredible that anyone could actually fight a battle here.[19]

No Canadians were more shocked than veterans of the great gas attack in April 1915. This should have been, for these men at least, familiar territory. "I thought that I knew every phase of that old ground in 1915," wrote Brigadier-General George Tuxford, a battalion commander in the earlier clash who now led the Third Brigade, "but now I could not recognize it at all. The whole country side seemed to have been turned over and blasted out of all recognition. Of the handful of brick buildings on the Gravenstafel Ridge which had formed the 5th Battalion H.Qrs. it was now impossible to find a single brick." Paul Villiers, now a thirty-three-year-old major serving at First Division headquarters, had fought at Second Ypres with the Third Brigade.

> I was interested to see how changed the country was since 1915, when I was last here. I had been prepared for a change, but not for the change that I saw. Of Wieltje there was not one stone left upon another. If it had not been for a notice board which said "Here stood Wieltje" one would have passed on without knowing it. The country itself was a wreck of its former self. Gone were the pleasant meadows, farm houses and copses. Nothing but a wilderness of mud and shell holes, dead bodies, and blasted trees.[20]

If the rear areas were shocking, the front line was an even bigger eye-opener. There was no line per se, none of the trenches to which the Canadians had become accustomed. It was impossible to do any amount of digging because the whole area "was simply a mass of mud and water," in the words of Private Pat Burns of the 46th Battalion. "We tried to dig down for protection [but] you couldn't go any further than one foot and you'd strike water." The front was merely a loosely connected series of shell holes, filled with cold, murky water, often with bodies or parts of bodies floating in them. Huddled in these miserable craters, which offered precious little protection from either the elements or enemy shell fire, mud became an integral part of their lives: it soaked their equipment; they slept in it; food tasted of it. Recalled one veteran:

> Your clothes were wet all the time, but there was nothing to be done about it. It was part of the job, and it had to be done, and it was done. Every morning you got your rum just before stand-to. They'd give you a good slug of rum and that would warm you up, but half an hour after you had it the effects were gone, because you were wet practically through.

The quartermaster of the 42nd Battalion weighed the mud-plastered greatcoat of a soldier just back from a tour of the front lines: it weighed fifty pounds![21]

Comforts were few and far between. Private Percy Hellings of the 46th Battalion in later years recalled one rare delight:

> They brought up some long underwear—long johns. Boy, did they ever feel good, I'm telling you. It was just pull your clothes off and pull 'em on. All these guys in the mud and under fire trying to find a dry spot so you could get your feet out of the mud. You'd get a groundsheet so you wouldn't get mud all through your underwear. It would be funny if someone were taking a picture, I guess, but we didn't think nothing about it. We were often glad of that underwear. By golly it was cold.

Few suffered more than the Canadian Highland battalions, still stubbornly wearing their kilts. Pride took a back seat to practicality, however, and the Highlanders were only too happy to pull on their longies, so that "instead of our knees showing our long underwear was showing," recalled John MacKenzie of the 72nd (Seaforth Highlanders of Canada) Battalion. "However, with the cold that was there, and the wet, we just didn't care, and there was nobody looking at us." The Highlanders usually needed only one visit to the front before trading their kilts for trousers at the first opportunity.[22]

In this environment, trench foot briefly threatened to pose a problem. Trench foot was an ailment which resulted from prolonged exposure to wet and cold and produced symptoms similar to frostbite.

During the winter of 1915-16 it reached epidemic proportions in the BEF, despite the insistence of medical authorities that it could be prevented. One commander who took to heart their advice was Major-General Arthur Currie of the First Canadian Division. He took stringent measures to curb trench foot, and they worked admirably: throughout that long, cold winter, no division in the BEF boasted a better record in the prevention of trench foot. Now, as Corps commander, General Currie had no intention of allowing his troops to succumb to trench foot at Passchendaele. Each man was required to take with him into the battle zone three pairs of socks, and a clean, dry pair was issued every two days. They were also ordered to regularly rub their feet with liberal quantities of whale oil. Although some soldiers told comical stories of men hopping about with one boot on and one off, trying to apply the whale oil, with shells and bullets whizzing by, rigorous enforcement of the rules paid dividends: trench foot did not emerge as a serious health hazard here.

As if the Canadians did not have enough problems, between the ever-present mud and the incessant shelling, the Germans added a new wrinkle. Through most of 1917, the Allies and the Germans had taken turns winning temporary superiority in the air: from mid-October to mid-November, it was the enemy's turn to dominate the sky. As mentioned earlier, this disadvantage impaired the performance of the Canadian artillery at Passchendaele. It also affected the infantry, who found themselves being bombed and machine-gunned by German aircraft at all hours of the day or night. It was disconcerting, as Jack Quelch, a sniper in the 44th (Manitoba) Battalion, admitted in a letter home:

> I will say this, that only Hiney [sic] has some dashed airmen and planes, and nothing to be laughed at by our airmen. He has a new formation now, he comes over with one big Gotha with [an] escort of half a dozen small & fast fighting machines. The Gotha is a big [aircraft] and does the bombing. I have seen this formation come over Ypres three times a day and drop several dozen large bombs at a time. One that you could drop a team and loading of grain into the hole and lose.[23]

There was nowhere to hide. The Canadians found themselves at the mercy of German flyers en route to the front or to the rear, in the front lines or in their billets. Night raids were particularly unnerving; the great height of the giant Gotha bombers "gave the feeling that they were hovering directly above, searching out and preying on the individual. It was hard to remove the delusion that one was being singled out by an invisible demon in the sky. Few things were more trying to morale." Of course, in the next great war, this experience would be commonplace; in the Great War of 1914–18 it was considered a "new form of terrorism."[24]

"At Passchendaele our air force was practically nil." It was a common complaint among the Canadians. Stanley Baker of the 54th (Central Ontario) Battalion recalled how members of his unit "lined up at the cook wagon, and German planes drove us away five times before we got our breakfast." Joe O'Neill of the 19th (Central Ontario) Battalion remembered seeing an enemy plane swoop so low "you could see the buttons on his uniform, we were so close, and he leaned over the side of the plane and he waved at us, and we waved at him."[25]

Lieutenant Stanley Quinton of the 78th (Winnipeg Grenadiers) Battalion decided to do something about it. Fed up with being strafed, the twenty-nine-year-old subaltern, with the help of his batman, rigged up a device that would enable him to fire four rifle-grenades simultaneously. In broad daylight, Quinton and the batman crawled into no man's land and waited in ambush for a wayward German aircraft. It was, Quinton admitted, "an ambitious undertaking, as the range of grenades is distinctly limited." He had no opportunity to test his contraption, waiting all day in vain for a plane to venture close enough to spring his ambush. When darkness fell, Quinton and the enlisted man stole back to their lines. Their mission failed, but it illustrates the anger and frustration felt by the Canadians.[26]

They would have been even more uncomfortable had they known that the Germans were expecting them. The Canadians' reputation had preceded them: from their first brilliant battle here in the Ypres salient in 1915, through the capture of Vimy Ridge and Hill 70 earlier this year, they had won the grudging admiration of their enemy. In fact, German staff officers in Flanders "considered the Canadians to be the best troops the British had."[27] The presence of the Canadian Corps could mean only one thing: another attack on Passchendaele.

And now the defenders, the 11th Bavarian Division, sat secure in their pillboxes on this long, low ridge. Confidently, they peered down on the Canadians mired in the mud below. The enemy would be ready and waiting.

11 / "A Truly Magnificent Performance"

Zero hour, 5:40 A.M., Friday, 26 October 1917.

It was a misty, overcast morning. Rain had fallen sporadically through the night, as it would continue to do all day long. In the semi-darkness, the Canadians crouched in waterlogged shell holes or shallow ditches that served as jumping-off lines, awaiting the moment when their officers would stand up and blow whistles, signalling the start of the attack. The daily rum ration, for those lucky enough to have received it, helped take the edge off the chilly air. In the final, nervous hours prior to zero, many of these young men, like Private Pat Burns of the 46th (South Saskatchewan) Battalion, turned to prayer for solace. "I never prayed so hard in my life," Burns later admitted. "I got down on my knees and I prayed to God to bring me through. My whole life went before me and I couldn't see any future. I really prayed, believe me."[1]

The Canadians faced an undeniably difficult task. Due to the swamp formed by the flooded Ravebeek, the Corps would be forced to make a two-pronged assault. On the left, Major-General Lipsett's Third Division would employ two brigades but, due to the constricted front, only three battalions could take part in the attack. On the division's left, the Eighth Brigade would deploy a single battalion, the 4th Canadian Mounted Rifles (CMR), while on the right, the Ninth Brigade would be attacking with two battalions, the 43rd (Cameron Highlanders of Canada) and 58th (Central Ontario). Their intermediate objective, designated on Corps maps as the Dotted Red Line, lay 600 yards away; the final objective, the Red Line, was 1,200 yards from the jumping-off positions. The key to the entire operation was the Bellevue Spur, where the Anzacs had come to grief earlier in the month. General Lipsett called the spur "about the strongest position I have ever seen," describing it as "a fortress with numbers of concrete machine gun emplacements and concrete dugouts placed checkerwise on the forward and reverse slopes so as to be mutually supporting."[2]

On the Corps right was Major-General Watson's Fourth Division. So narrow was this flooded front that only one battalion, the 46th (South Saskatchewan), could make the assault, with the 50th (Calgary) Battalion in close support. These units, which belonged to the Tenth Brigade, were to take, in conjunction with neighbouring

Australian troops, Decline Copse, a shattered wood that lay 600 yards distant, beside the Ypres-Roulers railway. Decline Copse, a veritable maze of camouflaged defences, was strongly held, as the Australians had discovered on 12 October.

The artillery spared no effort to assist the infantry. For the previous four days, the guns of the Canadian Corps had bombarded the Germans each morning and afternoon, "to wear down the enemy and mislead him as to the actual time of the forthcoming attack." For zero day, an elaborate program had been prepared, consisting of six separate barrages:

"A" barrage—two-thirds of the available 18-pounders

"B-1" barrage—the balance of the 18-pounders, firing 100 yards ahead of the "A" barrage

"B-2" barrage—4.5-inch howitzers, 100-50 yards ahead of "B-1"

"C" barrage—machine-guns, 100 yards ahead of "B-2"

"D" barrage—medium howitzers, 100 yards ahead of "C"

"E" barrage—heavy howitzers, 200 yards ahead of "D"

In normal conditions, the creeping barrage would move in hundred-yard lifts every four minutes; because of the mud at Passchendaele, it moved at half-speed. The 18-pounders, which were directly supporting the infantry, would increase their range fifty yards every four minutes, while the remainder of the guns shifted their fire in hundred-yard lifts at eight-minute intervals.[3]

The bombardment opened precisely at zero hour. It was an unsettling experience, even for the many veterans among the Canadians waiting to go over the top. Private Arthur Turner of the 50th Battalion would long remember the shrapnel shells exploding "right over our heads. The concussion was terrific, it made me feel as if my chest was being ripped open. The shells would explode over our heads, but the shrapnel shot forward on to the Germans." The enemy artillery soon responded. Not only was the resultant din deafening, the earth literally shook with the violence of the innumerable explosions. One survivor likened it to "a big jelly pot of wet mud and water shaking or rather quivering under the fire of the guns."[4]

On the extreme left of the Canadian attack, the 4th CMR faced "the bloodiest battle in their history." The men could not know that, of course, but there were plenty of omens. Moving into the front line two nights earlier proved to be "one of the worst reliefs the Battalion ever experienced," in the words of the regimental history. The night had been pitch black and raining heavily, and chaos ensued: the

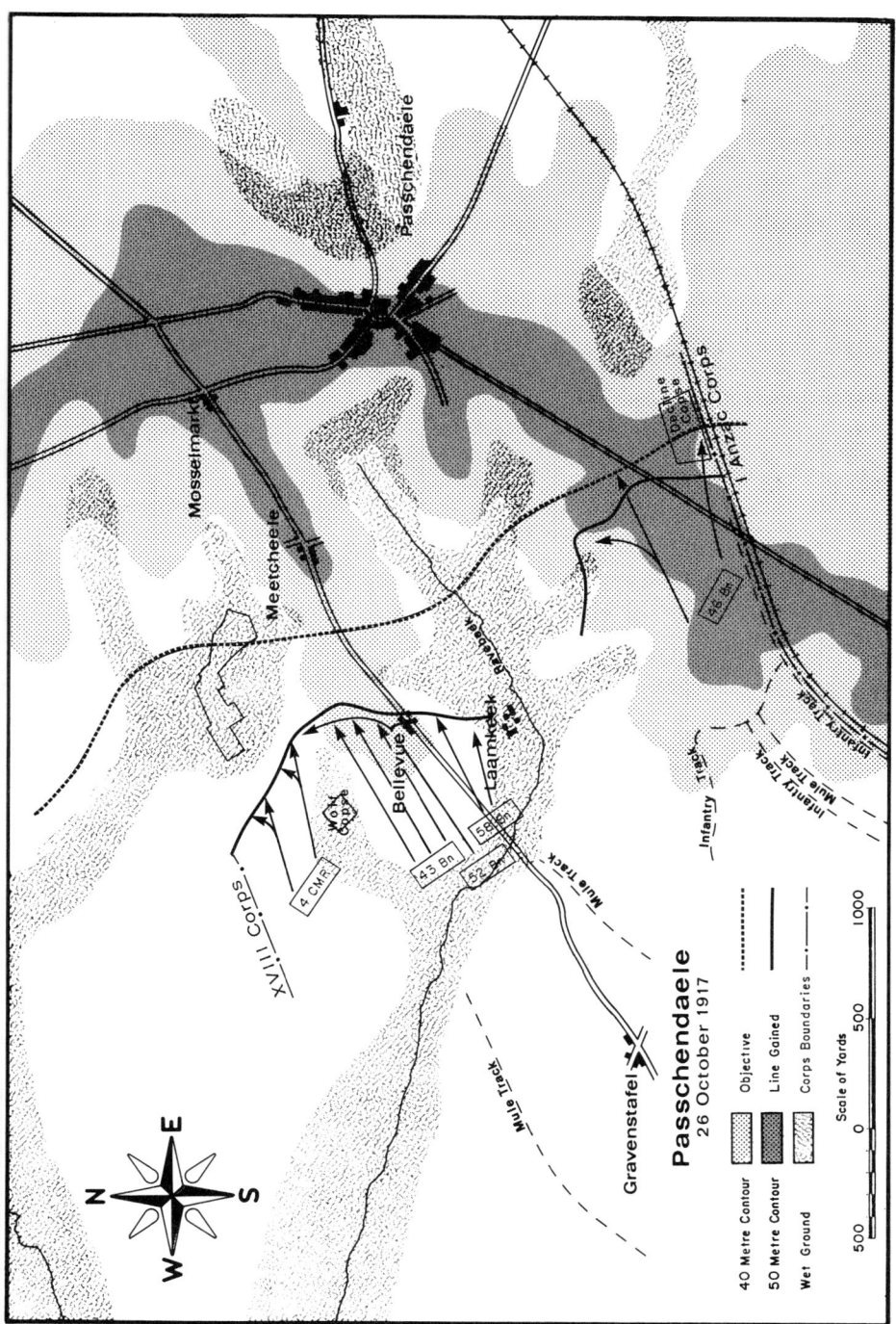

companies became intermixed and the battalion's water and food rations had been lost en route. To make matters worse, reconnaissance on arrival produced the unsettling "discovery that their attack had to be launched across a bog."[5]

At 5:48 A.M., zero plus eight minutes, the 4th CMR went over the top and straight into a living nightmare. It had begun to "drizzle" by now, and Lieutenant-Colonel W.R. Patterson was alarmed to see that the Canadian artillery barrage "was erratic and not uniform," as he later reported, "causing a number of casualties in our left leading company." Shelled by their own guns, raked by German machine-gun fire, the Canadians found themselves struggling through what one 4th CMR man called "porridge, a ghastly, dreadful porridge, thigh-deep, in which if you got it on the shoulder blade with a bullet that merely knocked you unconscious for two minutes you drowned. We lost lots of men who simply drowned because they were knocked over or stunned and couldn't get recovered before they'd sunk in the mud." It was a horror that would be repeated countless times on this battlefield.[6]

As the losses mounted, the attack bogged down, and not solely because of the mud. The Germans had more than a little to do with it; their pillbox defences appeared to be marvellously effective on the 4th CMR front. Indeed, the battalion's attack foundered in front of a pillbox supported by a pair of machine-guns in a nearby shell hole. Khaki-clad corpses sprawled in the mud attested to the deadly accuracy of the enemy fire. No one, it seemed, could get to within fifty yards of the pillbox.

With failure staring the battalion in the face, a single young soldier saved the day. Private Tommy Holmes was an unlikely looking hero: just nineteen, his boyish countenance highlighted by a beaming smile, he looked like he should have been at home attending school and playing softball rather than being here, in this abattoir in a foreign land. It was his first time in combat, but he acted like a veteran. Jumping up, he slipped and slid through the mud, scrambling from shell hole to shell hole, bullets dancing at his feet. Word of his one-man attack soon spread. "What's going on?" someone would ask. "Some crazy guy!" would be the reply. "Look! Look at him!"[7]

They watched in amazement as young Holmes leap-frogged closer and closer to the enemy machine-guns. Finally he was within bomb-throwing range. Holmes had only one Mills bomb with him— his aim would have to be good. It was. He lofted the grenade into the air with impressive accuracy: it landed between the two guns and the ensuing explosion wiped out both crews. But Holmes wasn't finished yet. He worked his way back to his admiring comrades, secured another bomb, then returned to deal with the pillbox. Still under heavy fire, but somehow unscathed, Tommy Holmes made his way around it, then threw the grenade into the rear entrance. Moments later, nineteen Germans emerged with their hands in the air.

Private Holmes later was awarded the Victoria Cross, the Empire's highest award for bravery in the face of the enemy. Holmes, however, took his heroism matter-of-factly. Afterward, when asked if he realized what he had done, he shrugged, "Well, no. I thought everybody did that sort of thing."[8]

The 4th CMR, inspired by Holmes's bravery, surged forward. Ignoring murderous machine-gun fire, the Canadians floundered through the mud and reached their intermediate objective, Wolf Copse. Two platoons pressed on to Woodland Plantation, but the position was too exposed and they were withdrawn. The battalion now found itself in a bad situation; British troops on the left had been stopped in their tracks, while on the right, as we shall see, the attack of the Ninth Brigade was faring poorly. Under merciless fire not only from the front but both flanks as well, Colonel Patterson realized that there was little point in continuing on to the final objective: it would merely invite disaster. As it was, the 4th CMR had been grievously hurt. Only five of the sixteen officers who had started out survived; one company had no officers still standing. Patterson ordered his men to dig in where they were, and by eleven o'clock that morning the battalion's modest gains had been consolidated. During the afternoon, reinforcements from the 1st CMR arrived to help hold the line.

It was in mid-afternoon that something remarkable happened. Around three o'clock, the Canadians were surprised to see a lone figure in front of them. It proved to be the padre of the 4th CMR, Captain W.H. Davis. With a handkerchief tied to his walking stick, Captain Davis struggled across the muddy, pockmarked ground, searching out the wounded, both Canadian and German. An injured officer asked Davis what he was doing. "I was getting *anxious* about you," he replied with a smile.[9]

Gradually, an astonished silence fell over this part of the bloody battlefield. Occasionally, there would be a burst of gunfire nearby, and Davis would angrily wave his walking stick. Then he would continue his work: at each wounded man, he would plunge the soldier's rifle into the mud and hang his helmet from the gun butt. This went on for long minutes. A few cautious Canadians joined Davis, then a few Germans came forward to help out. A clearing house was set up at a ruined pillbox. Here, Germans carried wounded Canadians and Canadians carried wounded Germans. The injured men were exchanged, along with the odd cigarette, both sides keeping a wary eye on each other.

The unofficial ceasefire lasted about half an hour. Then renewed shooting shattered the silence in this sector, and the killing resumed. Captain Davis's humanitarian gesture earned him not only the Military Cross, but the gratitude of a great many Canadian and German soldiers.[10]

Grimly, the 4th CMR held its position, despite fierce enemy fire and at least one counter-attack. It had rounded up 200 prisoners and taken twelve machine-guns, but the cost was considerable: by the time the battalion was relieved the following day, it had suffered 321 casualties. Major G.F. McFarland, the unit's second-in-command, summed up the feelings of many when he wrote in a letter to a friend:

> I have experienced my first battle, and it was pure hell. Even yet I am dazed, and I doubt if I could give you a coherent account of it. We are out of the line now, and it is a blessed relief to be away from the continuous roar of the guns. You have no idea how it gets on your nerves.

But Major McFarland was intensely proud of his men: "their conduct was beyond all praise."[11]

While the 4th CMR had at least gained a partial success, an even more desperate struggle was taking place to the right, where the Canadians came perilously close to a defeat reminiscent of that suffered by the Anzacs earlier at the Bellevue Spur.

Brigadier-General F.W. Hill's Ninth Brigade deployed two battalions to the right of the 4th CMR, and both enjoyed early but illusory success. The barbed wire which had halted the Anzacs before them had been well cut by the Canadian artillery, and the 43rd (Cameron Highlanders of Canada) and 58th (Central Ontario) battalions quickly overcame the initial line of pillboxes. Having reached their intermediate objective with relatively light losses, the Canadians might have suspected that it had been all too easy. And so it was, until the Germans brought down intense artillery fire on their own abandoned forward positions. The enemy gunners had them ranged perfectly. With nowhere to hide, the Canadians could not endure this deadly accurate fire for long; by mid-morning they had been forced to relinquish most of their gains.

There was but one saving feature. Lieutenant Robert Shankland of the 43rd, with about fifty men—his own platoon and remnants of others—and two machine-guns, stubbornly refused to give up a toehold on the Bellevue Spur, just north of the Mosselmarkt road. As the morning wore on, the Germans focused their full attention on this brave little band. Counter-attack followed counter-attack, but the Canadians clung tenaciously to their slimy shell holes on the crest of the spur. Lieutenant Shankland, manning one of the machine-guns, later remembered dispersing an enemy attack: "along the skyline of the ridge down came fifty men and wheeled left, and when they wheeled they couldn't have wheeled more direct on [t]his gun, so I gave them one burst of fire, and that was enough."[12] But the lieutenant knew that his men could not hold on without reinforcements. After assuring himself that the position was secure, for the time being, Shankland went for help, running the terrible gauntlet of fire that separated him from the Canadian lines.

Plastered with mud from head to foot and nearly exhausted, but uninjured, Shankland reported to the headquarters of a reserve battalion, the 52nd (Ontario). Shankland's story came as a revelation; it had been presumed that the Ninth Brigade's attack had been a complete failure. But there was no time to waste: a company under Captain Christopher O'Kelly was promptly dispatched to aid the beleaguered Canadians on the spur.

It was a decisive move. With no artillery support, Captain O'Kelly's company left its reserve position and braved a thousand yards of open ground, slogging through deep mud and enduring heavy fire to reach Shankland's tiny force. The timing was impeccable: the Germans were in the midst of another counter-attack when O'Kelly and his men reached the scene. They took the Germans by the flank and routed them. O'Kelly had only just begun to fight, however. He organized and personally led attacks on a number of nearby pillboxes, and within a short time the situation was markedly better. Six pillboxes were taken, along with 100 prisoners and ten machine-guns. Additional reinforcements from the 52nd Battalion arrived soon after to secure this success. By the following morning, the 52nd had taken the intermediate objective and pushed to within 300 yards of the Ninth Brigade's final objectives, bagging 275 prisoners and twenty-one machine-guns in the process.[13]

Two Victoria Crosses came out of this action. One was awarded to Lieutenant Shankland,* the other to Captain O'Kelly. Thanks to

---

* By a curious coincidence, Shankland lived on the same street in Winnipeg as two previous winners of the Victoria Cross: Company Sergeant-Major F.W. Hall, who won it at Second Ypres in April 1915, and Corporal Leo Clarke, who won it at the Somme in September 1916. Pine Street was later renamed Valour Road in honour of these three heroes.

their leadership, and to the bravery of the men under them, the Ninth Brigade had overcome adversity and taken a large part of the Bellevue Spur. The brigade commander, General Hill, was justified in writing a few days later: "I feel it was a fine performance. We had the nut to crack & we did it."[14]

Nevertheless, 26 October had been a close call for the Third Division. The Canadians had literally snatched victory from the jaws of defeat, to use the time-worn cliché. Ironically, a similar scenario developed on the Fourth Division's front that day; the only differences were that the Fourth actually came closer to failure and took longer to restore the situation.

The 46th (South Saskatchewan) Battalion led the assault. Ground conditions were, here as elsewhere, terrible, as Private Don McKerchar vividly recalled: "We were wading in mud and falling in shell holes. Just unbelievable.... If you were a casualty... you'd probably drown in the mud and dirt—many of them, all kinds, drowned in this mud." But the mud proved to be a blessing in disguise. "A lot of the shells," McKerchar remembered, "would bury in the soft mud—many of them were duds—and if they did explode, they were down so deep that the shrapnel wasn't too effective."[15]

The 46th Battalion soon found itself under not only German shell fire but Canadian, too. Lieutenant-Colonel Herbert Dawson later complained that many of his battalion's "losses were due to our own Artillery. The barrage was very wide, and caught Companies advancing...." It was not pleasant, said Private Percy Hellings, "getting shelled from both sides—a pretty rough situation. They were coming down just like rain."[16]

Enemy machine-gun fire was equally galling, and terribly effective. Bullets ripped through the ranks of the advancing Canadians, cutting the battalion to ribbons. A bullet ended Private Hellings's war after he had struggled only "twenty feet," by his own estimate. His left arm and hand mangled, Hellings was later declared medically unfit and shipped home.[17]

Not far away, Private Ernie Harris was living his premonition. Believing that Passchendaele would be his last trip, Private Harris seemed to have a charmed life. Within thirty yards of the jumping-off line, he discovered that he was the sole survivor of his platoon. Joining another platoon, he slogged his way to the objective, a low rise near Decline Copse. Harris was the only man in this group to get there. While waiting for reinforcements, he used Mill bombs to knock out a pair of pillboxes, then sat down to wait for help to arrive. It was not long in coming; a captain directed Harris and six others to occupy and hold one of the pillboxes. Before they could do so, a shell exploded in their midst, and "blew the seven of us up," Harris recalled. "I was about the height of a one-and-a-half storey house. I remember going up but I don't remember coming down." Once more, Harris was the only survivor. But his premonition had been borne out: this was his last trip. Wounded in seven places, Harris soon returned to Canada as disabled.[18]

The casualties were incredible. The 46th Battalion would lose 70 per cent of its attacking strength this day.* Private Pat Burns was among the lucky few to escape injury:

> I went over with . . . fifteen men in the machine-gun section, and every man was hit beside me, and a fellow by the name of Piercey and I were the only survivors that got to the objective. We jumped in a big hole. I had the machine-gun, which I knew nothing about, and all the ammunition we could carry—and there we were, holding the front line.[19]

Amazingly, the 46th Battalion—or, rather, what was left of it—took its objectives. By 7:10 A.M., Colonel Dawson later reported, his men had occupied Decline Copse. But taking it was one thing; holding it would be something else again.

It was painfully clear that the Germans had no intention of forfeiting Decline Copse without a fight. Two hastily organized counter-attacks were beaten back by the remnants of the 46th, with help from the 50th (Calgary) Battalion. The mud made it impossible to dig in, and the Canadians were forced to seek shelter in shell holes to escape the punishing enfilade fire coming from the vicinity of Lamkeek. As the day wore on, it became apparent that the Germans were marshalling their forces for another big counter-attack.

The enemy attacked at 4:43 P.M. They came from three directions: Crest Farm, Passchendaele, and Tiber House. Behind a heavy barrage, hundreds of grey-clad German soldiers converged on the Canadian position. The heavily outnumbered Canadians fired SOS flares, calling for a counter-barrage by their own guns. But there was a breakdown in communications somewhere along the line. Nearly twenty critical minutes passed before the Canadian artillery responded to the SOS, and by then it was too late.

---

* The nominal strength of a Canadian infantry battalion in the Great War was 35 officers and 996 other ranks. However, it was standard practice to designate a portion of these men as "left out of battle"; in the event of disaster, the battalion could be more easily reconstituted around this group. At Passchendaele, the average Canadian battalion went into battle approximately 600 strong.

It was a hopeless situation. There were too many Germans and too few Canadians. Seventeen-year-old Private Gordon Brown of the 46th squeezed off several shots at the swarming enemy soldiers. At ten yards, Private Brown threw his Mills bomb at the Germans, then scrambled out of his shell hole and ran for his life. "Boy oh boy, the bullets were flying!" he would recall. "I could see the bullets hitting the ground all around me. One of my puttees was cut off, there were bullets through my pant-legs, bullets through my uniform here and there, but none of them touched me."[20]

Private Don McKerchar had a similar experience. He and a lance-corporal named Dyck had been sent to cover the battalion's left flank; they were cut off when the Germans counter-attacked. Surrounded by the enemy, McKerchar and Dyck decided to make a run for it. Stumbling, slipping, and sliding, with bullets whizzing about them, they somehow scampered to safety. Afterward, they joked that as they fled they could hear the German bullets twice, "once when they passed us, and again when we caught up to them!"[21]

The Canadian small-arms fire was too weak and scattered to slow the Germans, much less stop them, and the 46th crumbled in the face of the enemy onslaught. For the first time in their experience, and probably the only time for the men of this brave battalion, panic gripped the handful of survivors. "You'd never believe how scared a person can be," one of them later confessed. "I didn't know anything, I couldn't see anything—just run, run, run—I never stopped running till...an officer stuck his revolver in my face and said, 'Halt!'"[22]

One such officer was Major John Hope. The very sight of him was an inspiration to the tired and frightened men of the 46th. "Dressed immaculately—you'd think he'd just stepped out of a band-box!" recalled Private Pat Burns. Another heroic figure was Captain William Kennedy. He was the only officer left between the two left-hand companies, which had been decimated: he had a mere forty-five men left, and a lance-corporal was his sole non-commissioned officer (NCO). Kennedy later called this tense moment in the battle "about the hottest corner we were ever in."[23]

These determined officers rallied the shattered remains of the 46th Battalion. In the meantime, the German attack ran out of steam: the enemy had no easy time manoeuvring in the mud, and they ran into the massed fire of the 10th Canadian Machine-Gun Company, which was supporting the 46th. The Germans withered in the face of this furious fusilade, and then the 46th resumed its own attack, led by the redoubtable Major Hope. "We can't lose that place," he called out. "The 46th has never lost an inch of ground yet!"[24] Waving his revolver, the major led a wild charge up the slippery, sodden slope. The Canadians made up in ferocity what they lacked in numbers and took back the rise near Decline Copse, though they were unable to recapture that shattered wood.

The 46th Battalion paid dearly for its determination. Of the 600 men who took part in the attack, more than 70 per cent of them became casualties: the toll amounted to eighteen officers and 426 other ranks. Soon after being relieved, the battalion paraded for its commanding officer, Colonel Dawson, who appeared after his adjutant had assembled the men. "Where's the rest of them?" inquired the colonel, as he surveyed the small group standing before him. "That's all you have, sir," shrugged the adjutant. "There are no more left." Dawson broke down in tears.[25]

There remained, despite the sacrifice of the 46th, the problem of Decline Copse. Brigadier-General Edward Hilliam, commanding the Tenth Brigade, declared that it must be taken "at all costs,"[26] and handed the assignment to his two remaining battalions, the 44th (Manitoba) and the 47th (British Columbia), which relieved the 46th and 50th late on 26 October. Lieutenant-Colonel M. Francis of the 47th and his counterpart with the 44th, Lieutenant-Colonel R.D. Davies, consulted and agreed to renew the attack that very night, with the 47th leading and the 44th in support.

The night assault was seemingly successful. At midnight, a bloodied runner appeared at the pillbox which the two colonels were using as a joint headquarters. He had good news: "Captain Lindsell of the 47th reports that he has retaken Decline Copse."[27] This information was quickly flashed to General Hilliam at Tenth Brigade headquarters and to neighbouring Australian units. Colonel Francis broke out a bottle of Scotch to celebrate.

The celebration was short-lived. Soon after, an irate Australian officer appeared at the headquarters pillbox. "I'm lookin' for the bloke as clyms 'e took Decline Copse just now." Francis acknowledged that he was responsible, and the Australian explained that, on receiving the report of its capture, he had taken a patrol to Decline Copse, where he encountered the "'ole blinkin' German Army." The Australians fled in a hail of bullets, and the officer's annoyance was unmistakable as he recounted how he had been forced to crawl to safety "like a bloody snike."[28]

What had gone wrong? When the Australian left, Colonel Francis dispatched runners to determine the status of Decline Copse. It was not until after three in the morning that the confusion was cleared up.

The 47th had, in the darkness, mistaken a small wood for Decline Copse, which remained in enemy hands. However, by now, "it was too late to arrange an attack before daylight," in the opinion of Colonel Francis.[29]

Colonel Davies decided that it was up to his 44th Battalion to vindicate the Canadians in the eyes of the Australians. That morning, he and his staff drew up a plan of attack which he presented to General Hilliam; when the brigadier approved, the 44th prepared to storm Decline Copse that very evening.

The assault went in at 10 P.M. on 27 October. It was a stirring success. The 44th, attacking with bayonets fixed, took the Germans by surprise. Good thing, too, for Colonel Davies rated the artillery support as poor, complaining that the Canadian shells fell "to the left and in our area," leaving the enemy unscathed.[30] The battalion captured Decline Copse in a stiff, bloody battle in which the men from Manitoba used their bayonets freely, a form of fighting for which the Germans showed little stomach. But they were not quite ready to concede the copse to the Canadians; a counter-attack the next night recaptured part of it, the Germans taking advantage of a relief of the 44th by the 85th (Nova Scotia Highlanders) Battalion. However, the Canadians rallied and promptly pushed the Germans out. Decline Copse was, once and for all, in Canadian hands.

So ended the first phase of operations for the Canadian Corps at Passchendaele. The Canadians were entitled to be pleased with their efforts. Though they generally fell short of their assigned objectives, they had gained sufficiently solid footing for the next scheduled attack. Considering the conditions of mud, it is nothing short of remarkable that they were able to achieve even a partial success. General Currie called it "a truly magnificent performance," and his British superiors were just as generous in their praise of the Canadians. Sir Douglas Haig commented that "the performance of the 3rd Canadian Division in particular was remarkably fine," while Sir Herbert Plumer told Currie that he was "simply delighted."[31]

Moreover, the Canadian Corps had scored the only appreciable success in either the Second or Fifth Army. Elsewhere on the Second Army's front, only the Australians, operating on the immediate right of the Canadians, had managed to advance. On the Australian right, however, X Corps had been repulsed in its attack on Gheluvelt. On the left of the Canadians, Fifth Army had attacked with two corps, XVIII—adjacent the Canadians—and XIV; both had been stopped in their tracks. Sir Hubert Gough later admitted that "very little progress was made" by his army on 26 October, and he blamed the battlefield conditions. The ground, he wrote, "was getting absolutely impossible. Men of the strongest physique could hardly move forward at all and became easy victims to the enemy's snipers. Stumbling forward as best they could, their rifles also soon became so caked and clogged with mud as to be useless."[32] Yet, the Canadians had faced the same conditions, and persevered.

Indeed, Gough was so distressed by the results of this attack that he again recommended to Haig that future operations be postponed, at least until the first frost hardened the ground. But the commander-in-chief, seeing what the Canadian Corps had accomplished, disagreed.

> In my opinion, today's operation at the decisive point (Passchendaele) had been so successful that I was entirely opposed to any idea of abandoning the operations till frost set in! If the wet continues, a day or two's delay may be advisable before we launched the next attack.[33]

To be sure, there were few front-line soldiers—Canadian, British, or Australian—who could relate to Haig's optimism. Jack Quelch, a sniper in the 44th (Manitoba) Battalion, made no effort to conceal his revulsion as he wrote home on 29 October:

> We have just completed... one of the worst trips in the lines since I have been in France. I have seen and been in some dirty holes in this country but this was the worst. The facts seen and done here by the troops can live up the imagination [sic] of any man. I thought I had seen a few thousand guns while I have been in France but have never seen the mass of guns there are in this place and the incessant bombardment.... I have seen a few hundred dead too, but this is the worst, its an ungodly hole. From the front line to three miles back there is, well I think I will leave it at that. They are lying all over, shell holes full of water and corpses. Hineys [sic] shell fire is the worst I have yet seen.[34]

There was, of course, a price in blood to be paid for the Canadians' courageous performance. Their casualties from 26 to 28 October totalled 2,481, not unduly large amid the carnage on the Western Front. But most of them had been incurred by seven battalions, with an average battle strength of 600 men each. Losses of that magnitude were unusually and distressingly heavy.

Herein lies an astounding success story scripted by the stretcher-bearers. In the twenty-four-hour period from 6 A.M. on 26 October through the same time on 27 October, the Canadian Corps medical service treated 1,207 wounded Canadians and fifty-five injured Germans. Surprisingly, "the whole Corps Front was cleared [of wounded] in 12 hours." This was a feat of almost superhuman proportions on the part of the stretcher-bearers provided by the field ambulances and reserve infantry battalions. Theirs was an unenviable task, "squelching and sliding down shell holes at almost every step, burdened with the stretcher, and soaked with fine rain, the visual sense sickened with the desolation and slime, with corpses of man and beast...." Under shell fire much of the time, they found themselves "in some places thigh-deep in mud" and were forced at times to carry "in squads of 10 men to a stretcher," according to Lieutenant-Colonel H.S. Donaldson of the 3rd Canadian Field Ambulance.[35]

Their arms and legs aching, many of them nearing the point of utter exhaustion, the stretcher-bearers managed to maintain their sense of humour. They joked that the ideal bearer was "broad across the back and narrow between the eyes." The self-denigrating humour aside, the work performed by these men was difficult in ways not easy to measure, as Private Arthur Turner of the 50th (Calgary) Battalion discovered. "It was heartbreaking," he recalled, to see not only the dead but the injured, who had been 'torn to pieces'.... When we got them out, the Doctor would look them over. Sometimes he would say, 'Set him down over there, boys.' And we knew what that meant."[36]

But the chances of surviving their wounds were impressively good. That so few of the wounded perished at Passchendaele is attributable to the fine work of the medics of the Canadian Corps. For example, the 8th Canadian Field Ambulance, which operated a dressing station at Vlamertinghe Mill until 2 November, treated a total of 3,270 wounded soldiers, of whom only a handful died, "not more than nine or ten," in the words of the ambulance's commanding officer, Lieutenant-Colonel J.N. Gunn. Overworked as were the doctors and nurses, every case had to be treated individually, as Colonel Gunn later wrote,

> each being attended to according to his particular needs, most of them being stripped of their muddy and blood-stained clothing and made warm and comfortable in pyjamas, many of them needing the most delicate handling in relieving and protecting fractured limbs, every solitary man (excepting where the peculiar seriousness of his wound prohibited this) receiving his hot coffee or cocoa with cake or biscuits, not forgetting that greatest of boons to the wounded soldier—a cigarette.

Clerical work was vital, too, and "every man had fixed to him, before leaving, his official medical card, showing his full particulars, giving an exact description of his wounds, and stating any special treatment that had been administered." Full records were kept at the dressing station, with reports being sent to various headquarters and to each man's unit.[37]

Adding to their difficulties was the fact that the Canadian dressing stations and field hospitals were well within range of enemy artillery. Consequently, they were often shelled, but the medical people accepted the danger matter-of-factly. Captain Harold McGill of the 5th Canadian Field Ambulance warned his fiancée, a nurse in London, that their plans for a December wedding might be spoiled. "Do not indulge too much in your day dreaming," McGill wrote, "for if one of Bertha Krupp's messengers ever takes me you will have to revise all your program, or at least substitute somebody in my place in the scheme."[38] It was with such stoicism that the medics went about their life-saving work. And there would be much to do before this battle ended.

12/Another Step Closer

Preparations for the next Canadian attack were already under way. Of vital importance was "a major job of housekeeping," as the Canadian official history put it. "To ensure the delivery of ammunition, rations and other supplies to the forward troops, engineers and pioneers set to building a track of planks, corduroy and fascines in each brigade sector, to carry brigade mule-trains, 250 strong."[1] The first assault, while falling short of the Red Line objectives in most places, had nevertheless carried the Canadian Corps onto higher and slightly drier ground; the Corps was now in a position to take the remaining objectives of 26 October, as well as the Blue Line six to seven hundred yards beyond. The latter included strongpoints such as Vienna Cottage and Crest Farm, in front of the Fourth Division, and Meetcheele and Vapour Farm in the Third Division's sector. As before, Sir William Birdwood's I Anzac Corps would operate on the Canadian right, while Sir Ivor Maxse's XVIII Corps would attempt to assist on the left.

The key, once again, would be the Bellevue Spur, and it was plain that the Germans would spare no effort to hold onto it. A Corps intelligence report, based on an interview with a co-operative prisoner belonging to the 11th Bavarian Division, sounded ominous:

> The greatest importance was attached to the Bellevue Spur which was to be held at all costs and which the battalion commander of the Prisoner stated must not under any consideration fall into our possession.... Prisoner thinks that every effort will be made to regain the lost ground, which is considered of the highest importance to the enemy.[2]

Before the second Canadian attack could be carried out, the proceedings were marred by a confrontation between the Corps commander, Currie, and the Fifth Army's Sir Hubert Gough. The gentlemanly but stubborn Currie had great difficulty concealing his contempt for Gough, and he was still stewing over the Fifth Army's poor showing on 26 October when Sir Hubert paid a visit to Canadian Corps headquarters on the twenty-ninth. A terse entry in Currie's diary sums up their meeting: "Gen. Gough called to ask me to postpone, refused to do so and confirmed refusal again at 7 P.M."[3] The reader will recall that ten days earlier Gough had wanted Currie to advance his plans; now, on the eve of the next operation, he sought a postponement. Currie's refusal to co-operate is understandable: his was the main effort, all his preparations had been completed, and, in any event, he expected little assistance from the Fifth Army. His decision would be amply justified.

Zero hour on Tuesday, 30 October, was 5:50 A.M. At that moment, 420 guns of all calibres opened fire along the Canadian Corps front. If the Canadians had one thing in their favour this day, it was the weather. For the past three days it had not rained, each day being cool but clear; while the ground was not noticeably better, at least it was no worse than it had been during the first assault.

The Canadians attacked under "a blood-red sky."[4] On the right, the Fourth Division had more room to manoeuvre and General Watson was able to employ three battalions: from right to left, the 85th (Nova Scotia Highlanders), the 78th (Winnipeg Grenadiers), and the 72nd (Seaforth Highlanders of Canada), all belonging to Brigadier-General J.H. MacBrien's Twelfth Brigade.

The 85th Battalion had already had one scrap with the Germans. It had happened on the night of 28/29 October, when the 85th relieved the 44th (Manitoba) Battalion near Decline Copse. In the midst of the relief, the Germans had attacked and recaptured a portion of the shattered, battered wood. The two Canadian battalions quickly counter-attacked, and drove the Germans out. The coup de grâce was a bayonet charge delivered by Captain Ross MacKenzie's D Company of the 85th. At the moment of success, Captain MacKenzie had been felled by a bullet in the abdomen. Despite intense pain, he refused treatment. "You can do nothing for me," the dying officer told his men, "go and help some one where it will do some good."[5]

It was the kind of spirit that stood the 85th in good stead on 30 October. The Nova Scotians went over the top and disconcertingly discovered that they were receiving virtually no help from the artillery. The barrage was later described as "not at all satisfactory," and surviving officers agreed that if they had it to do over again, "they would prefer to attempt it by surprise without any barrage." Its only effect, concluded the battalion report, "appeared to be to give the enemy warning that an attack was pending."[6]

The Germans, members of the 238th Infantry Division, put the warning to good use. No sooner had the Canadians clambered out of their shell holes than they were greeted by withering machine-gun and rifle fire. So intense was this hail of bullets that "anyone who attempted to walk upright instantly became a casualty." One survivor later testified: "I thought that morning that I was hit a dozen times, but actually I never had a mark when I got over. I came out . . .

with four holes through my clothes and not a scratch on my hide." He was lucky; more than half of the 85th became casualties in the next few hours.[7]

A fierce fire fight ensued. The determined Canadians brought their Lewis machine-guns into action; under this covering fire, the infantrymen ran and jumped from shell hole to shell hole, edging closer and closer to the enemy line. The losses on both sides were heavy. It is difficult to say how long this furious fight lasted; participants put its duration at anywhere from ten to thirty minutes. What is not in doubt is the move that proved to be decisive. Major Percival Anderson, the battalion's second-in-command, led forward a reserve platoon and the Germans, apparently mistaking the movement for a major assault in the making, suddenly broke and fled, with the Nova Scotians hot on their heels. By 6:35 A.M., just three-quarters of an hour after zero, the 85th Battalion was on its Blue Line objective.

In the centre of the Twelfth Brigade attack was the 78th (Winnipeg Grenadiers) Battalion. Assaulting in four waves fifty yards apart, the battalion encountered terrific small-arms fire. Within minutes, the assault stalled; all company commanders were casualties. Its ranks riddled, the 78th wavered. Major John McEwan, this battalion's second-in-command, saw what was happening and acted without hesitation. Rushing forward, he led the remnants of the Grenadiers on a wild charge that carried them to their final objective, 800 yards distant. His clothing was shredded, but Major McEwan was miraculously uninjured; he received the Distinguished Service Order (DSO) for his heroic performance.

German shell fire was sporadic and generally ineffective on this front. The enemy guns were slow to answer the SOS signals, and most of their shells fell behind the attacking Canadians. Private Archie Brown was one of the few members of the 78th to be injured by German shrapnel. He recalled that he had struggled perhaps fifty yards

> when something exploded, and the next thing I remembered I was in a shell hole, and my leg was around my neck. I untangled myself, noticed that... there was a hole in my steel helmet [and] blood running down my face from a gouge in my forehead, but otherwise I seemed to be intact, and about one hundred yards ahead I could see the troops moving forward and, by the looks of the way it was behind, I figured it was safer to go ahead. So I stepped along and caught up to my unit.

Brown caught up to them just in time to help repel a counter-attack,

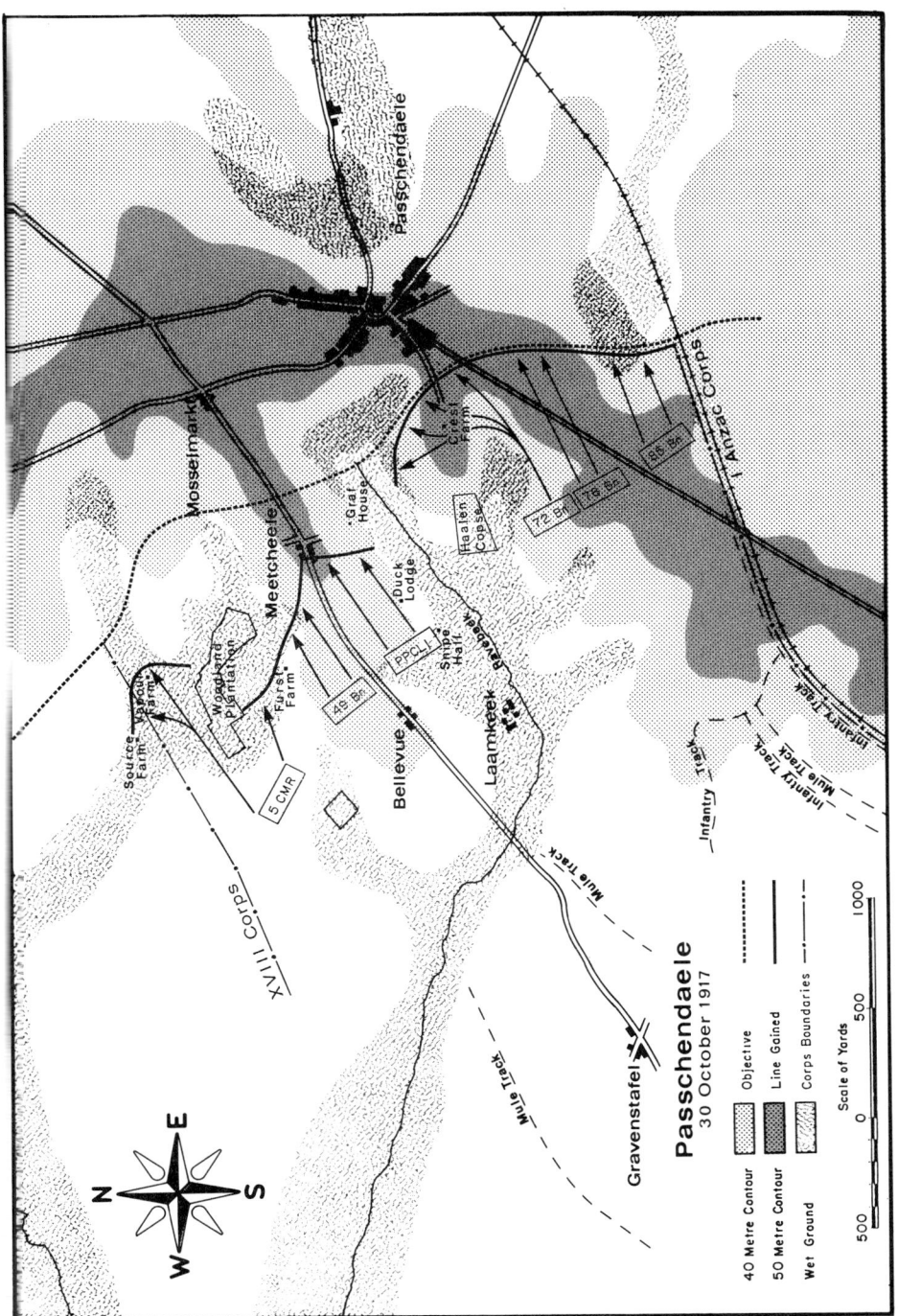

one of three attempted by the Germans during the day. But the 78th was here to stay. By seven-thirty that morning the battalion had dug in: the ground here was sufficiently dry to allow the survivors to construct real trenches. "The average depth was six feet and average width three feet. C.T.'s [communication trenches] and Saps were constructed and latrines dug." The battalion commander, Lieutenant-Colonel J. Kirkaldy, who was later wounded during a front-line inspection, proudly wrote: "It was a fine operation and the men were better than ever."[8]

The 85th and 78th had both achieved fine successes, but the day's outstanding action belonged to the 72nd (Seaforth Highlanders of Canada) Battalion, operating on the brigade left. Its objective was Crest Farm, a strongpoint defended by twenty-four machine-guns. The operation went like clockwork, prompting Sir Douglas Haig to label it "a feat of arms which would go down in the annals of British history as one of the great achievements of a single unit."[9]

But it was far from easy. The battalion's front was so flooded that the officer commanding, Lieutenant-Colonel J.A. Clark, was forced to funnel his three attacking companies through an opening only fifty yards wide. Moving through this gap in single file, the attackers fanned out on the solid ground beyond and struck for their assigned goals. They were fortunate enough to have plenty of help. "The artillery and machine gun barrage," states the regimental history, "was everything that could be desired."[10]

A Company swung to the left, storming Haalen Copse. It fell following a brief but bloody battle: "at least fifty Huns were killed, twenty-five taken prisoner, and four machine guns captured." The bravery and initiative of one man stood out. Private P.M. Gillis, seeing his company come under enfilade fire from a German machine-gun, went ahead of the Canadian artillery barrage, attacked the gun, and knocked it out.[11]

Crest Farm fell to B Company. Here, the Canadians killed at least forty of the enemy and captured thirty more, including the commander of the strongpoint, who told his captors that "your men attacked so closely upon the barrage that they seemed to be mixed up with their own shell-fire! My guns had no time to get properly into action." One of the highlights of this action was the work of Lance-Corporal S. Irwin, who was in charge of a Lewis-gun section. Corporal Irwin spotted three enemy machine-guns in position to enfilade A Company at Haalen Copse; they were deliberately holding their fire until the Canadians came within point-blank range. Irwin gave them no opportunity to spring their trap. He quickly worked his way around behind them, sprang to his feet, and, firing his Lewis gun from the shoulder, wiped out the three surprised gun crews in a few bloody seconds.[12]

On the right of the battalion, C Company took the high ground east of Crest Farm, killing at least fifty Germans and capturing twenty-five others. A patrol was dispatched toward Passchendaele, which the Canadians—like the Australians on 12 October—found to be virtually deserted. From this vantage point, the patrol had a commanding view of the whole battlefield and could see German troops fleeing "in all directions."[13] However, the patrol was in a vulnerable position and was wisely withdrawn later in the morning.

By nine-thirty, the 72nd Battalion had consolidated its gains. The cost to this point had been remarkably light, but that was about to change. The Germans brought the battalion under a protracted bombardment, "the most intense enemy shell-fire that any member of the Battalion had ever experienced." It lasted eighteen grim hours, but the 72nd was made of stern stuff. That night, the Germans mounted a company-strength counter-attack on Crest Farm. They were routed, and at daylight thirty survivors surrendered.[14]

The Twelfth Brigade had achieved success everywhere. Its three assaulting battalions were solidly entrenched on their Blue Line objectives, though northwest of Crest Farm the ground was so badly flooded that the Canadians consolidated short of the final objective. The cost had been considerable. Two battalions, the 78th and 85th, had lost more than 50 per cent of their attacking strength: the 78th suffered 356 casualties, while there were 397 in the 85th. Losses were somewhat lighter in the 72nd Battalion, numbering 275. This is a reflection of the artillery support rendered on 30 October: the 85th had the heaviest casualties and the least help from the artillery; the 72nd received the most effective assistance from the gunners, and lost far fewer men.[15]

On the other side of the Ravebeek, the results were rather disappointing by comparison. The Third Division again found itself in hot water—figuratively speaking, of course—and fell short of its objectives. As on the twenty-sixth, General Lipsett was able to utilize three battalions from two brigades. On his right, Brigadier-General Hugh Dyer's Seventh Brigade attacked with Princess Patricia's Canadian Light Infantry (PPCLI) and the 49th (Edmonton Regiment) Battalion, while on the left, J.H. Elmsley's Eighth Brigade was represented by the 5th Canadian Mounted Rifles (CMR). Theirs was a horror show relieved only by incredible heroism: these three battalions would win four Victoria Crosses this day.

The PPCLI had scored an impressive preliminary success. Moving into the front line early on 29 October, the battalion faced the prospect of attacking with an enemy strongpoint on its flank, a pillbox named Snipe Hall, which had caused many casualties in the Ninth Brigade in the previous assault. Captain M.M. Macpherson, commanding 4 Company* of the PPCLI, reconnoitred the position and decided to mount an immediate attack, relying on the element of surprise. It worked beautifully. By dawn, Snipe Hall and its garrison were in Canadian hands.

Having straightened out the line and removed a key enemy fortification on its flank, the PPCLI was ready for the main operation of 30 October. The battalion's intermediate objective was a strongpoint named Duck Lodge; with the 49th Battalion on the left, it was to take Meetcheele, then capture Graf House. The assignment proved to be beyond its capabilities.

One man who was most unhappy with this operation was the officer commanding the PPCLI, Lieutenant-Colonel Agar Adamson. A veteran of the Boer War, Adamson was, at age fifty-two, somewhat older than usual for a battalion commander in the Canadian Corps. Colonel Adamson, a Toronto businessman in peacetime, was appalled at the conditions his men would be fighting under. "The ground beggars description," he complained in a letter written shortly afterward. "There is absolutely no cover and while it did not rain it might just as well have done so as far as the ground was concerned." Adamson flatly rejected putting his troops on a timetable, explaining that "it was useless to lay down any mode of attack to troops going over unknown and swamped lands, pitted with shellholes filled with water."[16]

The PPCLI attacked with all four of its companies, two forward and two in close support. Each man carried 270 rounds of small-arms ammunition, a flare, two iron rations and one day's fresh rations, three sandbags, two rifle grenades, and a shovel. Following close behind the barrage, moving at the rate of fifty yards every four minutes—which Colonel Adamson called "curious" but "about right for the heavy going"—the battalion history wryly remarked that it was probably the slowest attack ever staged: "The speed of 750 yards an hour must surely be the low record for a charge in all the history of war."[17]

Lacking cover, plodding through deep mud and icy water, the PPCLI soon found itself in a storm of fire. Casualties mounted rapidly:

* Battalions designated their four companies either by letters, A, B, C, and D, or by numbers, 1, 2, 3, and 4.

a horrified witness recalled that the Princess Pats "were just mowed down like wheat."[18] Within an hour, almost every officer had been killed or wounded. But the battalion pressed on to its intermediate objective, Duck Lodge, taking it by seven o'clock. Ahead lay its next objective, Meetcheele; as we shall see, the neighbouring 49th Battalion was so badly battered by this point that it was incapable of co-operating in this operation. If Meetcheele was to be captured, the PPCLI would have to do it alone.

Debouching from Duck Lodge, the Patricias forged onward, in the teeth of galling small-arms fire. The key to Meetcheele, a ruined little village on the road to Passchendaele, was a pillbox that stood on the outskirts. It proved to be a heavily defended position, and 3 Company—now commanded by a sergeant-major and reduced to only forty men—was soon pinned down by heavy machine-gun fire. But, as was so often the case at Passchendaele, Canadian initiative and courage conquered adversity.

Seeing the Patricias pinned down, Lieutenant Hugh MacKenzie of the 7th Canadian Machine-Gun Company hurried forward to take charge. Lieutenant MacKenzie quickly sized up the situation and produced a plan. He detailed several parties to manoeuvre around the pillbox to take it from the flank and rear. At the same time, he would lead a diversionary frontal attack which he surely realized would be tantamount to suicide.

As it turned out, one man took the pillbox. Sergeant George Mullin, thanks to MacKenzie's diversion, was able to get into position to rush the strongpoint. Using Mills bombs, he wiped out a sniper's post in front of the pillbox, then braved a hail of fire to climb on top of it, where he shot two machine-gunners with his revolver. Then Mullin rushed the entrance. The sight of this wide-eyed man, his clothing cut to ribbons, was too much for the rest of the garrison: ten Germans surrendered to him. The pillbox, and Meetcheele, now belonged to the PPCLI.

Both Sergeant Mullin and Lieutenant MacKenzie were subsequently awarded the Victoria Cross. However, MacKenzie's award was posthumous; he had been killed just moments before the pillbox fell.

At this point, Colonel Adamson called off further operations. Graf House, a fortified farm to the northeast, would have to be left in German hands for the time being; it was more important, Adamson decided, to consolidate the gains already won at such terrible cost. The battalion was sadly depleted: there were fewer than 200 survivors. The PPCLI had suffered a near-catastrophic 363 casualties, losing 80 per cent of the officers and 60 per cent of the other ranks who had taken part in the attack. Among the dead was Major Talbot Papineau, one of the most popular officers in the regiment. Just prior to leading his company over the top, Major Papineau had said to a fellow major, H.W. Niven, "You know, Hughie, this is suicide." Prophetic words, indeed.[19]

The Patricias braced for the inevitable counter-attacks. They did not have long to wait: the first was mounted around eight o'clock that morning; it was destroyed by the Canadian artillery before the enemy infantry could come close to the PPCLI's weak line. There were two more attacks before noon; both were repulsed by the artillery and the battalion's Lewis guns. During the afternoon, reinforcements from the Royal Canadian Regiment (RCR) arrived to help the Patricias hold their ground. The RCR also brought up badly needed water and ammunition, and helped remove many of the wounded.

The position remained precarious for the rest of the day. Snipers on both sides did deadly work, but by midnight it appeared that the PPCLI had managed to consolidate the blood-stained, muddy ground around Meetcheele. Major H.E. Sulivan, in command of the front line, sent an optimistic report to battalion headquarters at 1:30 A.M.:

> I find our line consisting of shell holes running about level with the pill-box [in front of Meetcheele]. Well held in small separate posts. Capt. Wood of the RCR has brought up his Coy. of 30 Other Ranks and has dug in 50 yards behind PillBox.... We have 6 Lewis Guns in working order and hold the crest of the ridge. The enemy have apparently dug themselves in 200 yds. in front of us. One of their patrols had just come up to our line but were beaten off. I figure I can hold this line against any counter-attack they put across. The sniping from our left is the worst feature....

Twenty minutes later, Major Sulivan was fatally wounded by a sniper's bullet in the chest.[20]

The following day, 31 October, passed quietly. The Patricias were in Meetcheele to stay, but Colonel Adamson was embittered and angry about the operation. He confided in a letter to his wife:

> The ground we gained... is of some importance, as the ridge we took is a commanding one and I do not expect the Army (although they ordered us to do so) thought we would be able to hold it, even if able to take it. The higher authorities are wearing themselves out in expressing to us their appreciation of our efforts, but I cannot help wondering if the position gained was worth the awful sacrifice of life.

However, within a few days, he had toned down his criticism. "The more I think of our assault the more wonderful it appears," he wrote his wife. "We were given the almost impossible to do and did it."[21]

On the left of the PPCLI was an even more tragic tale. Here, the 49th (Edmonton Regiment) Battalion endured the worst day in its history. Its misery began with the opening bombardment. The Canadian barrage was "short, irregular and ineffective," according to the officer commanding the 49th, Lieutenant-Colonel R.H. Palmer. "Our heavies were constantly short...a number of casualties were caused by our guns before the men left the Jumping Off Line." The German artillery responded immediately, and the battalion was immersed in a deluge of high explosives and small-arms fire. Colonel Palmer watched helplessly as his right-front company "lost practically all its effective strength" in a matter of minutes.[22]

In the midst of this bloody shambles, Private Cecil John Kinross rose to the occasion. Nicknamed "Hoodoo" by his comrades, Private Kinross had a reputation of being "incorrigible"; he "loathed parades" and "his appearance was usually disgraceful," recalled one of his officers. "He was strictly a front line soldier," and he proved it on 30 October. Seeing his company stalled before a stubborn machine-gun post, Kinross swiftly shed his equipment, save for his rifle and an extra bandolier of ammunition. Crawling forward, he managed to outflank the enemy and shoot the six-man crew.[23]

It was a Victoria Cross-winning performance, but bravery alone was not enough to enable the Edmontons to press their attack. Reaching the intermediate objective, Furst Farm, it was apparent to Colonel Palmer that the 49th could go no farther. He ordered his men to dig in. "During the morning sniping was severe," he later wrote, "and movement of any kind difficult owing to heavy shell fire." Two companies of the RCR were allotted to him during the afternoon, in hopes of resuming the attack. But the colonel insisted that this would be impossible, and "the operation was cancelled."[24]

The 49th Battalion had fallen far short of its final objectives, and it had paid dearly for the ground it did take. Entering the battle with twenty-one officers and 567 other ranks, its losses on 30 October totalled a staggering 443.[25] The casualty rate of 75 per cent was the worst in the battalion's history.*

---

* Among the 49th Battalion dead was thirty-year-old Alex Decoteau, felled by a sniper's bullet. Decoteau, a full-blooded Indian from the Red Pheasant Reserve in west-central Saskatchewan, was buried near Ypres. "Believing that without an Indian burial Decoteau's spirit was left to wander the earth," a colourful ceremony was held by his tribe in August 1985—sixty-eight years after his death—to lay his spirit to rest.[26]

It was on the left of the Canadian Corps that a truly amazing achievement was engineered on 30 October. The 5th Canadian Mounted Rifles (CMR) had been entrusted with several crucial objectives, including Vapour Farm and Vine Cottage. That the regiment succeeded so well was due largely to the leadership and courage of one man, Acting Major George Pearkes.

The twenty-nine-year-old Pearkes was, ironically, one of the first casualties in the battalion. "It was hardly daylight," he recalled, when the 5th CMR went over the top that fateful morning. German artillery responded speedily to the Canadian bombardment in this sector, and Pearkes, commanding C Company, had no sooner stood up to lead the charge when he was struck by a jagged chunk of shrapnel. The blow knocked him down, but he remained conscious. "Now I've got it!" he thought, as he examined the ugly gouge in his left thigh. Sensing some hesitation among his men, Pearkes decided to ignore the injury. "I've got to go on for a while anyway, wounded or not," he told himself. Struggling to his feet, he waved his men forward and set out across no man's land.[27]

It was tough going. His leg stiffened, but he was able to walk unaided. That he did so is a tribute to his determination: the terrible ground conditions posed a significant obstacle to able-bodied men, and even more so for a wounded man. Pearkes never forgot the scene.

> Our principal concern during the first few minutes of the attack was to adjust ourselves to the light and the darkness and how best to navigate round the shell holes. The mud was a terrible handicap to us. On the other hand, the mud saved many from the enemy's artillery fire because the shells buried themselves in the mud and if they did explode the mud deadened the effect of the explosion and the fragments of the shell.

The water-filled shell holes proved to be deadly. "I'm certain," said Pearkes, "that there were men who were wounded, fell into the shell holes, and were drowned." Just as alarming, Pearkes realized that he and his men were not keeping pace with the creeping barrage, even at the slow-motion rate of fifty yards every four minutes.[28]

The 5th CMR soon found itself subjected to punishing enfilade fire from the left. Pearkes was not really surprised. The previous night he had visited the British battalion assigned to guard the Canadian flank. This was the Artists' Rifles of the 190th Brigade, 63rd (Royal Naval) Division. Pearkes discovered that the Artists' Rifles had never before been in action; a company commander politely asked him what a barrage was like. "They were nice young men," Pearkes would say, "but...it was not very reassuring to know that on one's left were quite inexperienced troops who would be playing an important part."[29] In fact, the Artists never had a chance to help their Canadian cousins; they were decimated within minutes of zero hour, freeing the Germans opposite them to focus their fire on the exposed flank of the 5th CMR.

The Canadians forged onward, braving the machine-gun fire riddling their ranks, and reached their intermediate objective. Because the plan of attack prescribed a forty-five-minute pause at this point, the attackers had the opportunity to rest and reorganize, as well as catch up to the barrage. However, when the advance resumed, Pearkes was shocked to see that the artillery support being provided "seemed very thin."[30]

Pearkes and the remnants of C Company pressed forward. The few Germans they encountered showed little inclination to face Canadian steel at close quarters, and surrendered swiftly. But the machine-gun and sniper fire continued unabated, particularly from the left, and Pearkes determined to do something about it. He detailed a lieutenant named Otty and a small party of other ranks to attack Source Farm, a strongpoint in the neighbouring British sector. As Pearkes explained, "Unless this was being screened, we couldn't get on."[31] Lieutenant Otty did more than just screen it; he took and held it, though he was killed later in the day.

The left flank more or less secure, Pearkes, with perhaps three dozen men, all that was left of C Company, stormed Vapour Farm. Taking it at bayonet point, they found that it was rather elegantly named because, in Pearkes's words, "there was no farm there at all...it was [just] a rotten haystack."[32] There was precious little cover for the Canadians, who had to seek shelter in nearby shell holes. They were now being enfiladed from the right, where A Company had been stopped short of its objective, a fortified sniping post named Vine Cottage. Pearkes hoped to duplicate his Source Farm success and dispatched a party of riflemen to take Vine Cottage. But the position proved to be too strong, the attack failed, and Pearkes could spare no more men for another effort. With only fifty men, from both C and A companies, Pearkes knew that he would be hard pressed to hold Vapour Farm.

Pearkes was a heroic figure, and looked the part. "My wound had stiffened up and it wasn't hurting and I'd forgotten about it," he modestly recalled. But the very sight of their blood-stained leader inspired his brave little band. "I could see blood on him," remembered Private A. Molyneux. "I could see where his pants were torn but he was still going." Another would say of Pearkes, "I... would have followed him through Hell if I had to."³³

Pearkes was under no illusions: his position was desperate. He outlined the situation in a message to battalion headquarters in the early afternoon: "Ammunition running short. Do not think we can hold out much longer without being relieved. Both flanks still in the air."³⁴

Help was on the way, but it would be a long time getting there. Any reinforcements had to run a gauntlet of galling small-arms fire, which had already ruined a rescue bid at mid-morning by a company of the 2nd CMR. Cut to pieces by enfilade fire from the left, the would-be rescuers were forced to take "cover in shell holes, from where they returned the fire of the German riflemen and machine gunners," until darkness enabled them to withdraw safely. Another company of the 2nd CMR tried again during the afternoon: only ten men made it to Pearkes's isolated post. It would be nightfall before substantial reinforcements arrived. In the meantime, Pearkes had to hang on.³⁵

The first counter-attack was delivered against him just before noon. Two more followed in the afternoon. "How we stopped them, I don't know," Pearkes said later. "We attributed it largely to the effective fire of our own machine-guns who were in rear and in position.... But the Germans were obviously in the same exhausted condition as our men had been, and there was no spirit or drive in their counter-attack." By now, most of his men had been wounded, and their supply of ammunition was running dangerously low. Pearkes, however, stubbornly refused to abandon either Vapour Farm or Source Farm. "To have gone back and given up everything which we had gained that morning didn't seem very sensible, particularly as, if we had started to drift back, we'd have had more casualties. So the best thing to do was to stay."³⁶

And so they stayed, and fought, and won. That evening, they were finally relieved by two companies of the 2nd CMR, and Pearkes happily led his handful of wounded and weary heroes to the rear, gingerly stepping around the shell holes and the dead. There was a Victoria Cross in the major's immediate future, along with promotion to battalion command. But rewards were the last thing on his mind at that moment. "I certainly felt no more heroic than anybody else after it was all over. The only feelings were those of relief and weariness, and glad we made it through."³⁷

The 5th CMR was a mere shadow of its former self. In the space of twelve hours, it had lost two-thirds of its attacking strength. Going into battle with twenty-five officers and 565 other ranks, the battalion suffered 416 casualties.[38] Only the 49th Battalion had suffered more severely; but while the 49th had been stopped short of its allotted objectives, the 5th CMR had taken most of its assigned goals, plus one in the neighbouring British sector. It had been an notable feat of arms.

Consideration was briefly given to a possible withdrawal from the exposed position won by the 5th CMR. However, General Currie, who had the final say, was opposed to such a move, pointing out that if it was abandoned it would have to be recaptured before further operations could continue against Passchendaele. He realized that his men were "entirely isolated with a morass behind them, both flanks in the air, and the enemy in a commanding position immediately in front of them." But Currie argued that a partial success was better than none at all, and stressed "the importance of hanging on with the utmost determination to any portions of the enemy's position which have been gained." The decision to hold this ground would soon pay dividends.[39]

It had been a costly day for the Canadian Corps. Losses for 30 October amounted to 2,321: 884 killed, 1,420 wounded, and eight taken prisoner.

Once again, the stretcher-bearers performed magnificently. "By 4 p.m. both sides [of the Ravebeek] were reported clear," states a Corps medical report. "As a matter of fact for two hours before that time, cases had been simply dribbling in, and the main part of the Forward evacuation was completed." Yet, carrying the wounded was still a daunting task, for the mud remained a major problem. Major George Kilpatrick, the chaplain of the 42nd (Royal Highlanders of Canada) Battalion, experienced this difficulty:

> The doctor and I were in a pillbox right behind the front line, and word came in that a fellow was wounded out on the left flank, and I went out with another fellow to bring him in. Now, it was only four hundred yards, but when we got that fellow back to our position, I was absolutely and utterly done in. Yet these stretcher-bearers were going from the front line to Waterloo Redoubt, which was three miles behind the lines, over these indescribable conditions. They were doing it six and seven times a day, which means a mileage of nearly twenty miles a day under those appalling conditions. I don't know how the human frame stood up to it, and their courage and cheerfulness and care for the wounded was simply beyond words.[40]

But, sadly, delivery to the medics did not guarantee survival. Though they performed admirably, the doctors could not always save the wounded men brought in to them. One such case was a member of the 85th Battalion, Private Alexander Taylor, a twenty-year-old from Bridgewater, Nova Scotia. His diary tells part of the story:

> *30 October:* "Got wounded this morning. Rather badly in leg and foot. Carried out thru heavy shell fire. Got dressed at F.A. [field ambulance] and took auto to C.C.S. [casualty clearing station] where I got fixed up again."
>
> *31 October:* "Took ambulance train this afternoon and arrived at Etaples about four. Some tired and my wounds pretty painful."
>
> *1 November:* "Still at Etaples. Doctor is sending me to Blighty [England] in a day or so."
>
> *2 November:* "Still at the 56th Gen Hosp at Etap[le]s. Feeling pretty miserable and in quite a bit of pain."
>
> *3 November:* "Feeling a little better today, but off my feed. Moved to ward 51 in afternoon."
>
> *4 November:* "Had a good day. Read quite a bit and resting quite comfortable—head me to Blighty."
>
> *5 November:* "Feeling pretty good still. Not got much appetite tho."
>
> *6 November:* "Read a little bit and wrote a card."[41]

Private Taylor's diary ends there. Complications apparently set in, likely an infection, and he died 9 November. He is buried in Belgium, as are so many others from Canada and elsewhere in the British Empire.

The "Welsh Wizard": Prime Minister David Lloyd George.

Courtesy of The Trustees of the Imperial War Museum, London/ Q70208.

General Sir William Robertson.

Courtesy of The Trustees of the Imperial War Museum, London/ Q69626.

Field-Marshal Sir Douglas Haig.

Courtesy of The Trustees of the Imperial War Museum, London/ Q3254.

General Sir Herbert Plumer *(left)* with King George V.

Courtesy of The Trustees of the Imperial War Museum, London/ Q9227.

General Sir Hubert Gough.

Courtesy of The Trustees of the Imperial War Museum, London/ Q35825B.

Lieutenant-General Sir Arthur Currie.

Courtesy of the Provincial Archives of British Columbia/HP72344.

The Flanders offensive begins: a captured German strongpoint, 5 August 1917, showing the devastation wrought by the British bombardment.

Courtesy of The Trustees of the Imperial War Museum, London/Q2679.

A British soldier tries on a breastplate selected from German body armour salvaged in mid-August 1917.

Courtesy of The Trustees of the Imperial War Museum, London/Q2733.

The opponents: Scottish troops wearing waterproof capes, en route to the front lines, 5 August 1917...

Courtesy of The Trustees of the Imperial War Museum, London/Q2677.

... German soldiers in an observation post await the next British attack.

Courtesy of The Trustees of the Imperial War Museum, London/Q23934.

A German shell bursting in the Ypres salient during the fighting on 22 August 1917.

Courtesy of The Trustees of the Imperial War Museum, London/Q5901.

A British mule train negotiates the heavily cratered Menin Road, near Gheluvelt, in early September 1917.

Courtesy of The Trustees of the Imperial War Museum, London/Q11761.

The village of Passchendaele in September 1917, when it was still in German hands. By the time the Canadians captured it, in November, little but rubble remained.

Courtesy of The Trustees of the Imperial War Museum, London/Q45460.

Aerial view of the battlefield, about half a mile southwest of Passchendaele, 10 October 1917. The squarish objects are pillboxes, the zig-zag lines rudimentary trenches.

Courtesy of Public Archives Canada/RG9 III C3, Volume 4091, Folder 26, File 1.

Parties of Canadian pioneers and German prisoners laying duckboards, or "bath mats."

Courtesy of Public Archives Canada/PA 2084.

Canadian artillerymen manhandling a field gun.

Courtesy of B.H. "Jack" Turner Collection, Public Archives of Prince Edward Island/2767-151.

The desolation of the battlefield of Passchendaele.
Courtesy of Public Archives Canada/PA 2165, 2167.

The Canadian front line at Passchendaele, 31 October 1917. (Aerial photograph, Second Army Intelligence, 1 November.) Contrast the devastation in the foreground, to the rear of the Canadians, with the relatively intact landscape in the background, to the rear of the Germans. Note also the remarkably flat lay of the land; Passchendaele Ridge is barely discernible from this angle.

Courtesy of Public Archives Canada/RG9 III C3, Volume 4183, Folder 36, File 5.

An abandoned tank amid the desolation at Passchendaele.
Courtesy of Public Archives Canada/PA 2195.

The front line: members of the 16th Canadian Machine-Gun Company.
Courtesy of Public Archives Canada/PA 2162.

A Gallery of Heroes

Private Tommy Holmes, VC, 4th Canadian Mounted Rifles.

Courtesy of Public Archives Canada/PA 2352.

Private Cecil Kinross, VC, 49th (Edmonton Regiment) Battalion, *left*, and Corporal (Sergeant at the time of this photograph) Colin Barron, VC, 3rd (Toronto Regiment) Battalion.

Courtesy of Public Archives Canada/PA 6672.

Sergeant (Lieutenant at the time of this photograph) George Mullin, VC, Princess Patricia's Canadian Light Infantry.

Courtesy of Public Archives Canada/PA 6946.

Lieutenant Hugh MacKenzie, VC, 7th Canadian Machine-Gun Company.

Courtesy of Public Archives Canada/C 33427.

Captain Christopher O'Kelly, VC, 52nd (Ontario) Battalion.

Courtesy of Public Archives Canada/PA 6819.

Major George Pearkes, VC, 5th Canadian Mounted Rifles.

Courtesy of Public Archives Canada/PA 2364.

Lieutenant Robert Shankland, VC, 43rd (Cameron Highlanders of Canada) Battalion.

Courtesy of Public Archives Canada/C 32496.

Private James Robertson, VC, 27th (Winnipeg) Battalion.

Courtesy of Public Archives Canada/C 26832.

The Menin road, outside Ypres.

Courtesy of B.H. "Jack" Turner Collection, Public Archives of Prince Edward Island/2767-129.

German prisoners and Canadian soldiers receiving refreshments en route to the rear.

Courtesy of Public Archives Canada/PA 2155.

Canadian soldiers and captured pillboxes.

Upper: Courtesy of B.H. "Jack" Turner Collection, Public Archives of Prince Edward Island/2767-154.

Lower: Courtesy of Public Archives Canada/PA 2210.

Evacuating the wounded.

Above: Courtesy of Public Archives Canada/PA 2229.

Opposite: Courtesy of Public Archives Canada/PA 2140.

13 / "At All Costs"

By any measure, 30 October had been a day of significant success for the Canadian Corps. As the Canadian official history notes, "The step by step battle was gradually accomplishing its purpose."[1] The Corps had achieved gains of up to a thousand yards, and was now poised to take Passchendaele village and the surrounding high ground.

General Currie had mixed feelings about the fighting on the thirtieth. While he was undoubtedly pleased with the progress made by his own troops, he was most upset with the performance of the British on his left. Sir Hubert Gough admitted that his Fifth Army "could not get far forward—an advance of 300 yards or so being the limit of the day's advances." Currie was not sympathetic. "Imperials on flank failed again as they did on the 26th," he fumed privately. "This checked our progress on left very much."[2]

On the other hand, Sir Douglas Haig was more optimistic than ever. The Canadians, he said, had "completed the difficult task assigned them in a wholly admirable manner." As he commented in his diary, the Canadian attack had moved "our line closer to the ridge on which the Passchendaele village stands. The operation was most successful and we are now round the village on the south west and north-west." In a long letter to Sir William Robertson, on 31 October, Haig wrote that

> it is my intention to continue the offensive on the Flanders front for several weeks yet. The situation there, despite the advanced season and the delays caused by bad weather, is still favourable for a considerable and important further measure of success. From the positions already reached I see no reason to doubt that PASSCHENDAELE and the high ground round it will be in our possession by the middle of November, if not sooner....
>
> The political, moral and strategical advantages of gaining this ridge have been stated by me in previous memoranda. I may point out here, however, that tactically possession of the ridge will be of extraordinary value at the opening of next year's campaign, while as a defensive line for the winter it offers very great advantages, giving us dry trenches, excellent cover in rear of them, and secure flanks.[3]

According to General Currie's time-table, the Canadians would have six full days to prepare for the resumption of operations. Having canvassed his subordinates for their views, Currie concluded that several tactical changes would be in order. In their first two attacks, the Canadian bombardment had begun at zero hour, with the infantry jumping off eight minutes later, "in deference to the wishes of the [British] troops on the flank," Currie explained. However, "this was found to be far too long, and heavy casualties were incurred from the German barrage during this long wait." Currie cut the interval to two minutes for the 6 November attack, "in order to give the assaulting troops a flying start and get them clear of the jumping off line before the German barrage comes down on it." In a similar vein, Currie objected to the British preference for a long pause—half an hour to forty-five minutes—at the intermediate objective. Currie contended that it was unnecessary:

> Such a pause exposes the troops to loss from machine gun fire at 1,000 or 1,200 yards range, which is now a prominent feature of German tactics. It also gives time for the men to get cold and stiff and makes it difficult sometimes to get them going again. With the slow rate of barrage, such as 8 minutes to 100 yards, there is usually time enough for units in the second line to leap-frog the leading ones without making a specially long pause for the purpose.[4]

Currie, to his credit, refused to be tied to standard practice. It shows not only his refreshing independent thinking, and a willingness to depart from the norm, it demonstrates that the Canadian Corps, while serving in the BEF, was not just another corps. Its special status, and Currie's, was earlier indicated by Haig's inclination to consult with the Canadian and persuade him to accept the Passchendaele assignment, something the field-marshal would have done with no other corps commander. It cannot be surprising, then, that the Canadians cultivated a growing belief that, while they were intensely proud to be part of the Empire, they were more than mere colonials doing the bidding of their King. If this budding sense of nationalism eluded the average Canadian soldier—whose primary concern in the field was, after all, survival—it was very much impressed on the senior officers of the Corps, many of whom were sympathetic toward and would be influential in the post-war bid to achieve full autonomy for Canada and the Empire's other dominions.

The by now familiar preparations resumed throughout the salient. As zero day neared, an eyewitness was able to write:

> Railway troops had worked unceasingly, pushing forward the

light tracks that carried the narrow-gauge lines up past Wieltje. Plank roads had been repaired and extended. Many hundreds of yards of duck-boards had been added to the straggling shell-pocked trails that led to the forward line.... By night and by day, through mud and slime, guns of all calibres had been slowly advanced to new positions.[5]

The results of this activity were most impressive. L.V. Shier, a young, starry-eyed lieutenant in the 20th (Central Ontario) Battalion, was overwhelmed with the material preparations in the Canadian Corps sector:

In a slight depression between two of the "ridges" are our lighter guns, the 18 pds & the 4.5's. These are arranged in 5 or 6 rows 50 or 75 yards apart stretching away as far as the eye can see. The heavier guns, 6" & 8" & 9.2" howitzers are nearly as numerous and are ranged in depth according to their size. There seems to be no limit to the number of guns. Further back still are rows of even heavier guns 12 and 15 inch howitzers and long range naval guns. There are not just guns here & there but regular batteries of them.

The amount of material is appalling. Shells of all sizes, bath mats, wire—everything without limit. Going backwards & forwards from the various dumps are endless streams of pack mules carrying up shells to the guns.

Hundreds of men are working night and day building & extending the roads, laying bath mats & carrying up material.[6]

It was an awesome sight, to be sure, but it must also have been consoling for these soldiers to know of the efforts being made on their behalf.

The work was as tiring and backbreaking as ever. Much of it was being carried out under the very nose of the enemy, and shell fire sometimes made work impossible. According to the diary of a major of engineers, Richard Smith, 3 November was such a day: "Heavy shelling, no one working."[7]

No less dangerous were the pack trains. Lance-Corporal Donald Fraser, a machine-gunner, was assigned to a carrying party on 4 November, to his ultimate regret.

The horse I was leading... had several cans of water balanced on each side. Spacing out about 25 feet, the party of about 12 to 15 men and horses moved up past Poti[j]ze into the range of guns, not being able to move far from the road on account of the mud.

157

While going up the Gravenstafel Ridge it was observed the enemy was sending over salvos every few minutes, and I expected we would have to halt and lay low until shelling ceased. However, the officer in charge, who was a new man, thought otherwise, and we proceeded up the dangerous spot. I was second from the end. The first lot passed safely, but the salvo came over with disastrous results when the final four entered the shelled area. The fellow behind me was killed, also his horse. The fellow ahead was also killed and his horse likewise. The fellow ahead of him was severely wounded and his horse killed. The shell burst threw my horse and myself from one side of the road to the other, my face being buried in the mud at the side of the road. I was completely dazed, and when I came to, trying to get up I found I was pinned down by the horse lying across my thighs. The horse was dead. Struggling to get free I finally squirmed from underneath and got up. How my legs were not damaged is a puzzle to me. I felt I was wounded but did not know where. My face burned as if hot wires were jammed into it. I was peppered in the face and hands with small pieces of shrapnel. Another salvo came over and the bursts this time so disturbed the air that I could hardly breathe. I quickly headed down the road and it was then that I noticed for the first time that my right arm, shattered at the shoulder, was dangling in front of me and twisted around.[8]

Corporal Fraser's war was over. Sent to a nearby Australian casualty clearing station, he was in hospital in England two days later. His wounds were so serious that he was invalided home to Canada in June 1918.

The attack scheduled for 6 November would be unique in one aspect: it would be an all-Canadian show. Only the Canadian Corps would be attacking; elsewhere on the Second Army's front, artillery demonstrations and simulated attacks would be staged. (To assist the Canadians—and, possibly, to answer some of General Currie's concerns about his left flank—Sir Douglas Haig had once again altered the boundary between the Second and Fifth armies, placing XVIII Corps on the Canadian left under Second Army jurisdiction on 31 October. The move effectively removed Sir Hubert Gough from any further role in the Flanders campaign. XVIII Corps was relieved on 2 November by Sir Claud Jacob's II Corps.)

Fresh troops were being brought in to carry out the operation. The Third and Fourth divisions were replaced in early November by the First and Second divisions of Major-General Macdonell and

Major-General Burstall, respectively. The newcomers were brought by rail as far as Ypres, then marched by battalions into the salient to take their places in or near the front lines. The last reliefs took place by 4 A.M. on Tuesday, 6 November, only two hours before zero.

General Currie personally greeted many of the incoming units. As before, he forthrightly explained what their task would be and what they faced. Typical was his address to Brigadier-General William Griesbach's First Brigade. With the four battalions formed in a square, Currie stood on a table and spoke to the men, "simply, sincerely, as soldier to soldier," according to war correspondent Fred McKenzie, who recorded the Corps commander's words:

> The Commander-in-Chief has called on us to do a big job. It has got to be done. It is going to be your business to make the final assault and capture the ridge. I promise you that you will not be called upon to advance—as you never will be —until everything has been done that can be done to clear the way for you. After that it is up to you, and I leave it to you with confidence.

The assembled troops responded with "cheer after cheer," observed McKenzie.[9]

These men would have at least one important advantage over their comrades in the earlier operations. If the attacks of 26 and 30 October had done nothing else, they had stripped the enemy's pillbox defence of its mystique and, therefore, much of its effectiveness. That these defences were impressive-looking cannot be denied. Major George Kilpatrick, the chaplain of the 42nd (Royal Highlanders of Canada) Battalion, considered that they were "practically indestructible. A 9.2 shell only chips them. Nothing less than a direct hit from a 12" or 15" gun is any good." Major Kilpatrick had reason to appreciate the solid construction of a captured pillbox being used as an aid post. "It stood like a rock; a 5.9[-inch shell] got a direct hit on us and the concussion was terrific but it simply bounced off the wall."[10]

But these pillboxes were soon to become death traps for the defenders. A Ninth Brigade report offered the following observations about the enemy's pillboxes:

> There are two kinds, square and oblong. The square Pill Box is small, and has one entrance at the rear, and has one compartment only. The Oblong Pill Box has two entrances, and two or three compartments; the three compartment type has a ventilator shaft to the centre room. Some Pill Boxes have loopholes for enfilading

fire, one on either side, or according to the physical features of the ground. Others have no loopholes, but a platform over the doorway from which guns are fired over the top of the Box. In the rear of many is a trench.

In general, the idea of the Pill Box is shelter from shell fire, and to enable the use of the machine gun before any time elapses and the attackers arrive, as well as economy in manpower.

The majority have no loopholes, and guns are fired from corners where platforms are not provided.

The garrison varies from 15-30 (sometimes more).

The Oblong Pill Boxes contain 5 machine guns each....

The general idea on which we captured nine Pill Boxes and one fortified farm on BELLEVUE SPUR being that (in our case without any barrage) of working up by making all possible use of ground to within, where possible, rifle grenade distance of the Pill Boxes, then creating a diversion by means of showers of rifle grenades, machine gun fire, etc. under cover of which a small party—three or four will often be enough—to get to the blind side of the Pill Box, when hand bombs were thrown in, and the whole rushed in.[11]

These words spelled doom for the pillboxes at Passchendaele.

In the meantime, desultory fighting continued on the Canadian Corps front. Both sides patrolled aggressively and staged several small-scale attacks, though with little success.

A night patrol gave Will Bird, a twenty-seven-year-old corporal in the 42nd (Royal Highlanders of Canada) Battalion, a memorable experience. The 42nd had relieved the battered and bloodied 49th Battalion and PPCLI on 31 October, and Corporal Bird and his platoon commander promptly set off on a patrol near Furst Farm. The smell, Bird remembered, "was nauseating, with a putrid stench that had both of us close to gagging." As they slowly made their way through and around the muddy shell holes, a flare suddenly lit up the sky. The two Canadians threw themselves face-first into the mud, and as they did so, Bird saw an alarming sight: directly ahead, there was a row of coal-scuttle helmets. They had run into an enemy patrol! The flare faded, and darkness shrouded them once more. Then another flare was fired, turning night into day for several agonizingly long seconds. As this one faded, Bird stole another quick look at the Germans, and was surprised to see that they had not moved. His curiosity piqued, Bird crawled over to investigate. He found all the Germans were dead, apparently killed by the concussion of an overhead explosion, their bodies wedged in the mud so that most were still upright.[12]

Bird's battalion also staged an unsuccessful attack, in an attempt to take an objective left over from the thirtieth. The strongpoint at Graf House prevented the Canadians from uniting their front, so the 42nd Battalion organized a night assault to take it, as the chaplain, Major Kilpatrick, recalled:

> There were seven parties of about ten men apiece detailed various aspects of this approach and attack. Five of these got lost in the pitch darkness and in the unmarked mud territory, but two of them arrived, chief being that under [Lieutenant] Meyer T. Cohen. Meyer T. Cohen advanced on Graf House with [Lance-] Corporal [W.J.] Taylor and twenty-five other ranks. They attacked Graf House and the garrison fled, but only temporarily. They came back with two tremendous counter-attacks, and in the second of these Cohen was shot dead with a bullet through the abdomen. All the ammunition was gone. There were only four men left, but they held Graf House, and when the reinforcements came up there was little Meyer dead at his gun and the Germans lying about him. That attack on Graf House had a very serious effect on the German plans because they had three huge raiding parties ready to advance on our flank, and this attack on Graf House disorganized the whole thing so that Meyer didn't die in vain. It was a magnificent last stand.[13]

However, the 42nd was finally forced to abandon the position, and Graf House was added to the list of objectives to be taken on 6 November.

The Germans, too, were active. On Saturday, 3 November, they staged a heavy bombardment combined with a half-hearted attack along the Canadian line. General Currie recorded the result in a terse entry in his diary: "Repulsed leaving few prisoners in our hands."[14]

But there was ample evidence of German determination to hold Passchendaele. On the third, the enemy moved in fresh forces to face the Canadians. The 11th Division, newly arrived from Champagne in northern France, took over most of line in the Canadian Corps sector, between the Ypres-Roulers railway and the Mosselmarkt road. The balance of the defences were manned by the 4th Division. At the same time, the German high command issued orders that Passchendaele must "be held or, if lost, recaptured at all costs."[15]

14/Bayonets and Bombs

The Canadians took Passchendaele on Tuesday, 6 November.

Once more, the weather improved a bit between attacks. After 31 October, it remained cool and misty each day, but with no heavy rains to worsen ground conditions. On the morning of 6 November, Captain Harold McGill, stationed at a field hospital near Ypres, wrote his fiancée: "The weather lately has not been at all bad for the time of year. It is very much better than that we had at this time last year.... There has been no rain for the past several days."[1] It would rain on the sixth, but not until later in the day, when it was too late to be a factor.

The night before the attack was deceptively calm, as historian D.J. Goodspeed has written:

> Towards morning the overcast sky cleared, the stars showed through, and a bright full moon shone down on Passchendaele. A brisk wind, rising just before the dawn, brushed away the ground mist. Periodically during the night, golden shower signals had broken out above the enemy's front, but apart from this, the whole forward area seemed deserted. Looking out over the barren waste of gleaming mud, pocked with water-filled shell-holes, the men...lay quietly in the cold, waiting for the barrage which with the dawn would begin the battle.[2]

Zero hour was 6 A.M. For two minutes, every available gun in the Canadian Corps sector fired on the enemy defences in the Passchendaele area. Then the barrage began to creep forward, and the Canadian infantrymen were on their feet and slogging through the mud toward their objectives. These were designated along the Corps front as the Green Line, appearing on maps as a rough semicircle about one thousand yards deep. Among the objectives this day were the ruins of Passchendaele, Mosselmarkt, and Goudberg.

As before, the Corps was employing elements of two divisions in this operation. On the left was General Macdonell's First Division, while the right was the responsibility of the Second Division, under General Burstall. The First Division attacked with three battalions, all belonging to Billy Griesbach's First Brigade. The left-hand battalion, the 3rd (Toronto Regiment), was to complete the conquest of the Bellevue Spur by taking the strongpoint known as Vine Cottage. At the same time, the 1st (Western Ontario) and 2nd (Eastern Ontario)

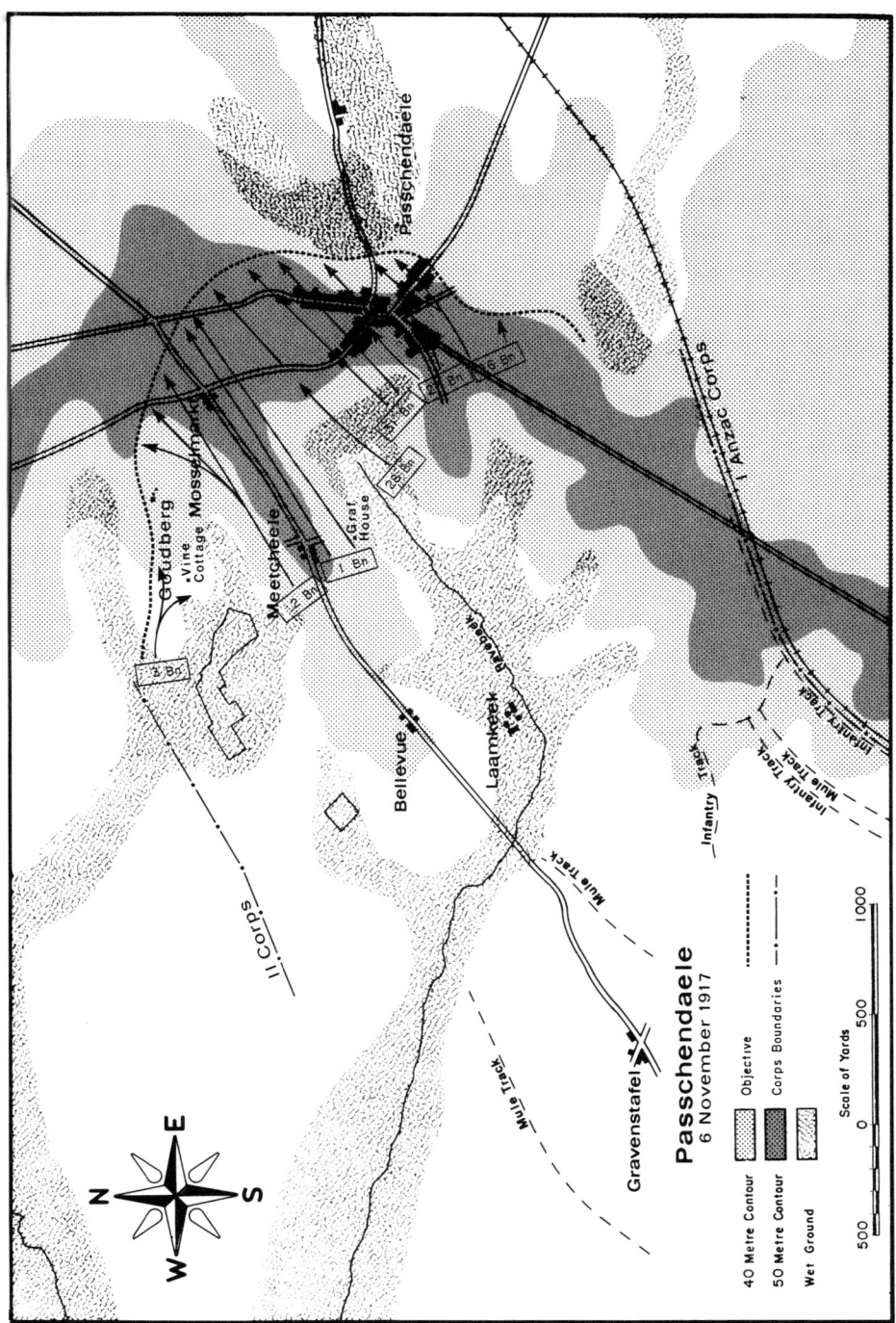

battalions were to strike side-by-side at the hamlet of Mosselmarkt, north of Passchendaele.

Vine Cottage, despite its pastoral designation, was a powerful position. Not only was it heavily defended by several pillboxes and machine-gun posts, it was naturally strong, surrounded by a veritable swamp: the limited approaches were expertly covered by overlapping fields of fire. Still, the 3rd Battalion got off to a good start. By keeping close behind the barrage, the Torontonians were on top of the defenders before many could respond. Two pillboxes were knocked out, and a third produced more than forty prisoners. It appeared, momentarily, that the battalion was on its way to an easy success.

But the impression was both mistaken and fleeting. Within minutes of jumping off, the 3rd Battalion was pinned down by deadly fire from three machine-guns in a fortified post. Casualties began to pile up rapidly as the Canadians floundered in the mud to meet this new challenge. They made several attempts to rush the enemy gunners, but the men were mown down each time, without even getting close. What had seemed to be certain success suddenly seemed like sure failure.

Enter Corporal Colin Fraser Barron. Carefully cradling his rifle to protect it from the mud, Corporal Barron began to crawl forward. There was no cover, and it appeared to those watching that Barron's approach would certainly be discovered. Miraculously undetected, he crept to within point-blank range of the enemy post. Tossing several bombs, Barron opened fire on the surprised and stunned gunners. Four were killed outright, and the rest fled. But they did not get far, as Barron shot them down with one of their own machine-guns. For his bravery, Barron would be awarded the Victoria Cross.

The tide turned again. The 3rd Battalion swarmed over the swampy ground. Vine Cottage fell, and the troops pushed on toward Goudberg. En route, the battalion encountered many more machine-guns. These were manned bravely and skilfully, but the Canadians dealt with them quickly and decisively. Often, the gunners would fire right up until the last possible moment before raising their hands in surrender. But, as the 3rd Battalion's history notes, the tactic did not work: "the attackers, infuriated by the casualties these guns had inflicted on their comrades, gave no quarter but put the machine-gunners to the bayonet." By mid-morning, Goudberg was in Canadian hands, at the cost of 240 dead, wounded, and missing.[3]

The attack by the 1st and 2nd battalions went surprisingly smoothly. The most serious difficulty of the day was sustained by the

2nd Battalion prior to the operation. Moving into the front lines during the night, the battalion discovered that due to extensive flooding it could occupy only a third of the 300-yard front allocated to it. As a result, the attacking companies had to double up, presenting a splendid target to the German artillery. At four in the morning the worst happened: a routine enemy bombardment fell on the battalion, causing extensive casualties. Many of these were officers. Indeed, the 2nd Battalion would lose all but one of its officers on 6 November, but its training paid off. Before moving to Passchendaele it had undergone, with the rest of the First Division, intensive practice that enabled platoon and other small unit commanders to exercise "their initiative in dealing with unforeseen situations... N.C.O.'s and Senior Privates were given opportunities to handle a Platoon so that, in the event of casualties, no confusion would occur."[4] Accordingly, the 2nd Battalion was able to function effectively despite the loss of its officers, taking all its objectives on the sixth.

Surprise was a major element in the success here. Captured Germans later confirmed that the Canadian attack was "most unexpected." There were other factors, too. The 1st Battalion reported that "the mud was not as bad as expected," and the German artillery was remarkably ineffective. The defenders fired green SOS flares as soon as the attack began, but it was not until 6:17 A.M. that the enemy guns replied—and their defensive barrage fell, in most instances, far behind the attacking Canadians. The first prisoners arrived at 1st Battalion headquarters at 6:10, just eight minutes after the troops went over the top. The only bother met by the 1st Battalion occurred on the flank, rather than the front. Heavy machine-gun fire from Graf House on the right inflicted some casualties, but this strongpoint was quickly eliminated. Trench mortars fired at close range neutralized it and forced the enemy machine-gunners into the open—"none of the crews escaped."[5]

Mosselmarkt fell with only token resistance. Most of the defenders had been killed by the Canadian barrage, which Major Walt Sparling, the officer commanding the 1st Battalion, called "most satisfactory." A strongpoint on the outskirts of the hamlet might have caused problems had the garrison been more determined, but the four officers and fifty other ranks "surrendered without resistance" to the 1st Battalion, which also boasted among its prizes this day a 77-millimetre field gun and 200 rounds of ammunition.[6]

By 7:45 A.M., the 1st and 2nd battalions were on the Green Line and consolidating their gains. Together with the 3rd Battalion to their left, these units of the First Division had performed impressively.

General Macdonell, the division commander, commented that "the old Div'n never showed to better advantage & our splendid men won through. You can't beat them."[7]

However, the First Division's exploits were to be overshadowed by the neighbouring Second Division, which had been given the task of taking Passchendaele village. General Burstall committed to this battle four battalions from two brigades. On his right was the 26th (New Brunswick) Battalion, of Brigadier-General J.M. Ross's Fifth Brigade, while in order to the left came three battalions of H.D.B. Ketchen's Sixth Brigade—"the Iron Sixth," it was nicknamed—the 27th (Winnipeg), the 31st (Alberta), and the 28th (Northwest).

The 26th (New Brunswick) Battalion jumped off smartly and hugged the barrage. The bombardment, recalled Private G. Mc-Knight, "was terrific. I remember turning around and looking back, and everything seemed to be on fire." Lieutenant A.L. Barry would later write, "The noise was deafening." For the first time in the battle for Passchendaele, the Canadian gunners would win rave reviews for their efforts across the Corps front. The 26th's report would say: "The work of the Artillery throughout was splendid."[8]

That is not to say the day passed without mishaps, as Lieutenant Barry would attest. This was his introduction to combat; he had only arrived on the Continent in September. As he led his platoon of the 26th forward, a shell exploded directly in front of him. "It could only have happened by one of our 8-inch shells entering the ground behind me, passing underneath and exploding in the soft mud in front. The plunge of the explosion was forward, thus saving my life." Barry fell into the yawning, five-foot-deep hole, and then—"I am not ashamed to tell this"—panic set in, and he "started back toward Ypres. I must have gone 50 yards mowing men out of my way," before he was able to get a grip on himself and return to the head of his platoon. His only regret, he later remarked, was "that the 50-yard dash was not clocked. I am sure I established a record for a heavy track."[9]

Despite the fine work of the artillery, losses mounted quickly. G.K.K. Holder of A Company recalled: "We went in there with a hundred and thirty men, and came out with thirty. It was mostly shell fire, very little machine-gun fire."[10] The 26th Battalion's casualties numbered nearly 300, including all of the company commanders. But the New Brunswickers were not to be denied. At 7:35 A.M., barely an hour and a half after zero, three white flares signalled that the 26th had reached the Green Line and held the high ground immediately south of Passchendaele.

The village was the goal of the three battalions from the Iron Sixth. By now, there was not much left to capture, as one eyewitness observed that day:

As I saw it this morning through the smoke of gun fire and a wet mist, it was less than I had seen before, a week or two ago, with just one ruin there—the ruin of its church—a black of mass of slaughtered masonry and nothing else; not a house left, not a huddle of brick on that shell-swept height.[11]

To reach this pile of rubble, the Canadians had to struggle across a swampy morass. The 28th (Northwest) Battalion, emerging from the valley of the sodden Ravebeek, had a particularly tough time; its commanding officer, Lieutenant-Colonel Alex Ross, recalled that "the ground in the early stages of the attack was in places knee-deep in mud and water, sometimes waist-deep," though it got better as the battalion scaled the modest heights to the village. Despite the difficult conditions, the Canadians kept pace with the creeping barrage, which moved, as before, at the rate of fifty yards every four minutes, and stormed the enemy defences. They did so with deadly efficiency, as one prisoner despondently related: "The Canadians came over practically with their barrage and attacked so suddenly that we had no opportunity to use our guns."[12]

There was, however, isolated resistance, most of it coming from stoutly defended pillboxes and machine-gun emplacements. The 31st (Alberta) Battalion, in the centre of the Sixth Brigade's attack, clashed with a number of these strongpoints, which often became concrete coffins for the occupants. Repeatedly, the battalion employed the tactics which had proven so successful: splitting into several small parties, one would pin down the defenders with small-arms fire and grenades, while the others worked their way around to take the pillbox from the flank or rear. Still, individuals distinguished themselves. Lieutenant J.A. Cameron's platoon was pinned down by an enemy strongpoint before the barrage reached it. Rushing through his own artillery fire, Lieutenant Cameron went on a one-man rampage, bayonetting several Germans and capturing twelve others, along with a machine-gun. Another officer, Lieutenant H. Kennedy, single-handedly took a pillbox and the three officers and thirty-four other ranks manning it. So swiftly did the 31st overcome the defences that German plans were completely disrupted: among the dozen prisoners in one pillbox were a pair of embarrassed battalion commanders who were in the midst of preparing a counter-attack on the Canadians.[13]*

---

* German aircraft continued to harry the Canadians. As the Sixth Brigade later reported, "The 31st Battalion had left their greatcoats in our jumping-off trenches, in order to be more lightly equipped for the advance. Enemy planes evidently mistook these [coats] for troops in the trenches and shell holes and swept them heavily with Machine Guns."[14]

The most serious setback of the day faced the 27th (Winnipeg) Battalion, on the right of the brigade attack. Its left-hand platoon ran into a German machine-gun emplacement surrounded by uncut barbed wire. Three times the Canadians charged, and three times they were repulsed with heavy losses. Things looked bleak, until Private James Robertson took matters into his own hands. While the rest of the platoon used rifle and machine-gun fire to force the Germans to keep their heads down, Private Robertson launched a one-man assault. He jumped up, dashed across the bullet-swept ground, hurdled the barbed wire, and waded into the enemy with bayonet fixed. He killed some of the gunners and forced the rest to flee, some of whom he cut down with their machine-gun. For his heroism, Private Robertson received the Victoria Cross, the last of nine to be awarded Canadians at Passchendaele. But it would be a posthumous award: Robertson was killed later in the day while helping to rescue wounded comrades exposed to enemy fire.

Bravery also paved the way for the left-hand battalion, the 28th. Private H. Badger, who was "looking for a good fight," recounted that he was one of the first to reach the foremost enemy positions, "and was indeed very disappointed when they surrendered without wanting to fight." Forging ahead alone, Private Badger took on a pair of pillboxes. Jumping from shell hole to shell hole, firing his rifle with remarkable accuracy—"I emptied my magazine and only missed twice (fault sanded bolt)"—he manoeuvred into position to bomb the nearest one, then called on the defenders to surrender. Several Germans emerged "with their hands in the air," but Badger cold-bloodedly dispatched them: "There was no mercy in me and I bayoneted six Fritzies as fast as they came out." The other pillbox surrendered shortly afterward, and this time Badger took prisoners, an officer and five other ranks. One of them pointed out a nearby strongpoint, so Badger marched everyone over there and demanded its surrender: two more officers and seven other ranks were added to his collection of prisoners. Within minutes, "other Fritzies came running up to me," and Badger found himself holding three officers and twenty-one other ranks. Before he could lead them to the rear, a Canadian shell exploded in their midst, killing two Germans and wounding a third. Badger was also hit by shrapnel, "on the left shoulder, right neck, and right leg." Despite his painful injuries, Badger escorted the Germans back to the nearest prisoner cages, en route putting them to work collecting Canadian wounded and carrying them to an aid post.[15]

Irresistibly, the three battalions of the Iron Sixth fought their way into Passchendaele. With bayonets and bombs, the Canadians cleared the defenders from the rubble-filled cellars. But the struggle was somewhat anticlimactic, as the 28th Battalion's history relates: "The Germans had little stomach for hand-to-hand fighting and our shellfire had been terrific, our advance so rapid, that the enemy was dazed, broken and ready to surrender."[16]

By 7:40 A.M., Passchendaele was in Canadian hands. Commented a captured German officer, "With an army of men like these I could get anywhere."[17]

The fighting did not end with the fall of the village, however. Many Germans fled rather than surrender. With the Canadians in hot pursuit, few of them got away, as Private W.E. Turner of the 27th Battalion recalled:

> We went through the village and down to the swamp on the other side. Some of the Germans had tried to get away and they were trying to get across this swamp, but they couldn't. They were just going too slowly in there. Things weren't too rough at the time and we weren't feeling too bad about it, and we shouted for them to come back. But they wouldn't, so there was nothing that we could do, we had to finish them off. We gave them a chance, but they wouldn't take it.[18]

A rare sight greeted the Canadians in and around Passchendaele. In sharp contrast to the muddy, shell-shocked, pockmarked desolation about them, they could see in the distant north "a beautiful rolling country of green fields, good roads, orderly farms, villages, and towns."[19] It was now that the troops realized what they had been fighting for: from this high ground, though it was a mere 165 feet above sea level, they saw that the Germans had enjoyed a remarkable and commanding view from this part of Passchendaele Ridge. Ypres was clearly visible, six miles away.

It started to rain during the afternoon. A drizzle at first, it became progressively heavier as the day wore on. The Canadians braced for the counter-attacks they had come to expect, but none materialized. With the coming of darkness, "an ominous quiet brooded over the battle-scarred region."[20]

At Canadian Corps headquarters, General Currie again had mixed thoughts about the day's work. While he considered the operation of 6 November to have been "eminently successful," as, indeed, it was, Currie was plainly as perplexed as he was proud. "The situation," he wrote a Canadian cabinet minister on the seventh, "was that certain tactical features had to be taken. Canadians were brought in to do the job; so far they have done the job mighty well." Doubts about Passchendaele would continue to plague him, and he would, in the weeks and months ahead, become more outspoken in his criticism of the venture. In the meantime, however, he could only contemplate the latest casualty toll. The Corps' losses for 6 November numbered 2,238, including 734 dead.[21]

The casualties, while not as heavy as in the two late October attacks, had been numerous enough. This was evidenced by the 28th Battalion which, after being relieved on 7 November, had paraded and held a roll-call. After suffering 250 casualties the previous day, "there weren't too many of us left to answer our names," remarked Corporal H.C. Baker. "My impression was that we had won the ridge but lost the battalion...."[22]

The reaction at GHQ was predictable. That evening, Currie received a call from Lieutenant-General Sir Launcelot Kiggell, Haig's chief of staff, who was seeking assurance that Passchendaele had, in fact, been captured. When Currie confirmed it, a relieved Kiggell muttered, "Thank God."[23]

Field-Marshal Haig was most pleased. Through Sir Herbert Plumer, he sent congratulations to the Canadians. "The ground gained is of great importance," he telegraphed Second Army headquarters. "Please convey to General Currie and his troops my warm appreciation of the gallant manner in which they have overcome all difficulties and carried out the task assigned them." Later that night, he wrote in his diary:

> The operations were completely successful. Passchendaele was taken, as also were Mosselmarkt and Goudberg. The whole position had been most methodically fortified—yet our troops succeeded in capturing all their objectives early in the day with small loss—"under 700 men" [Haig was obviously referring to early fatality reports]. The left Battalion of the 2nd Division had hard fighting. 21 officers and 408 other ranks were taken prisoner. To-day was a very important success.[24]

Not everyone at GHQ saw it that way. More pessimistic was Haig's intelligence chief, Brigadier-General Charteris, who wrote that "the whole of the ridge is now in our hands. We have now got to where, with good weather, we should have been in early September, and with two months in front of us to carry on the operation and clear the coast. Now, from the purely local point of view, it is a rather barren victory...."[25]

15/"They Are Wonderful Troops"

The loss of Passchendaele came as a bitter blow to the Germans. Admitting that "German losses around Passchendaele were once again considerable," the German official account credits the Canadians with a "meaningful" success, "inasmuch as the rise in the ground gave good observation into the German artillery positions. The British had a favourable base for further attacks.... A speedy renewal of their offensive had to be reckoned with."[1] The Germans pondered the possibility of mounting a major counter-attack on Passchendaele on 7 November, but this was cancelled by Oberste Heerseleitung (OHL), the high command, due to the difficulty involved in such an undertaking, the uncertainty of adequate artillery support, and doubts whether the available infantry could carry out the operation. Instead of attacking, the Germans contented themselves with a prolonged bombardment of the Canadians in and around Passchendaele.

And what a bombardment it was. The 28th (Northwest) Battalion bore the brunt of twelve hours of heavy shelling. According to the officer commanding the 28th, Lieutenant-Colonel Alex Ross, the barrage was "one of the worst ever experienced by our Unit on a battle front." The battalion had suffered comparatively few casualties in the assault on 6 November; most of its 250 dead and wounded were incurred during the bombardment on the seventh. Evacuation of the injured was out of the question. Receiving reports of heavy losses among prisoners and walking wounded headed for the rear, Colonel Ross issued orders forbidding anyone from leaving the battle zone. "The front-line at that time," he later explained, "was unquestionably the safest place."[2]

When the enemy shelling eased and allowed the evacuation of the Canadian wounded to proceed, the same old problems presented themselves. The rainfall on the sixth made the mud that much worse, and caused considerable suffering, as Colonel Ross recounted:

> Often no less than eight men were required for a single stretcher, and even then it was killing work. The nature of the ground was such that sure footing was impossible and time and again the poor wounded would be hurled to the ground. Their agonies were unspeakable and even after they had reached the dressing stations their difficulties were not ended for the ambulances could not get forward through the mire; often the carrying process had to be continued farther back for a further two miles.[3]

It was no easier on the ever-present carrying parties charged with bringing forward water, food, and ammunition. W.A. Bottrill, a subaltern in the 4th (Central Ontario) Battalion, would never forget his experience in command of fifty men burdened with 25,000 rounds of small-arms ammunition, two men to a box of 1,000 rounds.

> I have no way of knowing what length of time I spent on a stretch of road that probably was less than a mile, but I must have been on it for several hours. There would be a spurt of intense artillery fire, and we were beginning to lose some of our own people. It became such utter confusion. Time and memory and everything else simply dissolved into nothing. I have no way of knowing precisely and exactly how many casualties we suffered, but it ended up with one corporal, two men, and myself.

Between them, they had only a single box of ammunition, but it was delivered safely.[4]

Fresh troops were soon moved onto the ridge. The first reliefs were carried out on 7/8 November, and the scene that greeted the newcomers was somewhat shocking. The 13th (Royal Highlanders of Canada) Battalion took over a portion of the First Division's front lines north of Passchendaele. Says the regimental history: "The mud was in many places waist deep, torn and twisted wire lay everywhere, water filled shell holes were numerous, while all about lay the bodies of the dead, the whole area presenting a picture of desolation and horror hard to equal and impossible to surpass." The 22nd (French Canadian) Battalion relieved the battered and shell-shocked 28th Battalion in front of Passchendaele. A signaller, A.J. Lapointe, was sickened by the conditions he and his comrades encountered:

> In a flooded trench, the bloated bodies of some German soldiers are floating. Here and there, too, arms and legs of dead men stick out from the mud, and awful faces appear, blackened by days and weeks under the beating sun. I try to turn from these dreadful sights, but wherever I look dead bodies emerge, shapelessly, from their shroud of mud.

So desolate was the place that Private Lapointe lamented, "It would seem that life could never return to these fields of abundant death."[5]

But there was one more battle in store for the Canadian Corps. General Currie, hosting a corps commanders' conference on 8 November, agreed to undertake another attack, as he commented in a brief entry in his diary: "Situation reviewed and plans for next operation approved."[6] What would prove to be the fourth and final phase of the Canadian operations at Passchendaele was intended to secure the gains already made. Scheduled for 10 November, the attack was aimed at the high ground north of the village: the objectives included Vindictive Crossroads, 1,000 yards from Passchendaele, and Hill 52, the highest point on the ridge, a half-mile beyond the crossroads. The main thrust would be made by two battalions of Brigadier-General Frederick Loomis's Second Brigade, supported on the right by a battalion of the Fourth Brigade and on the left by a British brigade.

The weather would prove to be the worst to accompany any Canadian operations on this front. At zero hour on Saturday, 10 November—6:05 A.M.—it was "misty and with low clouds." But within an hour a driving rainstorm swept the battlefield. The rain fell so heavily at times that the Canadians found it impossible to walk; many literally had to crawl to reach their objectives.[7]

The German artillery caused havoc, too. The 7th (1st British Columbia Regiment) and the 8th (90th Winnipeg Rifles) battalions, which were to spearhead the Second Brigade's attack, had no sooner assembled along their jumping-off line—signalled to brigade headquarters at 3:40 A.M. by the code word "Texas"—than they came under intense shelling. "The enemy had evidently concluded that our attack was in preparation," suggests the Second Brigade's report. Around five o'clock the bombardment intensified, and the troops were forced to endure this "terrific fire for about one hour." The barrage, which ended just a few minutes before zero, caused 132 casualties in the two battalions.[8]

It did not, however, deter the Canadians. And it was ironic to note that, once the attack was under way, the German guns were noticeable only by their silence. The Canadian barrage began precisely at 6:05 A.M., and the infantry went over the top three minutes later, but fifteen precious minutes passed before the enemy artillery responded to the SOS flares frantically fired by the desperate defenders.*

Vindictive Crossroads, the primary objective, was quickly captured by the 7th Battalion. But it was not easy. One company lost all of its officers in the attack; a platoon, decimated by machine-gun fire, was left with only a lance-corporal and seven other ranks. Having taken the crossroads, the battalion came under heavy fire from a nearby trench, and Lieutenant G. Carmichael's 1 Company, ignoring the rain that was now falling in torrents, attacked and captured the position, along with twenty prisoners. Then two

---

* The line opposite the Canadians was now held by the 4th Division and elements of the 44th Reserve Division which had relieved the exhausted 11th Division the previous day.

machine-guns in a pillbox fired on the Canadians and pinned them down in their hard-won positions. Private Crosby Dorais promptly took on the pillbox with his Lewis gun: he not only neutralized it, but prevented enemy reinforcements from reaching it. With the time bought by Private Dorais, the 7th Battalion organized another attack. Storming the pillbox, the Canadians added eighteen prisoners and two machine-guns to their prize collection.[9]

However, the 7th could go no farther. Its heavy losses precluded further operations, and the brigade commander, General Loomis, wisely committed a reserve battalion, the 10th (Canadians), to the attack. With difficulty, the 10th passed through the 7th and, despite the pouring rain and steady shelling, pressed forward. By dawn the next morning, Hill 52 was in Canadians hands, and Loomis could report "that we commanded the whole slope to our right front."[10]

To the right of the Second Brigade, the 20th (Central Ontario) Battalion supported brilliantly. So smoothly did its operation proceed that the regimental history later called it a "walk-over." At 7:10 A.M., little more than an hour after zero, Captain A.D. Fisken, commanding 2 Company, dispatched the following message to battalion headquarters:

> No. 2 Company LEFT, No. 3 Company CENTRE, No. 1 Company RIGHT. We have consolidated objectives with post 150 yards in front. Nearest enemy observed 1,000 yards in front. 7th Canadian Infantry Battalion in touch on LEFT. RIGHT FLANK all O.K. Enemy planes active. Old wire 100 yards in front of Company. Our Artillery splendid. One Company strength 50 approximate. Ground dry. Have field of Fire 200 yards in front.

Later that morning, a gap was discovered between the 7th and 20th Battalions, and Captain Fisken sent two platoons to fill it. These troops ran into a previously undetected pillbox that had sat silently through the attack. Until now. The Canadians dealt with it in a textbook operation: "The rifle sections... covered by the fire of the rifle grenade and Lewis Gun Sections, approached by rushes, maintaining a rifle duel with the enemy at each halt. As soon as they were close enough they charged with the bayonet, capturing the 'pillbox' and twenty-five prisoners."[11]

There was, unfortunately, trouble on the left, though it was no fault of the Canadians. The 8th (90th Winnipeg Rifles) Battalion had, in fact, carried out a flawless attack, taking Venture Farm and four 77-millimetre guns. "Am on my objective on all points," a company commander reported at 7:15 A.M.[12] However, there were

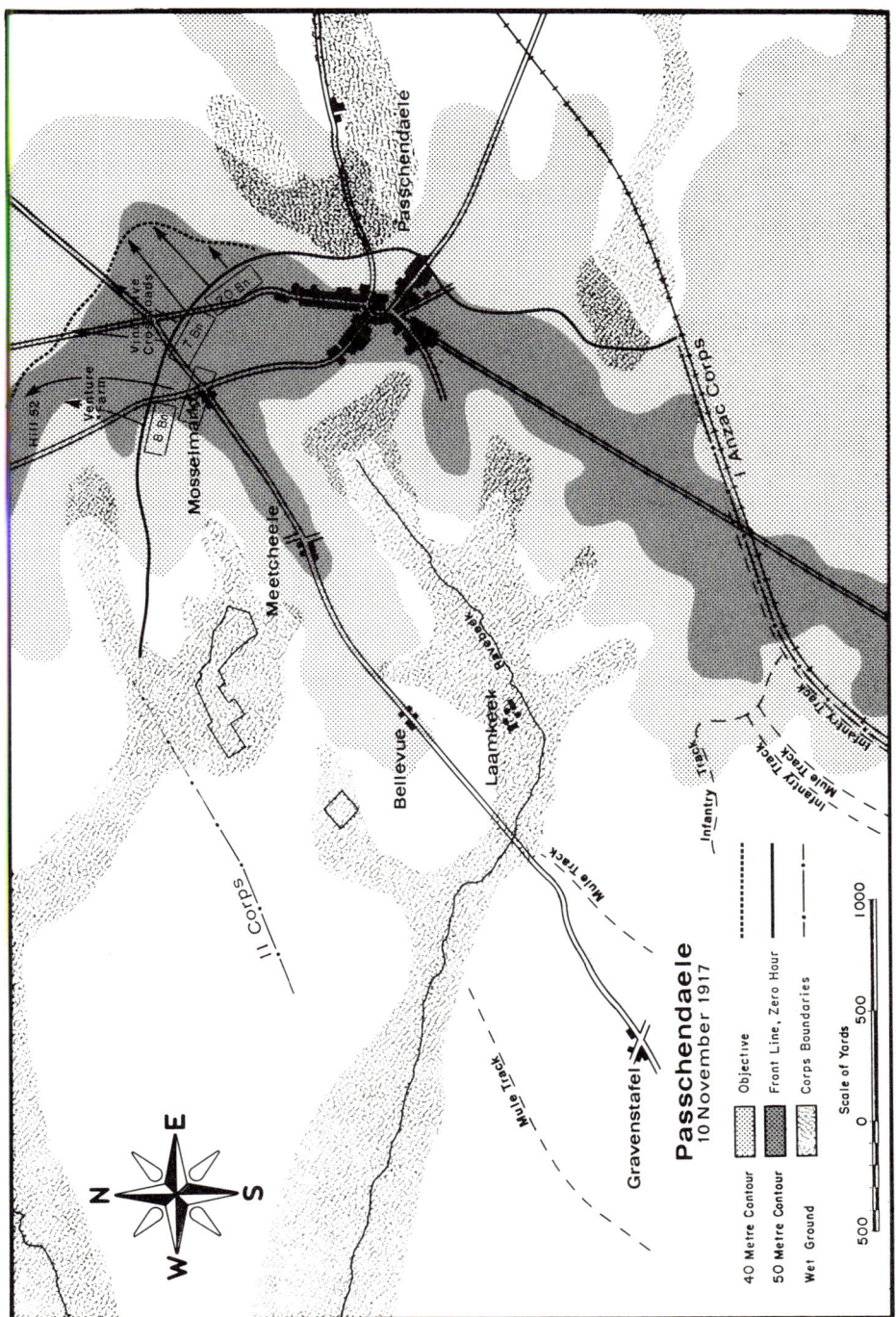

problems to the left of the 8th Battalion, where British troops guarding the Canadian flank failed miserably.

The assault by the 3rd Brigade of the British 1st Division, II Corps, appeared to have succeeded, initially. But in the confusion that was commonplace in these conditions, two attacking battalions—the South Wales Borderers and the Royal Munster Fusiliers—diverged, and a German counter-attack happened to hit this crucial gap, with predictable results: the Borderers and Fusiliers were routed with heavy losses. Their defeat opened the Canadian flank to terrible enfilade fire.

The Canadian commander, General Currie, was completely disgusted. He fumed that the British "retired in very bad and pronounced disorder, amounting to a panic."[13] It was not the last time he would complain about the performance of British troops in combat: he grew increasingly critical during 1918, though his complaints were not always justified. Currie's criticism also ruffled the feathers of more than a few senior British officers and led to often strained relations between the Canadian Corps staff and their Imperial brethren.

In this instance, Currie's angry words were understandable, because the British defeat threatened for a time to undermine the fine Canadian success. The 8th Battalion stabilized the situation by forming a defensive flank, with help from another Second Brigade unit, the 5th (Western Cavalry) Battalion. Nevertheless, the Canadians were now in an extremely vulnerable position, as their official history has noted:

> The frontage of the Anglo-Canadian attack, narrow enough to begin with and reduced by three-fifths by the failure on the left, allowed the enemy to concentrate an unusual weight of artillery against the new line. In all, the counter-batteries of five German corps were turned on the Canadian front.

The subsequent storm of shrapnel and high-explosive that swept across the Canadians was, according to General Currie, "the most severe and violent we ever experienced." An admiring Australian who witnessed the bombardment wrote in his diary: "If the Canadians can hold on they are wonderful troops."[14]

The Canadians were wonderful, and they did hold on. The shelling was at its worst from mid-morning until late in the afternoon, and the men of the 7th, 8th, 10th, and 20th battalions had precious little protection, "lying in water-soaked, half-filled shell holes or belly down in shallow trenches scooped out of mud. . . . Men were buried in the mud, dug out by their comrades and buried again, and again dug out." Private Thomas Rattray of the 10th (Canadians) Battalion considered himself to be "lucky" to live through it. "All my chums were killed down in that muddy trench," he recalled. "We did not know what hit us. I was the only survivor, though I did receive chest and leg wounds. Six men carried me out, walking up to their knees in mud, lugging me out."[15]

In the days that followed, the Germans mounted a series of poorly organized and half-hearted counter-attacks, more than two dozen in all, in hopes of matching their success against the neighbouring British. But it was not to be. Each time, the Germans were repulsed by small-arms and artillery fire, working in deadly combination. Typical is this account of an attack on the 19th (Central Ontario) Battalion:

> They came swarming overland on a clear afternoon, and were sighted. The S.O.S. went up, and the gunners found the range to a nicety. Shells fell in the very midst of dense formations, and pieces of Germans could be seen flying skywards. The enemy never even reached the barbed wire, and on attempting to retire were swept by machine guns and sniped out of existence.[16]

Canadian casualties on 10 November numbered 1,094, including 420 dead. But the worst was over. The Corps, having captured and consolidated Passchendaele, would soon be saying farewell to the Ypres salient.

16/Farewell to the Salient

The Flanders campaign came to a close soon afterward. A half-mile of ridge north of Passchendaele remained in enemy hands, but on 12 November, Sir Douglas Haig decided "that we must stop the offensive in Flanders, except for bombardment and simulated attacks for the next fortnight."[1]

The Canadians began leaving the salient on Wednesday, 14 November. Four days later, General Currie handed over responsibility for the Passchendaele sector to Lieutenant-General Sir Aylmer Hunter-Weston and his VIII Corps. The same day, 18 November, Currie departed for the Vimy Ridge front, familiar and more friendly territory where the Canadian Corps would spend the winter. Most of the Corps preceded him, except for the artillery of the First and Second divisions, which remained at Passchendaele for an extra week, and the Corps heavy artillery, which stayed until the middle of December.

Passchendaele had been a painful experience for all concerned. It will be recalled that General Currie predicted that it would cost the Corps 16,000 casualties to take Passchendaele. His forecast was incredibly accurate; the actual toll was 15,654.* Though all services suffered, the bulk of the losses were, as usual, incurred by "the poor bloody infantry." Casualties of 50 per cent or more were not uncommon among the attacking battalions, particularly during the first two phases of operations. The 46th (South Saskatchewan) Battalion lost 70 per cent of its strength on 26 October, while on the thirtieth the 49th (Edmonton Regiment) Battalion suffered a casualty rate of 75 per cent. Yet, casualties were also astonishingly high among battalions which did not attack but performed other tasks, such as holding the front line between operations and providing carrying parties, work details, and stretcher-bearers. The 42nd (Royal Highlanders of Canada) Battalion, in a primarily passive role—though it did mount the minor attack on Graf House on 2 November—lost 276 men. The Royal Canadian Regiment suffered 258 casualties. The 24th (Victoria Rifles of Canada) Battalion spent three days in the front lines prior to the attack of 6 November: its losses amounted to 234, including one company that was "almost annihilated" by heavy

* This figure comes from the Canadian official history, published in 1964. However, the British official history, which came out in 1948, put Canadian losses at 12,924. No explanation for the discrepancy is given. Currie, in 1920, estimated Corps casualties at "just under 17,000."[2]

shelling. The 87th (Canadian Grenadier Guards) Battalion, in four days in the front lines, enduring "the heaviest concentration of shelling during the whole of its experience," lost 176 men killed and wounded. The 102nd (Central Ontario) Battalion, the last infantry unit to leave Passchendaele, did two tours of the front lines and suffered 175 casualties.[3]

There were no regrets about leaving. A veteran of the 13th (Royal Highlanders of Canada) Battalion spoke for every Canadian when he said of the salient, "I hope to God I never see the cursed place again!"[4]

Exhaustion was rampant. "One can never forget the haggard looks of the men and officers... almost helpless with the fatigue of their work," commented Lieutenant-Colonel J.N. Gunn of the 8th Canadian Field Ambulance. Few of them even resembled soldiers. According to one observer, "All were almost unrecognizable. Everyone had three-day-old beards. Faces, hands and clothing were covered with mud. A few had no shoes, several had no putties [sic], many had no helmets, but none cared much."[5]

As they stumbled along the bath mats and muddy tracks that led to Ypres, some seemed to be sleep-walking. Proper billets were in short supply, but no one minded, as C.J. Albon of the 25th (Nova Scotia Rifles) Battalion testified:

> And that night when we got out to Ypres and there was no place to stay there, I remember falling into a little funk hole in the ground and, boy, it was a home. I didn't even take my greatcoat off. I just shoved my pack under my head and went to sleep, and it didn't take long. I woke in the morning, and I was laying in about three inches of water. Been raining all night. It didn't make any difference. I didn't know.

Private Ernie Jenner of the 46th (South Saskatchewan) Battalion recalled that he slept for eighteen hours after being relieved. Others simply did not awaken. Private N.O. Barton, an orderly with the 8th Field Ambulance, "was found dead in his bed one morning after having retired the night previous in apparently good health."[6]

These men had undergone a test of courage and endurance seldom seen on any battlefield, in any war. And they knew it, too. Corporal Fred Allen of the Royal Canadian Regiment wrote his mother in December: "I was in that Passchendaele affair. *Some* hot *joint* believe muh! All the old timers in the Regt. say it was much worse than the Somme." That feeling was unanimous. Private Jack Quelch of the 44th (Manitoba) Battalion remarked in a letter home:

"We were up to our necks in mud at the Somme this time last year and are not much better this year. In fact worse...." Added D.E. MacIntyre, a Fourth Brigade staff officer: "I believe that any Canadian soldier who was there will agree that the conditions at Passchendaele were the worst he ever saw." Private Arthur Turner of the 50th (Calgary) Battalion agreed:

> The Passchendaele trip was by far the worst in my experience. I learned to pray that trip. Not in a kneeling, sissy way, but with a vengeance, and a *demand* that I wanted my prayer answered.... *I found that it worked.*

The artillery shared these sentiments. Colonel J.S. Stewart, temporarily commanding the Fourth Division's artillery, commented: "No gunner without experience of Passchendaele really knew the horrors of war." Passchendaele was, in the words of Gunner Elmer Philpott, "really hell on earth."[7]

Many were angry. "Passchendaele was absolutely the height of stupidity," recalled E.O. Anderson of the 49th (Edmonton Regiment) Battalion. "We were just cannon fodder." G. Allen Bagley, a member of the 50th (Calgary) Battalion called it "the most awful thing you ever saw. We should never have been in there at all." James Johnson of the 5th Canadian Mounted Rifles declared: "It was an awful place. It was the worst, as far as conditions—terrible.... The troops didn't think much of Currie after this.... He wasn't very popular."[5]

Still, morale remained high. Years later, when O.J. Turner of the 54th (Central Ontario) Battalion was asked to recall Passchendaele, this quality among the Canadians stood out in his mind: "The conditions at Passchendaele were just about the worst that you could possibly have anywhere. And yet those men, they were just as cheerful as they could be, and they...were always in such good spirits, no matter what they went through."[9]

How was this possible? Perhaps, it can be attributed simply to the irrepressible exuberance of youth. But that explanation does not go far enough, according to several veterans of Passchendaele. There was, as Major Arnott Mordy of the 16th (Canadian Scottish) Battalion wrote in November 1917, an unmistakable sense of pride.

> This last show was about the hardest, owing to the weather conditions, etc., that we ever engaged in, and nothing but the indomitable pluck and grit of every one in it got us through. This may sound like blowing our own horn a bit, but it is the least that

can be said of those chaps whom we left behind there.... None of us will ever forget the Ypres salient.

G.R. Stevens, a member of Princess Patricia's Canadian Light Infantry, believed that "there was something, and I can only think it was discipline, that sustained us." Of course, discipline was something in which the Canadians were supposedly lacking. It is one of the more persistent myths of the Great War, but Passchendaele proved beyond any doubt that the Canadians were among the most disciplined troops in the world; they could not have succeeded otherwise.[10]*

Another interesting theory about Canadian morale was put forward by Sergeant John Brice, also of the PPCLI, who suggested in a letter home that Passchendaele epitomized a Canadian characteristic that was, possibly, unique:

> It is really remarkable that the better we are treated, the more grub we get, the greater the growling and cussing. Put us up to our waists in water, let it rain and be miserable, six on a loaf, and only bully-beef for dinner, and the troops will sing and make merry. It takes a bit of swallowing, but such is the case.[12]

The Canadians recovered quickly from their ordeal. They luxuriated in their new billets near Vimy Ridge; though modest, these quarters seemed palatial compared to Passchendaele's miseries. "I shall never forget," wrote Lieutenant E.R. Knight of the 49th (Edmonton Regiment) Battalion, "the joy of a well-cooked meal, clean clothes, a roaring fire and a bed." Not to mention a hot bath. The effect of such comforts was startling, according to the recollection of a young gunner named D.C. Higgins:

> I would say that people came out of Passchendaele simply numb.

---

* There were, to be sure, some free spirits among the Canadians. A recently arrived medical officer acquired a considerable collection of souvenirs while serving at an advanced dressing station. His tour of duty complete, he stuffed the souvenirs into a sandbag, handed it to his batman, and together they set out for a field-ambulance unit. The two of them stumbled through the darkness, falling into shell holes and choking on mud.
  At one point, the officer inquired of his batman, "Aren't you tired?" When the latter assured him that he was fine, the officer pressed: "Are you sure that bag of souvenirs isn't making you tired?" Again, the batman told him that it was no trouble at all. The officer was not convinced. "That bag must be making you tired. Whereabouts are you carrying it?"
  "I ain't carrying it," replied the batman. "I dropped it in the first shell hole after we started."[11]

> Numb! Mentally and physically. And I wouldn't have thought that many of us would have recovered from it. But, c'est la guerre—and one good leave does an awful lot for a man, you know.[13]

Leave did, indeed, mean much to these weary soldiers. In the case of Private Arthur Turner of the 50th Battalion, it produced an exquisite irony that he would never forget. Private Turner was granted leave on 15 November and spent the next two weeks in London. While in the British capital, he stopped at a restaurant for tea and biscuits. Forgetting that rationing was in effect, Turner asked for sugar for his tea; the waitress inquired whether he had his sugar coupons. "No," he replied weakly. An elderly man sitting at the next table, overhearing this exchange, leaned over and nudged Turner: "Say, young fellow, don't you know there's a war on?"[14]

London warmly welcomed the Canadians. The capture of Passchendaele had, after so many weeks and months of bad news, come as a great relief, a feat which received much play in the press. *The Times* called it a "very fine and gallant operation," claiming that "the Canadians had never shown greater doggedness or determination than in this attack." The *Daily Chronicle* described it as "fine and thrilling as an act of persistent courage," while the *Daily Express* told its readers that "Canada will hear with pride of the part played by her troops in this important advance." A Canadian living in England, Charles Armstrong, wrote Sir Arthur Currie on 12 November: "Everybody here is talking about it & it makes one feel very proud of the Corps."[15]

Certainly, no one was prouder than General Currie. The Canadians, he later wrote, had taken Passchendaele "by superhuman efforts." His men had "never worked so hard or fought with such grim determination." He also confessed that

> I do not know which branch of the service is entitled the most praise. The Infantry who stormed the hostile trenches and beat off the counterattacks, the Artillery who prepared the way for the Infantry and who supported the attacks, the Engineers and Pioneers who made the roads which enabled the guns to be brought forward, and thus made victory possible, the Medical Services who have always done so well but who excelled all past performances in these battles, the Supply people who never failed once in getting forward the rations, engineer material and munitions of all kinds, all gave evidence of the highest soldierly qualities and the determination to win.

Concluded Currie: "I firmly believe that the Canadians were the only troops that could have taken the position at that time of the year and under the conditions under which the attack had to be made."[16]

Britain's French and Belgian allies appreciated the Canadian sacrifice at Passchendaele. The French, Currie recalled, "immediately awarded me a croix de guerre with palms and did what they did not do for any other General in the war, namely: asked me to go to Paris to receive this decoration. I went and on November 23rd attended a banquet given in my honour by the French Government at the Hôtel Meurice in Paris. Monsieur [Gabriel] Han[o]taux, the French Minister of the Interior, proposed my health, and in his speech state that he hoped some time I would take the title Duke of Paeschendale [sic]."[17] Belgium, not to be outdone, awarded the Canadian commander two decorations, the Belgian Croix de Guerre and named him an officer in the Ordre de la Couronne, in January 1918.

Currie, typically, did not let these honours go to his head. While he was undoubtedly flattered by them, he was also a bit embarrassed at all the attention directed his way. The rewards, he realized, had been given to him "solely because it is my proud privilege to command the Canadian Corps."[18] He might also have felt a tinge of guilt, because he still doubted the validity of the battle so heroically waged and won by the Corps.

17/Death Struggle

Months later, a grisly sight greeted the British defenders of Passchendaele. In the spring of 1918, the ground thawed and many of the thousands of dead who had been buried, deliberately or otherwise, in the mud of the previous autumn rose to the surface.

Burial parties were formed, and the bodies were reinterred. The Newfoundlanders holding the line discovered among the corpses the remains of "a big Canadian who had grappled with a big German. Both had fought desperately, and had died in the mud in each other's arms." The Newfoundlanders tried to separate them, but it was impossible—their death struggle had been cemented by rigor mortis. Unable to pry them apart, the soldiers buried the Canadian and the German together. Mortal enemies in life, in death they now shared the same resting place.[1]

Part Four: Consequences

18/Watershed

Passchendaele was the watershed of World War I. Its consequences were enormous, though no one realized it at the time and few have recognized it since. But the spectre of this great clash haunted the participants for the rest of the war and directly influenced the key decisions and events that followed.

The Germans were simply staggered by the fighting in Flanders. The drain on their resources was unprecedented, as Crown Prince Rupprecht admitted: "86 divisions, 22 of them twice, the mass of our reserve of artillery and other weapons and formations, have taken part in this, the greatest of all our battles." Their casualties—which, due to shortcomings in German bookkeeping, can only be estimated—exceeded a quarter of a million, which drastically affected the manpower situation, according to Rupprecht's chief of staff, General Hermann von Kuhl:

> From the 1st November the average strength of the German battalions on the entire western front dwindled to 640 men [as opposed to the nominal strength of 1,000]. Except for the class of 1899, composed of 18-year-olds, only men who had been already severely wounded and such men who could be combed out from the eastern front were available for the replacement of casualties.... This state of affairs influenced the conduct of the war in a decisive manner.[1]

Von Kuhl concluded that "the Flanders battle wore down the German strength to a degree at which the damage could no longer be repaired. The German sword, heretofore sharp, was blunted." Erich Ludendorff, the de facto commander-in-chief on the Western Front, complained that, as a result of the losses in Flanders, "our infantry approximated more nearly in character... a militia, as our best men became casualties, and discipline declined." In the words of a postwar General Staff publication, "Germany had been brought near to certain destruction (*sicheren Untergang*) by the Flanders battle of 1917."[2]

The psychological impact cannot be overlooked. As Ludendorff later confessed, "it must be admitted that certain units no longer triumphed over the demoralizing effects of the defensive battle as they had done formerly." Von Kuhl commented:

> The suffering, privation and exertions which the soldiers had to

bear were inexpressible. Terrible was the spiritual burden on the lonely man in the shell hole, and terrible the strain on the nerves during the bombardments which continued day and night. The "Hell of Verdun" was exceeded by Flanders. The Battle of Flanders has been called "The Greatest Martyrdom of the World War."

Inevitably, word of these horrors reached home. "In millions of letters from the Western Front from April to November," wrote a corps commander, General Otto von Moser, "came the ever-rising bitter complaints of the almost unbearable hardships and bloody losses in the scarcely uninterrupted chain of battles.... A hundred thousand leave men told the Home Front by word of mouth the details of the ever-growing superiority of the enemy, particularly in weapons of destruction." For the first time, the Germans had to consider the unthinkable, the possibility that they could lose the war.[3]

On 11 November, the day after the final Canadian attack at Passchendaele, Ludendorff convened a conference of senior officers at Mons, Belgium. Ludendorff had been especially impressed with the Canadian operations, later writing: "On October 26 and 30 and November 6 and 10 the fighting was again of the severest description. The enemy charged like a wild bull...." Ludendorff realized that OHL, the German high command, now faced what he called "the decisive question: Should it utilize the favourable conditions of the spring to strike a great blow in the West or should it deliberately restrict itself to the defensive and make only subsidiary attacks, say in Macedonia or Italy?" It was an easy question to answer. In Ludendorff's opinion, "it had become apparent that the holding of the Western front purely by a defensive [policy] could no longer be counted on, in view of the enormous quantity of material of all kinds which the Entente had now at its disposal." The German commander knew, too, that his armies could not stand any more punishing blows such as that sustained at Passchendaele.

> Against the power of the hostile weapons the troops no longer displayed their old stubbornness in defense; they thought with horror of fresh defensive battles and longed for the war of movement.... The interests of the army were best served by the offensive; in defense it was bound naturally to succumb to the every-increasing hostile superiority in men and material. This feeling was shared by everybody.

There was another consideration of importance to Ludendorff. "The attack," he claimed, "is the strongest form of combat; it alone is decisive; military history proves it on every page. It is the symbol of superiority."[4]

Two factors played essential roles in Ludendorff's thinking: Russia and the United States. The U.S. had been at war since the previous April, but it would not be until well into 1918 that the Americans could arrive on the Continent in significant numbers. The Germans had to act quickly in order to negate this Allied advantage, and the means to act was provided by the demise of Russia, which freed hundreds of thousands of German troops serving on the eastern front. The Bolsheviks had come to power in revolution-stricken Russia on 7 November, just a few days before Ludendorff's Mons conference, and they were determined to bring peace to their country: by the end of the month they had agreed to an armistice with Germany. Although a peace treaty was not finalized until the following March, Russia was no longer an active participant in the war, and the Germans could begin shifting westward some of the eighty divisions on the eastern front.

Thus, Ludendorff's conclusion was inevitable. The Germans, he said, must launch "an attack that would bring about an early decision. This was possible only on the Western Front...." His main opponent was equally obvious: "We must beat the British."[5]

Soon afterward, planning was begun on *Kaiserschlact*, the "Emperor battle," on which hinged German hopes to win the war. And so Passchendaele prompted the soldiers of the Second Reich to go on the offensive, a desperate battle, one that the Germans could not win. That they came close was due in large part to the British prime minister, David Lloyd George, whose continued meddling in military matters played right into the enemy's hands.

19 / "Irregular Warfare"

Prime Minister Lloyd George considered Passchendaele to be a major British defeat, and used it as an excuse to intensify what historian John Terraine aptly calls "irregular warfare" against his generals. On 16 October, even as the Canadian Corps was preparing to take Passchendaele, the prime minister signalled his intentions with a cable of congratulations to Sir Douglas Haig.

> The War Cabinet desire to congratulate you and the troops under your command upon the achievements of the British Armies in Flanders in the great battle which has been raging since July 31st. Starting from positions in which every advantage rested with the enemy, and hampered and delayed from time to time by most unfavourable weather, you and your men have nevertheless driven the enemy back with such skill, courage and pertinacity, as have commanded the grateful admiration of the peoples of the British Empire and filled the enemy with alarm. I am personally glad to be the means of transmitting this message to you, and to your gallant troops, and desire to take this opportunity of renewing my assurance of confidence in your leadership, and in the devotion of those whom you command.[1]

Haig was suspicious, and rightly so. This was, he noted in his diary, "the first message of congratulation on any operations by the War Cabinet which has reached me since the War began! I wonder why the Prime Minister should suddenly have sent this message."[2]

His suspicions were well founded. The next evening, Lloyd George dined with General Sir Henry Wilson, the former liaison officer at Grand Quartier Général (GQG). "It became very clear to me to-night," Wilson wrote afterwards, "that Lloyd George means to get Robertson out, and means to curb the powers of the C. in C. in the field."[3]

In fact, the prime minister had already come close to forcing Robertson's resignation. On 11 October, Lloyd George told the CIGS that he intended to consult two senior officers, the above-mentioned Wilson and Lord French, the embittered former commander-in-chief of the BEF. They were, in the prime minister's view, "two of the ablest Generals in the British Army" but, as usual, he was being far from truthful. The wisecracking Wilson had cultivated powerful political allies, but was widely mistrusted throughout the army as an ambitious trouble-maker. French had, during his sixteen months in command of the BEF, demonstrated his incompetence; humiliated by his dismissal in December 1915, he harboured an ill-concealed grudge against Haig, who, he believed, had conspired to oust him. Lloyd George assured Robertson that his desire to consult Wilson and French on war policy "implied no want of confidence in the General Staff," that he merely wanted "to obtain a second opinion, just in the same way as a second doctor was called in when a serious case of illness occurred." The difference, of course, was that the prime minister would choose the diagnosis and prescription he preferred.[4]

Wully Robertson was no fool. He saw immediately that the prime minister's proposal indicated that he had lost confidence in his chief military adviser. Furious at Lloyd George's blatant dishonesty and underhanded methods, the CIGS came within an ace of resigning. He was talked out of it by close friends, but the hurt and anger were apparent when he later wrote Haig: "The fact is it is a *very* weak-kneed, craven-hearted cabinet, and L.G.... is allowed to run riot. We shall see what we shall see."[5]

The war cabinet met for three days of deliberations, beginning on 23 October. Lloyd George must have been ecstatic as he listened to his informal advisers. Using the occasion to get even with Haig, French—so venomous were his words that the cabinet secretary, Sir Maurice Hankey, observed, "There was envy, hatred and malice in the old boy's heart as he spoke"—charged that Haig "was always making the same mistake," and predicted that this would not end "until we break the Haig-Robertson ring." Wilson questioned the possibility of winning the war on the Western Front. "It is no use throwing 'decisive numbers at the decisive place'," he argued, using Robertson's favourite phrase, "...if the decisive numbers do not exist, if the decisive hour has not struck or if the decisive place is ill-chosen."[6]

Both Wilson and French urged the creation of a supreme council to direct the Allied war effort. The coincidence is too much; clearly the soldiers were being coached by the prime minister, whose partiality to this idea was known. Wilson, though, had first thought of it in July, when he proposed "a body composed of three soldiers, English, French, and Italian, with suitable staffs and full knowledge, who would be empowered to draw up plans of attack and defence along the whole line from Nieuport to Egypt." He had presented the proposal to Lloyd George on 23 August, adding, for obvious reasons, "three Prime Ministers" to this prestigious body. Lloyd George, he noted, "was rather taken" with the idea.[7]

Indeed, he liked it so much that he adopted it as his own. By the end of August he was openly speaking of what Hankey dubiously called "a new, and not very well-thought-out scheme for an Allied Council and General Staff in Paris to direct the war." In a letter to U.S. President Woodrow Wilson in early September, Lloyd George sought American support for "an Allied Body which had knowledge of the resources of all the Allies and which could prepare a single coordinated plan for utilising those resources in the most decisive manner...." The prime minister's intention was clear: he sought to remove from Haig and Robertson responsibility for the control of the British war effort. But the supreme council remained nothing more than an idea. Until Caporetto.[8]

Caporetto was one of the biggest disasters of the war. On 24 October, two days before the Canadians mounted their first attack at Passchendaele, the Italian army had been crushed by Austro-Hungarian forces bolstered by half a dozen German divisions drawn from the Russian front. The Italians lost 305,000 men, including 275,000 who simply surrendered. The subsequent chaotic retreat—something that the Italians were very good at—covered nearly a hundred miles before the demoralized Italian army could be rallied.

The magnitude of the Italian misadventure was soon apparent. At GHQ, Haig's intelligence chief, General Charteris, feared that "this Italian débâcle will give a tremendous stimulus to all opponents of our policy and plans here [on the Western Front]." He was quite right. On 27 October, Sir Maurice Hankey commented:

> Ll.G. of course is furious. The Germans have struck at the weak link, just as he himself wanted to do on (almost) the very same spot—a plan which the General Staff rejected with contempt. Meanwhile Haig's plan has completely failed, as Ll.G. always said it would. As though to add fuel to the flames Robertson tonight sent down a Memorandum of his policy, which practically amounted to a reaffirmation of his "slogging on the Western Front" plan. It annoyed Ll.G. intensely.[9]

Nothing better illustrates the prime minister's state of mind. He was completely oblivious to the very real incompetence of the Italian high command. It was ridiculous to presume that the Italians, even with British troops to aid them, could have inflicted a Caporetto on the Austrians, as he seemed to believe, or wanted to believe. Thirteen unsuccessful battles on the Isonzo should have indicated that there was something seriously wrong with the Italian army.

But Caporetto was a golden opportunity, and Lloyd George grasped it. On 27 October, the war cabinet, at the prime minister's insistence, directed two British divisions to be dispatched from

France and Italy; two more followed on 8 November, along with Sir Herbert Plumer as the British commander in Italy; another division was transferred on the fourteenth. These moves were made over the protests of GHQ. Haig sent his chief of staff, General Kiggell, to London to explain "that the proper way to save Italy was by renewing the attack on the western front."[10] Kiggell's pleas, predictably, fell on deaf ears.

Lloyd George chose this moment of crisis to launch his campaign for a supreme war council. Knowing that Haig and Robertson would be opposed, he told Hankey that he "considered himself strong enough to beat the generals on the central council plan." On 2 November his war cabinet "approved the scheme for an Inter-Allied Supreme Council and General Staff (Advisory) and Henry Wilson's appointment as British representative." The same day, the French government consented to send a delegation, together with British officials, to a high-level conference in Italy.[11]

The conference, in Rapallo on 6 and 7 November, was a complete success from Lloyd George's point of view. The French and Italians, as well as the Americans, agreed to join with the British to create the Supreme War Council, which would "watch over the general conduct of the War," while aiming at "the better co-ordination of military action on the Western Front."[12]

The council, which was based at Versailles, just outside Paris, had little impact on the war's direction. It would be as short-lived as it was ineffective, fading to obscurity before the middle of 1918. But its impotence should not be surprising. Even Lloyd George admitted that it was little more than a glorified committee, and assured critics in the House of Commons "that the Council will have no executive power, and that the final decisions in matters of strategy...will rest with the several Governments of the Allies." In any event, as the war correspondent, Charles Repington, perceptibly pointed out at the time, "war by committee will not wash."[13]

The Supreme War Council was Lloyd George's ultimate expression of contempt for his leading generals. It was to be an instrument that would wrest responsibility for war policy from the military and put it where the prime minister preferred, in political hands. As such, it would be a weapon in his private war with Haig and Robertson. This purpose was plain to all, including Haig's intelligence chief, Charteris, who noted that because the council would have "no executive powers," it would be "utter rubbish so far as fighting is concerned." Its formation, he realized, could only mean "that the Cabinet is going to oust D.H. or Robertson, or both."[14]

As if to rub salt in the soldiers' wounds, Lloyd George went public with his complaints about the military. On his way home from Rapallo, he stopped in Paris, where he addressed a luncheon on 12 November, the very day that Haig halted his offensive in Flanders. "We have won great victories," the prime minister sarcastically told his audience. "When I look at the appalling casualty lists I sometimes wish it had not been necessary to win so many." He went on to compare these Western Front victories with the recent fiasco in Italy:

> It is no good minimizing the extent of the Caporetto disaster. If you do, then you will never take adequate steps to repair it. When we advance a kilometre into the enemy's lines, snatch a small shattered village out of his cruel grip and capture a few hundreds of his soldiers we shout with unfeigned joy.... but what if we had advanced 50 miles beyond his lines, made 200,000 of his soldiers prisoners, and taken 2,500 of his best guns, with enormous quantities of munitions and stores?

Never was Lloyd George's contempt for British military leadership so clearly stated.[15]

Field-Marshal Haig had been forewarned of this speech, by no less a personage than the prime minister himself. Lloyd George had met Haig on 4 November, en route to Rapallo. According to Haig's diary, "he complained about attacks being made on him in the press, which he said were 'evidently inspired by the military.' He intended to make a speech and tell the public what courses he had proposed, and how, if he had had his way, the military situation would have been much better to-day but that the military advisers had prevented him from carrying out his intentions." Added Haig:

> L.G. is feeling that his position as Prime Minister is shaky and means to try to vindicate his conduct of the war in the eyes of the public and try to put the people against the soldiers. In fact, to pose as the saviour of his country, who has been hampered by bad advice given by the General Staff.

Haig possibly did not believe that Lloyd George would make such a speech, as evidenced by his concluding comment: "Quite a pleasant little man when one had him alone, but I should think most unreliable."[16]

Despite the warning, Haig was appalled when the prime minister did as promised. Calling the speech "most unpatriotic," Haig later told Lord Milner

> that if Lloyd George did not wish me to remain as Commander-in-Chief in the interests of the country, and in order to obtain

success in the war, it would be much better that I should go *at once*, rather than that Lloyd George should proceed with his policy of undermining the confidence which the troops now feel in their leaders, and eventually destroying the efficiency of the army as a fighting force. Morale in an army is a very delicate plant.[17]

He was not alone in deploring the Paris speech. Colonel Repington of *The Times* noted that Lloyd George had "castigated every one concerned in the past conduct of the war except himself, and exalted himself as the only wise man. A dreadful, self-righteous speech, with severe indictment of the soldiers...." Lord Derby, Lloyd George's secretary of state for war, called it "a great mistake. The effect upon the Army has been most unfortunate. They have lost confidence in their leaders and in the politicians. A feeling of unrest and anxiety has been caused." As we shall see, the prime minister was just getting warmed up.[18]

Haig had, coincidentally, arranged a spectacular demonstration of the importance of the Western Front. Unfortunately, it backfired, leaving Lloyd George more than ever convinced that he was dealing with hopeless incompetents.

A surprise attack by massed tanks had been in the works for weeks and months. First proposed in August by a Tank Corps desperately seeking an alternative to Flanders, Haig liked the idea but was talked out of it by his chief of staff, General Kiggell, who argued that "we must concentrate every man in the Ypres area" for the time being. As a result, it was not until after 9 October, when the weather at last precluded their use, that the tanks were withdrawn from Flanders. In the meantime, General Sir Julian Byng, a former commander of the Canadian Corps and now commanding the BEF's Third Army, pursued the proposal. Not only did the use of tanks appear attractive to the able Byng, the Tank Corps had identified the flat plain near Cambrai in northern France as particularly appropriate for tank warfare; Cambrai happened to be in the sector opposite the Third Army. In early October, Haig relented and approved the plan for a diversionary attack by the Third Army using tanks en masse. The commander-in-chief, Byng would recall, "told me he thought he could give me the Canadian Corps, and for thirty-six hours I had that possibility offered to me. However, I am sorry to say that thirty-six hours later the Canadian Corps was ordered up North." It is tantalizing to speculate on what might have been achieved at Cambrai had the Canadians been sent there rather than to Passchendaele. Instead of the fresh, powerful Canadian Corps, Byng was forced to employ worn-out divisions from Flanders whose ranks had been filled with recently arrived, inexperienced conscripts. Moreover, Haig was unable to provide Byng with a reserve with which to exploit any success: the five divisions transferred to Italy in later October-early November made that impossible. And the plan had changed from a diversionary attack, for Flanders had ended on 12 November, eight days before Byng's operation, which was now a large-scale raid that could also serve to ease pressure on the beleaguered Italian front.[19]

It was, at first, a stunning success. The Germans were taken completely by surprise. Led by 325 tanks, seven British divisions drove nearly five miles into the enemy lines, taking 4,000 prisoners, at a cost of 4,000 casualties. When the British public was informed of the victory, two days later, church bells rang out across the land. But the cheers turned to jeers on 30 November, when fourteen German divisions, many of them from Italy and Russia, counter-attacked and retook much of the ground lost ten days earlier. By the time the fighting ended on 7 December, the balance sheet was about equal: the British had lost 44,000 men and 158 guns; the Germans, 53,000 men and 145 guns.

Despite the disappointing conclusion, General Byng considered the operation to have been "a remarkably fine one." But Prime Minister Lloyd George disagreed. It could have been, he said, "one of the decisive battles of the war"; instead, it had turned into an "egregious muddle." In his opinion, "Passchendaele was directly responsible" for turning victory into defeat at Cambrai, by killing or maiming the men who should have been available as reserves. "One-fourth of the men flung away so profligately at Passchendaele would have sufficed to win this signal victory, and to exploit it." The prime minister, preferring to place all blame on Haig's shoulders, conveniently overlooked the divisions rushed to Italy in the wake of Caporetto, as well as the countless thousands already serving in the Mediterranean theatre. A subsequent inquiry into Cambrai cleared the BEF's senior officers of responsibility for the reverse, but Lloyd George did not buy the verdict. As far as he was concerned, Passchendaele had proven, and Cambrai had confirmed, the need to wrest control of the war away from the soldiers and put it in the hands of the politicians, where it belonged.[20]

Haig was far from discouraged by the outcome of events on the Western Front during 1917. Even as the Germans were preparing to launch their own major offensive the following spring, Haig was doing likewise. It was his intention to resume his campaign in Flanders as early as possible in 1918. He had decided on this course as long ago as August when, writing in a memorandum to the War

Office, he declared that "the right course to pursue, in my opinion, is undoubtedly to continue to press the enemy in Flanders without intermission and to the full extent of our powers, and if complete success is not gained before winter sets in, to renew the attack at the earliest possible moment next year."[21] There was no reason, in Haig's view, to change his plans.

He was sadly mistaken. Lloyd George was appalled to learn of the field-marshal's determination "to continue in the spring his Passchendaele attack, and thus throw away another 200,000 or 300,000 men." The prime minister was just as determined as his commander-in-chief: there must be no more Passchendaeles. To ensure it, he did four things to hamstring Haig: agreed to extend the BEF's share of the Western Front; restricted the manpower available to Haig; shifted the focus of British endeavours to the Middle East; and stepped up his campaign of conspiracy and intrigue against both Haig and Robertson. As one of his biographers has pointed out, Lloyd George seemed "determined to run the war in a makeshift, amateurish fashion. It nearly cost the Allies the loss of the war: in terms of human life it cost tens of thousands."[22]

The fighting in Flanders was still under way when the prime minister initiated the first step. At a conference, which Haig had not attended, in Boulogne on 25 September, Lloyd George had "approved in principle" an extension of the British front by nearly forty miles; Haig was to work out the details with his French counterpart, Pétain. When Haig found out about it, he called it "a great bombshell," and his relationship with Wully Robertson was gravely shaken. The field-marshal resisted the extension, telling Pétain that "it is impossible for me to take over the extra line, and also retain sufficient men to carry on an effective offensive next spring." Of course, this was precisely what Lloyd George had in mind, and when Haig continued to resist, political pressure was brought to bear. Haig was forced to bow to the inevitable, though he was able, with Pétain's help, to limit the extension to twenty-eight miles when it was finally carried out in January 1918. However, this proved to be the very sector that would bear the brunt of the great German offensive.[23]

Not only would the British have a longer line to hold, they would, thanks to Lloyd George, have fewer men with which to hold it. As early as 24 November, Haig had sent to London a letter warning of impending manpower shortages, predicting that unless substantial drafts were delivered to his armies, the BEF would be 40 per cent understrength by the end of March 1918. The War Office concurred. On 6 December, Sir Maurice Hankey noted that the War Office had warned that "if large numbers of men are not recruited and sent out at once Haig's army would not be able to hold the line."[24]

The warnings were ignored. Lloyd George, who insisted "that we were over-insured on the Western front," had no intention of sending more soldiers for Haig to senselessly slaughter. He attempted to justify his stance in his post-war memoirs:

> Our military leaders had acquired the habit of prodigality in their expenditure of life.... They lavished the lives placed at their disposal in foolish frontal attacks on impregnable lines, in spite of the lessons of every war since modern weapons were perfected.... Whilst hundreds of thousands were being destroyed in the insane egotism of Passchendaele, every message or memorandum from Haig was full of these insistencies on the importance of sending him more men to replace those he had sent to die in the mud.[25]

By the middle of December 1917, it was evident that a genuine manpower crisis was facing the BEF. At GHQ, General Charteris bitterly commented;

> Our danger is at home. D.H. has told the Cabinet that we must expect casualties at the rate of 100,000 per month next spring. We have plenty of men for even this if the Government care to make them available. But L.G. does not believe either Robertson or D.H., and nothing is being done.

The prime minister, in later years, contended that the soldiers' figures were "purely fanciful. They were not estimates carefully prepared by officials who understood the elements of accountancy but merely a succession of grouses from Generals who had failed to achieve what they had hoped for and had promised and were anxious to put the blame for their discomfiture on the politicians who had dared to predict the failure."[26]

Sir William Robertson found the prime minister's position both frustrating and infuriating. At one point, in a letter to Haig, he complained that "the P.M. was good enough to tell me the other day in Cabinet that he had been through my weekly summaries and had marked a curious collection of statements showing that I had underestimated the enemy's power. Nice occupation for him and his creatures, and a proof of the impossibility of honestly working with such a man...."[27]

To back his case, Lloyd George formed in December a special committee, with himself as chairman and carefully stocked with men who shared his views, to assess the manpower needs of all aspects of the war effort. Its recommendations were nothing short of incredible. The navy and air force were placed at the top of its priority list, followed by civilian industries—ship-building, munitions, food production, and forestry, in that order—with the army, which could be expected to do most of the fighting and therefore had the greatest need, at the very bottom! Robertson had requested 615,000 Class A conscripts for the army's 1918 operations, as well as the 449,000 men who were being trained at bases in Britain. Instead, Lloyd George's manpower committee offered only 100,000 Class A recruits, plus 100,000 more from lower categories of conscripts, and 120,000 youths who would reach military age during 1918. The committee concluded that with these forces "the Allies ought to be able to hold their own on the Western Front until the period when the increase of American strength begins to alter the balance of advantage in their favour."[28]

Insiders were deeply distressed at these developments, as were a few perceptive observers. One such was *The Times*'s correspondent, Colonel Repington, who lamented:

> This is terrible.... I have never felt so miserable since the war began, and the whole cause of the trouble is the shameful poltroonery and strategic incompetence of the War Cabinet. The country has only to be told the truth to accept any sacrifice, but L.G. dares not face the music, and the Tory dummies in his War Cabinet are mere ciphers. I can say very little because the editor of the *Times* often manipulates my criticisms or does not publish them.[29]*

Even some of Lloyd George's stalwart supporters were shocked. Among them was Winston Churchill, his minister of munitions, who warned the prime minister:

> I don't think we are doing enough for our army. Really I must make that point to you. We are not raising its strength as we ought. We ought to fill it up at once to full strength.... Please don't let vexation against past military blunders (which I share

---

* Repington resigned from *The Times* on 16 January, resurfacing at the rival *Morning Post* a few days later. He promptly published in the *Post* an article "exposing the failure of the War Cabinet to maintain the Army," which earned him the enmity of Prime Minister Lloyd George. In February, after Repington printed a detailed critique of the Supreme War Council, the prime minister ensured that he was charged with defying the censor; Repington was subsequently fined £100.[30]

> with you to the fullest) lead you to understate the gravity of the impending campaign, or keep the army short of what is needed.

By now, however, Lloyd George was not interested in this sort of advice. Nor was he willing to heed a protest from the Army Council, which accused the cabinet of taking "an unnecessarily grave risk of losing the war, and sacrificing to no purpose the British Army on the Western Front."[31]

The war cabinet approved the recommendations of Lloyd George's manpower committee, then dealt in an equally brazen manner with a related problem, that of understrength battalions in the BEF. By the end of 1917 there were few, if any, at full strength, and in early January 1918 the war cabinet came up with a simple solution: British divisions would be reduced from twelve to nine battalions— the French and Germans, it noted, had done so earlier in the war— with the surplus battalions being broken up to provide reinforcements for the remainder. At the stroke of a pen, 141 battalions were stricken from the BEF's order of battle.

The result was, John Terraine has written, "disorganization to a fearful degree."

> This entire astonishing and demoralizing exercise took time— time during which the roads of France were filled with British units seeking new homes in strange divisions, and during which an *esprit de corps* built up over years of common experience was thrown away, while all existing tactical principles and schemes had to be scrapped.[32]

And all of this took place practically on the eve of the greatest German offensive of the war.

Historians have been both puzzled and amazed by Lloyd George's actions at this critical time. One, Donald McCormick, has observed: "It may seem incredible that any statesman claiming to be a patriot could devise such a tortuous and frustrating policy which, in effect, meant endangering the lives of whole battalions of British soldiers and risking, even courting, defeat."[33]

How, then, could the prime minister justify his behaviour? The most obvious explanation, though it does not excuse him, is that Lloyd George was operating under a dangerous delusion. "Defensive action," he bluntly told his son, Richard, "is not nearly as difficult as offensive"—and, by implication, not so costly. It was an understandable conclusion for any amateur strategist who, like Lloyd George, had watched the British and French armies banging their heads against the brick wall known as the Western Front. But no professional soldier, British or German, believed that. "This argument," Sir William Robertson later wrote, "was so utterly fallacious as to be almost incredible." Erich Ludendorff agreed. "War consumes men; that is its nature," declared the German general. "The modern defensive battle is more costly than the attack...." But the truth was lost on Lloyd George and his cabinet colleagues, who wished to believe otherwise. Many, like Winston Churchill, welcomed the prospect of fighting a defensive battle for a change: "Let [the Germans] make the pockets, let them traipse across the crater fields, let them rejoice in the occasional capture of placeless names & sterile ridges...." The popular image of Passchendaele refused to go away.[34]

Complicating matters was Sir Douglas Haig's own ambivalence: he knew that the Germans were going to attack—every sign pointed to it—but he could not believe that they would be so rash. As early as 7 December 1917, after attending a conference of army commanders, Haig had written:

> The main topic I discussed was the organisation of our defensive lines, in view of the Russians having dropped out of the war. This will enable the Germans to employ some 30 [*sic*] more divisions on this front... *we must be prepared for a strong hostile offensive in the spring*.

But he was convinced that it would consist of "attacks of limited scope," explaining that "Germany having only one million men as reserves for this year's fighting, I doubted whether they would risk them in an attempt to 'break through.' If the Germans did attack it would be a gambler's throw...." It was a gamble he did not think they would take. "If you put the problem to any Staff College student you would get the same answer: 'An all-out attack by the Germans must end in ultimate disaster to them'." Of course, Haig was, as always, supremely confident in the capabilities of the BEF. The possibility of a British defeat was beyond his comprehension.[35]

As if this were not enough, Haig's notorious inability to verbally express himself killed any chance of the war cabinet reconsidering its manpower decision. On 7 January 1918, he addressed the cabinet in a last-ditch appeal for more men. "I stated that I thought that the coming four months would be the *critical period of the war*," he wrote. "Also that it seemed to me to be possible that the enemy would attack both the French and ourselves, and that he would hold reserves in hand ready to exploit wherever he might have gained a success."[36]

Unfortunately, as was so often the case, there was a wide gap between what Haig thought he had said and what others thought he had said. During the meeting, he was asked by a minister, "If you were Ludendorff, would you consider that a smashing offensive would have sufficient chance of success to justify the losses that would be incurred?" Haig replied, "If the Germans were wise they would think twice before making the attempt, because if they failed the position would be critical for them."[37]

Such an ambiguous answer was open to interpretation, and Wully Robertson realized how the politicians would take it. After the meeting, he told Haig that he had left the impression that "the Germans would not attack" at all. "So long as the Cabinet are of opinion that you can hold your front this year with 9-Battalion divisions (and even these will not be up to strength) I am afraid we cannot get any more men than those now promised, namely, 100,000 as against 600,000 [Class A men] we consider we require."[38]

Robertson was right. Although Haig promptly submitted a written report clarifying his position, it was too late, the damage had been done. As Robertson later wrote, "the Prime Minister tossed it aside with the remark that it was entirely inconsistent with what Sir Douglas had said verbally...."[39]

Worse, with these decisions now behind them, Lloyd George and his cabinet now turned a blind eye to the impending crisis on the Western Front. Faced with convincing evidence of a German build-up, the prime minister and his fellow politicians simply ignored it, satisfied that any attack could and would be repelled with ease by the BEF. Sir Frederick Maurice, the director of military operations at the War Office, noted with alarm this new attitude at the war cabinet's meeting of 11 January:

> War Cabinet. Told them that signs of a German offensive on Western front were increasing but it was not likely to take place before the end of February. Cabinet don't believe in this offensive and think Germans really mean to attack Italy or perhaps Salonika.[40]

This was merely the first of many such warnings Lloyd George's cabinet would ignore in early 1918.

Having stripped Haig's BEF of the capacity to mount an offensive, and seriously impeding its ability even to defend itself, Lloyd George and his cronies had committed a cardinal military sin, willingly, gleefully, handing over to the enemy the advantage of initiative. The British would now be responding to German actions, rather than vice versa. But the prime minister was now pursuing his long-cherished dream of knocking the props from under Germany. In his memoirs, he decried "our complete failure until too late to appreciate the fact that the weakest point of the Central Powers was in the Eastern and South-Eastern Fronts. Thus a war of attrition [on the Western Front] was substituted for a war of intelligence." Or, to put it another way, "We hammered at the breast plate of Achilles and neglected the heel."[41]

The prime minister had his eye on Palestine. It was there, he believed, that Turkey could be knocked out of the war. His enthusiasm for this far-off theatre was fired by the capture of Jerusalem on 9 December 1917 by British forces under General Sir Edmund Allenby. Sir William Robertson, knowing what Lloyd George had in mind for this theatre, did his best to dissuade him. In a memorandum, one of several he wrote on the subject, dated 26 December, Robertson warned "that the conquest of Palestine requires men and material which can be provided only at the expense of the Western Front," a dangerous proposition in view of "the possibility of the enemy attempting to force a decision on the Western Front... in early 1918, and the possibility of his succeeding in doing so if we do not concentrate our resources there."[42] It was, as far as Lloyd George was concerned, a painfully familiar refrain, and he was not much interested in it.

He responded with a clever manoeuvre. Knowing that Robertson would vigorously oppose the Palestine expedition, and not entirely trusting his political colleagues, Lloyd George arranged that the war cabinet refer the matter to the Supreme War Council, where it was certain to be more favourably viewed.

The Supreme War Council met at Versailles on 30 January through 2 February 1918. To Lloyd George's satisfaction, the council's military representatives had concluded that no decision could be expected on the Western Front in 1918 and recommended that "a decisive offensive should be undertaken against Turkey." The prime minister's delight was diminished considerably when Sir William Robertson addressed the council and bluntly declared "that to undertake the campaign in Palestine... will be very dangerous and detrimental to our prospects of winning the war." Despite Robertson's alarming words, the council approved the expedition to Palestine, with the proviso that it should be delayed by two months, by which time the situation on the Western Front might be more definite.[43]

Lloyd George's gambit had worked. Not only had Britain's allies endorsed his strategic intentions, they had ignored and isolated

Robertson and Haig, who were seemingly the only soldiers devoted to achieving victory on the Western Front. Thus, while the BEF faced grave peril in France and Flanders, with understrength and demoralized battalions holding an elongated line, there would be three-quarters of a million British troops sweating under the hot sun in the Middle East, too far away to respond to an emergency.

Haig went home from Versailles completely disgusted. The war council was a failure, he wrote, with "much time wasted due to much talking by civilians on military matters, of the basic principles of which they know nothing." Robertson sourly observed that "the theory that the principal enemy could be overthrown by the defeat of a minor one was not yet extinct." The absurdity of the situation was even apparent to General Allenby, the commander of the Palestine expedition. "I recognise," he wrote in February 1918, "that the West is the essential battle-ground, where victory will be decisive. Make sure of victory there."[44]

In any event, Wully Robertson's days as the CIGS were numbered. Even before the Versailles conference, the strain between him and Prime Minister Lloyd George was noticeable to all. Sir Frederick Maurice noted in his diary on 26 January: "Relations between LG and WR rapidly becoming impossible." But it was the meeting of the Supreme War Council that proved to be Robertson's undoing. Lloyd George was furious with the CIGS for publicly speaking out against the Palestine campaign, and angrily told him, according to Maurice's diary, that "he had no business to disagree with the Prime Minister before the foreigners." By the time the conference closed on 2 February, the two were barely on speaking terms, as Maurice commented: "LG-WR very distant. Present position cannot continue." Nor would it.[45]

Returning to London, Robertson attempted to force the issue. Seeing how Lloyd George had used to advantage the conflicting advice of the military representatives on the Supreme War Council against his own, Robertson suggested that General Wilson, the British representative, be subordinated to the CIGS. The situation, Robertson later wrote, was simply intolerable:

> It is the right of a government to select its own professional advisers and to change them as often as it please, but it ought not to appoint independent advisers in addition, for such a proceeding must produce divided responsibility, delay, friction, and confusion. No business, military or other, could be smoothly and efficiently conducted if the board of directors employed two

separate managers to advise them on the work of one and the same department.

Robertson knew that he was treading on thin ice. Lord Derby, the war secretary, had already warned him that Lloyd George was bitterly complaining that he could no longer "get on" with the CIGS.[45]

Events quickly came to a head. Lloyd George flatly rejected Robertson's recommendation to subordinate Wilson to him. Instead, he offered Robertson a choice: he could remain as the CIGS, but with reduced powers, or he could trade places with Wilson. Robertson realized that this was no panacea to the problem of dual advisers: "Whether I stayed in London or went to Versailles could make no difference to the pernicious arrangement which created two separate military advisers and executive officers." It was clear, he said, "that, wherever I might go, my advice would not be accepted unless it happened to be of the desired kind, and if that were so the period of my usefulness had evidently come to an end." And so it had. Robertson neither resigned nor was he fired; he simply ceased to serve. On 16 February, Sir Henry Wilson replaced him as the CIGS.[47]*

Robertson was deeply disillusioned. He confessed to the *Morning Post*'s Repington "that he found that he had more friends than he knew, but fewer on whom he could count than he expected." If he was expecting a show of support from his long-time ally, Sir Douglas Haig, he was doubly disappointed. Haig, meeting Robertson on 11 February, had merely urged that "it was his *duty* to go to Versailles," which Robertson refused to do. Certainly, Haig had no intention of resigning, as Lloyd George discovered in two meetings with the field-marshal. The prime minister, still living in fear of a political crisis, summoned Haig to London on 9 February to gauge his position. A somewhat relieved Lloyd George wrote that night:

> Haig was quite reasonable. He did not quite like H.W. coming here, and thought the army might be shocked; but he said that

---

* It proved to be an ironic appointment. Haig, who considered Wilson to be "a terrible intriguer," wrote later that month, "I still fear that he means to help Lloyd George detach troops from my Command to fight against the Turks." However, Wilson soon saw matters from Robertson's point of view. As quickly as possible, he installed a subordinate at the Supreme War Council, which soon faded into inconsequence. Later in the year, he came to the conclusion that the Western Front was, after all, the decisive theatre. When he prepared a report to that effect in July, Lloyd George was enraged, calling it "Wully *redivivus*," and Sir Maurice Hankey warned Wilson that the prime minister considered him to be "too much like Robertson."[48]

was a matter for the Government. In fact, his attitude was perfectly correct.

They met again on the seventeenth. According to the prime minister, they "discussed the whole position for hours. Haig put up no fight for Robertson. He clearly did not approve of his defiance of a decision come to by the Government.... Haig himself had no intention of resigning...."[49]

Haig's stand was not surprising. For months, he had doubted whether Robertson was the right man to deal with Lloyd George and his confederates. The previous June, it will be recalled, Haig had been appalled when the CIGS expressed reservations about the Flanders campaign. Also, Haig had felt betrayed by Robertson's failure to inform him promptly of September's Boulogne agreement to extend the BEF's holdings on the Western Front. The field-marshal summed up his feelings in a letter to Lady Haig:

> I, like you, feel sorry for Robertson, but then it seems to me (and I can write it to you privately) that he has not resolutely adhered to the policy of "concentration on the Western Front"—He has *said* that this is his policy, but has allowed all kinds of resources to be diverted to distant theatres at the bidding of his political masters. So I think he ought to have made a firm stand before.

Haig was being realistic, too. He must have known that his own resignation could not save Robertson.* Indeed, he would have been playing into Lloyd George's hands, because GHQ had been the target of the prime minister's vindictiveness since Passchendaele.[51]

It had begun with his speech in Paris on 12 November. That evening, Haig's intelligence chief, General Charteris, wrote:

> L.G. has opened his attack on the Army generally and on D.H. and Robertson in particular. I am told he will go for individuals on the Staff here, as the easiest way of hitting D.H. I discussed this with D.H. to-night and again offered my resignation, if he thinks it would strengthen his own position. He will not have it.

It was a most perceptive observation, but Haig was unable to save

---

* Not even King George was able to do that. Upon learning of Robertson's replacement, the King sent his private secretary, Lord Stamfordham, to tell Lloyd George that he "strongly deprecated" the action. The prime minister, who was no fan of royalty, irately replied "that he did not share the King's extremely favourable opinion of Sir William Robertson," and threatened to resign if Buckingham Palace interfered in any way. The King backed down.[50]

Charteris, who was one of Lloyd George's primary targets. Although he privately felt that Charteris was not the best man for the job—"it was a mistake for him to specialise in Intelligence work," Haig admitted in his diary—the field-marshal publicly defended him. "I cannot agree that Charteris should be made 'whipping-boy' for the charge of undue optimism brought against myself," he argued in a letter to Lord Derby. But it was no use: Lloyd George was determined to get rid of Charteris and what he considered to be his exaggerated reports of victories. At the end of December, on orders from London, Charteris was transferred to a minor post at GHQ. In mid-1918, he returned to England in poor health.[52]

Charteris was just one of several staff officers to be sacked in the wake of Passchendaele. Another was Sir Launcelot Kiggell, Haig's chief of staff. Interestingly, Kiggell is associated with one of the most famous stories of Passchendaele. Soon after the fighting ended, so the story goes, Kiggell was driven through Ypres to inspect the battlefront. On spying the sea of mud, he purportedly burst into tears and cried, "My God! Did we send men to fight in that?" An aide ruefully replied, "It's worse further up."[53] It is almost certainly apocryphal, perpetuated by writers trying to portray the British high command as blundering idiots. However, Haig was acquainted with the condition of the battlefield, as shown by his repeated apologies to the Canadian commander, Currie; if Haig knew, his chief of staff surely did, too.

Haig made a determined effort to keep Kiggell at GHQ. "I am very loth to part with Kigg's help and advice...," he wrote. "No one could possibly have discharged the duties of C.G.S. [chief of the General Staff] during the past two years of great difficulty better than Kiggell has."[54] But Haig failed, and Kiggell was returned to England, ostensibly due to bad health. In the meantime, the housecleaning at GHQ continued. Kiggell's deputy, Sir Richard Butler, was transferred to a corps command, while a number of others were recalled: the quartermaster-general, Sir Ronald Maxwell; Sir Robert Rice, chief engineer; Sir Arthur Slodgett, director-general of medical services.

It did not take a genius to realize what was going on: this wholesale shake-up was aimed at Haig. "I gather that the P.M. is dissatisfied," the field-marshal observed, with remarkable understatement, in a 9 December letter to Sir William Robertson. "If that means that I have lost his confidence, then in the interests of the cause let him replace me at once. But if he wishes me to remain, then all carping criticism should cease, and I should be both supported and trusted."[55] As usual, Haig was careful not to offer his resignation directly to Lloyd George.

He was wasting his ink, anyway. Robertson himself was doomed, of course, and Lloyd George was more determined than ever, in the wake of Passchendaele, to undermine Haig. Just a week later, on 16 December, Sir Maurice Hankey noted in his diary that "Ll.G.... wants to get rid of Haig and Robertson." The rumour mill soon sprang into action, as Lord Bertie, the British ambassador in Paris, remarked on 8 January 1918: "There are reports in what are supposed to be well-informed circles that Haig's position is so shaken that he is likely to fall." There was more than a little substance to the rumours. On 21 January, Lloyd George sent Hankey and the South African, General Smuts, to France with instructions "to 'vet' all generals for possible successors to Haig." They were unable to recommend a replacement, however, and Lloyd George was, for the time being, forced to defer his campaign against Haig, concluding that it was not "worth risking all the attacks in Parliament etc. that would have followed."[56]

Nevertheless, Lloyd George's machinations were taking their toll. On a previous visit to GHQ, in May 1917, Hankey had complained of the mood of what he called "unbounded and quite unjustified optimism" that permeated the place. Now, in January 1918, it was considerably changed. Hankey observed that the "atmosphere of complaisant optimism that formerly pervaded GHQ was conspicuous by its absence." Hankey, it seems, preferred depression to optimism in his staff officers.[57]

Thus, the British Expeditionary Force, demoralized and disorganized from top to bottom, faced what would prove to be its greatest crisis of the war.

20 / The Feud Continues

In his tireless efforts to spare the BEF another Passchendaele, Prime Minister Lloyd George's intrigue and interference resulted in a near disaster to British arms.

In February and early March 1918, there were unmistakable signs of preparations for a German offensive on the Western Front. But the prime minister and his war cabinet—not to mention Sir Henry Wilson, the new CIGS, who was intent on ingratiating himself with the politicians—resolutely refused to believe the mounting evidence, attributing it to disgruntled officers at the War Office and GHQ who sought to sidetrack the Palestine expedition and give Sir Douglas Haig the means to mount his offensive in Flanders. Freddy Maurice, the director of military operations at the War Office, recounted in his diary his repeated efforts to convince the cabinet of the crisis brewing on the Continent.

> *14 February:* "Evidence is accumulating that the enemy are preparing a big attack on the Cambrai front; it is not likely to be ready before the middle of March, but meanwhile all this squabbling is good preparation for it."
>
> *23 February:* "German divisions already moving up on Western front. This can only mean attack though most of War Cabinet think Germans won't attack because they said they would."
>
> *28 February:* "War Cabinet. Ministers still disinclined to believe in attack on Western front. Told them Germans would be ready by March 15th and that it was probably coming on Cambrai front. They still believe in an attack on Italy because nothing much is heard about it."
>
> *4 March:* "We may expect a big German attack on Cambrai front before very long now.... Told CIGS I thought attack certain. He says he is afraid it won't come and doesn't think Cambrai/St. Quentin front likely because of the devastated area and the Somme...."
>
> *12 March:* "Wilson tells War Cabinet that he puts no certainty that attack on us is coming. I have no doubts about it. The Germans are not piling up divisions in the West for fun."
>
> *13 March:* "Ministers still looking for attack anywhere but in the West."

Maurice sourly noted Lloyd George's preoccupation with Palestine, particularly when, on 22 February, Allenby's forces captured Jericho. Remarked a bitter Maurice: "LG delighted since he had heard of Jericho before Passchendaele. Jericho consists of a few mud hovels and 1 third rate hotel."[1]

Field-Marshal Haig, too, was having no luck trying to warn the politicians in London. On 14 March he met Lloyd George and one of his ministers, Andrew Bonar Law, at 10 Downing Street. "They did their best," related Haig, "to get me to say that the Germans would not attack." However, Haig insisted that "we must be prepared to meet *a very strong attack on a 50 mile front, and for this drafts are urgently required.*" These pleas were, naturally, ignored. Indeed, the prime minister only grudgingly acknowledged "the apparent imminence of a large attack" by the Germans on the Western Front. It was of little concern to him, obviously.[2]

In the meantime, Haig had to make do with the resources at hand. On paper, the BEF was an impressive force. Its total strength, including combat troops, administrative personnel, and labour units, as well as the formidable dominion contingents, stood at 1,850,967. That was a third of a million more than the same time a year earlier. But the figure is somewhat misleading. In terms of fighting troops, the BEF was actually weaker by 100,000; its current combat strength of 969,283 compared unfavourably to the 1,069,831 of a year before.[3] These forces were organized into four field armies, comprised of sixty-two divisions (including three cavalry): fifty British, four Canadian, five Australian, one New Zealand, and two Portuguese.

Haig sensibly allotted his strength according to the strategic significance of each sector held by the BEF. The strongest armies were Sir Herbert Plumer's Second, in Flanders, and Sir Henry Horne's First, which included the Canadian Corps about Vimy Ridge. These two armies contained about half the BEF's fighting troops, but they held only a third of the hundred-mile front under Haig's jurisdiction. At their backs lay the vital Channel ports; with no room to manoeuvre, it was imperative that they hold their ground. Farther south, where ground could be given without necessarily dire consequences, the other two armies were stretched dangerously thin. Sir Hubert Gough's Fifth Army, with seventeen divisions, held a line forty-five miles long; on his left, Sir Julian Byng's Third Army, fifteen divisions strong, held twenty-seven miles of trenches.

The weather once again bedevilled the British. Whereas rain had been the problem in 1917, in the spring of 1918 it was abnormally dry. This compounded the weakness of the twenty-eight miles of front taken over from the French in January and now held by Gough's Fifth Army. Much of this terrain was usually flooded and therefore impassable, particularly during the spring; but in March 1918 it was bone-dry, and the defences left by the departing French were woefully weak. The Fifth Army set to work to improve them, but time was short, as was the supply of labour troops. Haig, during a visit to Gough, "reminded him that whenever we had attacked we had always been able to break the enemy's front, and to advance well into the German system of defence. We must expect the Germans to do the same if they attacked in force. So his 'Reserve Lines' must have his attention." Attending an army commanders' conference on 2 March, Haig heard that—underlining it in his diary—"*the enemy is preparing to attack on the fronts of our Third and Fifth Armies.*"

> I emphasised the necessity for being ready to move as soon as possible to meet a big hostile offensive of prolonged duration. I also told Army commanders that I was very pleased at all I had seen on the fronts of the three Armies which I had recently visited. Plans were sound and thorough, and much work had already been done. I was only afraid that the enemy would find our front so very strong that he will hesitate to commit his Army to the attack with the almost certainty of losing very heavily.

Haig need not have worried. The Germans would not disappoint him.[4]

However, his concern grew as work in the Fifth Army's sector began to lag. Gough, he noted, "complained of the shortage of labour for the work" that had to be carried out, and Haig's discomfiture was even more pronounced when he inspected the Fifth Army front later in March. "On the whole I don't like the position," he confessed, and ordered another division moved from the north to reinforce Gough. But that was all he could do. "I have no more troops to send him without uncovering *vital* points elsewhere."[5]

British intelligence was excellent. On 19 March, Haig received "reports on the examination of certain prisoners showing that *the enemy's intention is to attack about March 20th or 21st.*" With the long-awaited offensive at last imminent, Haig seemed satisfied with his arrangements to meet it, remarking in a 20 March letter to Lady Haig that "all Reserves and other questions, such as moving up troops to support, have already been settled." Haig faced the coming challenge with supreme confidence in the prowess of his soldiers.[6]

The storm broke, as forecast, on 21 March 1918. The Germans had assembled sixty-four divisions opposite Byng and Gough's armies, forty of them on the Fifth Army's front. At 4:50 A.M., a tremendous bombardment burst upon the defenders. For nearly five hours, 6,473 enemy guns blasted the British entrenchments. At 9:40 A.M., the German infantry went over the top, aided by a heavy mist that blanketed the battlefield and blinded the British.

It was not until later in the day that the extent of the catastrophe was realized. Indeed, the initial reaction in London was disbelief, as Sir Freddy Maurice described in his diary: "Told Wilson the battle had started. He is still doubtful [and] told the Cabinet that this might be nothing more than a big raid."[7]

In fact, the Germans had scored a success unprecedented on the Western Front. The outnumbered and outgunned British were routed in several places along the line; whole battalions were virtually annihilated. In a few locations, the defenders were too far forward and suffered fearfully in the terrific bombardment that preceded the assault. But the major factor was the dual problem of a shortage of manpower and weak defences. The Fifth Army collapsed like a house of cards; on 21 March, Gough lost the unheard-of total of 383 guns as the shattered remains of his army retreated behind the River Somme. Byng's Third Army was not much better off; by midnight of the twenty-third it had lost 150 guns, and the right-hand half of its front had been demolished.

Haig was baffled by the poor performance of Gough's army, in particular. The planned fighting withdrawal had turned into something verging on a rout. "I cannot make out why the Fifth Army has gone so far back without making some kind of a stand," the field-marshal commented in his diary on 23 March.[8] The only consolation was that no ground of consequence was being lost; the only strategically significant locale was the great rail centre of Amiens, forty miles behind the lines. Haig, who had only eight divisions in reserve for his entire expeditionary force,* did what he could to assist Byng and Gough, and turned to the French for help.

He met Pétain, the French commander-in-chief, on 24 March. It was not a happy meeting. Earlier, they had agreed to assist each other

---

* He would not have had even that, if the Supreme War Council had had its way. Before concluding its meetings on 2 February, the council had agreed to the concept of a general reserve, which would be under the command of a French general, Ferdinand Foch. The plan was to have a certain number of British, French, and Italian divisions placed in this pool, which would then be available for use in emergencies such as Caporetto. The general reserve never got off the drawingboards, thanks to Haig and Pétain. Haig bluntly, and correctly, stated that he had no divisions to spare for it, while Pétain's professional jealousy for Foch precluded any co-operation by the French commander-in-chief. Prime Minister Lloyd George was most annoyed by Haig's obstinacy, but the field-marshal would be vindicated by events.

in the event of a major German attack, and Haig expected Pétain to live up to their informal agreement. The Frenchman refused. "Pétain struck me as very much upset, almost unbalanced and most anxious," observed Haig, who was alarmed to learn that the French reserves, rather than rushing to his assistance, were instead being sent to defend Paris. "I at once asked Pétain if he meant to abandon my flank. He nodded assent and added 'it is the only thing possible, if the enemy compelled the Allies to fall back still further'." Moreover, Pétain insisted that this was merely a diversionary attack, that the main German effort would be made against the French forces in Champagne.[9]

This was a stunning setback for Haig. It was bad enough to discover that "to keep touch with the British Army is no longer the basic principle of French strategy," but Haig was incensed at Pétain's refusal to recognize that the BEF was "*now confronting the weight* of the German Army single-handed."[10]

Pondering the gravity of the situation overnight, the field-marshal came to what was seemingly a startling conclusion. He decided that it was urgent "that General [Ferdinand] Foch or some other determined General who would fight, should be given supreme control of the operations in France. I knew ... that [Foch] was a man of great courage and decision as shown by the fighting at Ypres in October and November 1914." Until now, Haig had rejected the concept of a supreme commander, or generalissimo, stating that "Pétain and I get on very well, and no co-ordinating authority is necessary for us."* But this was, clearly, no longer the case. Haig realized that Pétain was succumbing to the pressure of the situation, and that the BEF was in danger of destruction unless he could find a way to get the French into the fight.[12]

There was no time to waste. An Anglo-French conference was convened at Doullens on 26 March, and Haig, by his own recollection, "at once recommended that Foch should *co-ordinate the action of all the Allied Armies on the Western Front.*" This recommendation was accepted, with surprisingly little debate, and General Foch found

---

* Interestingly, Prime Minister Lloyd George also opposed the appointment of a supreme commander. "It would not work," he declared in the House of Commons. "It would produce real friction, and might really produce not merely friction between the Armies, but friction between the nations and the Governments."[11] This is the same man whose memoirs are full of repeated references to the need for unified command, yet he rejected the only practicable solution in favour of the unwieldy Supreme War Council, which allowed him to interfere more or less freely with the conduct of the war.

himself in overall command of the Allied forces in France and Belgium. A second conference, held at GQG at Beauvais on 3 April, clarified his status. Foch would be entrusted with "the strategical direction of military operations," wrote Haig. "The C. in C. of British, French and American Armies will have full control of the tactical action of their respective Armies. Each C. in C. will have the right of appeal to his Government, if in his opinion his Army is endangered by reason of any order received from General Foch."[13]

This says much about Sir Douglas Haig. True, he was motivated by self-interest, the desire to save the BEF, but it required courage and considerable humility for a proud man to surrender some of his autonomy, especially to an ally he believed to be unreliable, at best. Ironically, Haig was not at all pleased with Foch, who was convinced by GQG intelligence predictions of an impending German offensive against the French, and committed his reserves reluctantly and piecemeal to aid the beleaguered BEF. But Foch's appointment was beneficial in one vital respect: unlike the weak-willed Pétain, who was ready to abandon the British in order to defend Paris, the supreme commander ensured that the Allies maintained a united front. In doing so, Foch guaranteed that the Germans would lose the war.

In the meantime, the enemy offensive was already running out of momentum. By 26 March, the German advance had slowed considerably, as General Charteris at GHQ noted:

> It is not so much our resistance during these last few days that stopped them, as the fact that their attack had advanced so far as any attack could without a halt to bring up supplies, ammunition, and men. We learnt the same lesson in all our own attacks.[14]

On the twenty-eighth the Germans were soundly defeated by a rejuvenated Third Army, and even the weary troops of Gough's Fifth Army were beginning to rally. However, Gough, already under a cloud for his poor performance at Passchendaele, was being made a scapegoat for the disaster that had befallen his army: he was replaced on 28 March by Sir Henry Rawlinson.

By 5 April, the Germans were forced to admit failure. They were finally stopped within nine miles of Amiens, nine tantalizing miles short of a victory that would have split asunder the British and French forces and, quite possibly, have won the war. But they were unable to overcome the technological limitations of this war, as noted above by General Charteris. Having no cavalry with which to exploit success, the Germans could advance only as fast and as far as the tired legs of their infantry could travel. Running short of supplies, and leaving most of their artillery far behind, the Germans were now discovering what the Allies had found so many times previously: that it was much easier for a defender to plug a hole in his lines than it was for an attacker to capitalize on the situation. Ludendorff reluctantly conceded "that the enemy's resistance was beyond our powers."[15]

But the BEF had paid a high price for Prime Minister Lloyd George's naïve belief that defence was easier and less costly than offence. British losses in late March-early April 1918 totalled a staggering 178,000. As Charteris acidly observed at the height of the offensive, "We are paying in blood for the follies of professional politicians."[16]

The Germans, however, were far from finished. Just four days later, on 9 April, Ludendorff unleashed another heavy attack, this time in Flanders. It had been the German commander's desire to strike here initially—sharing Haig's belief that it was a strategically vital sector—but the fear that ground conditions in March might be unsuitable forced him to look further south. Thanks to the dry spring, the ground was in surprisingly good shape for offensive operations in April. Attacking between Armentières and Bethune, east of the River Lys, the Germans were again aided by a thick mist that blinded the defenders. More important, the blow fell on two Portuguese divisions which fled during the preliminary bombardment, even hijacking British bicycles at gunpoint in their haste to escape. On the first day of this new offensive, the Germans advanced more than three miles.

Sir Douglas Haig had another crisis on his hands. He judiciously juggled his weary troops as, once again, Foch and the French were offering precious little assistance. GQG intelligence continued to insist that the French were the enemy's main target, that the Flanders attack was nothing more than a diversion. Haig was disgusted. "I found Foch most selfish and obstinate," he told his diary on 9 April. "I wonder if he is afraid to trust French Divisions in the battle front." Later, he bitterly complained of the supreme commander: "Foch seems to be unmethodical and takes a 'short view' of the situation. For instance, he does not look ahead and make a forecast of what may be required in a week in a certain area and arrange accordingly." When French forces were finally dispatched to Flanders, they performed poorly. This came as no surprise to Haig.

> But this I knew in August, 1914. The Somme battle confirmed my view that much of the French good name as efficient fighters

was the result of newspaper puffs. Then came Nivelle's fiasco in the spring of 1917, and for the rest of last year, the French Armies "rested." And now, when the result of the war depends on their "fighting spirit" many of their Divisions won't face the enemy.[17]

For several agonizing days, the situation seemed almost hopeless. Indeed, on 11 April, Haig issued a special order of uncharacteristic gravity:

> There is no other course open to us but to fight it out! Every position must be held to the last man: there must be no retirement. With our backs to the wall, and believing in the justice of our cause, each one of us must fight on to the end. The safety of our homes and the freedom of mankind alike depend on the conduct of each one of us at this critical moment.

Sir Frederick Maurice, visiting GHQ from the War Office on the fourteenth, commented that Haig "looks tired and worried."[18]

British hopes hit rock-bottom on 16 April. That was the date that Passchendaele was abandoned. The ridge that had been won at such cost and under such terrible conditions was handed back to the enemy without a fight; the German attack to the south threatened to cut off the defenders unless they were withdrawn. It was a painful decision for Haig, but one that he had been prepared to face for months. Back in November, when he closed his campaign, he had commented that the "position...may be difficult and costly to hold if seriously attacked," while a GHQ memorandum issued on 13 December described the enlarged salient as "unsuitable to fight a defensive battle in," and recommended a fighting retreat in the event of a powerful attack. Nevertheless, the decision to abandon Passchendaele caused considerable, and quite understandable, anger at Canadian Corps headquarters.[19]

However, the German offensive was losing steam. After their sterling success of 9 April, the enemy could manage only another eight miles in the days and weeks that followed. When their operations were formally ended on 29 April, the Germans had been stopped five miles short of Hazebrouck—like Amiens, a key rail centre, the capture of which would have been a severe if not fatal blow to the British.

The BEF paid dearly for its dogged determination in these defensive battles. The fighting in Flanders during April 1918 cost another 76,300 British casualties. In forty days on the defensive during March and April, the BEF had sustained staggering losses: 239,793. By comparison, the British had lost 244,897 during 105 days of offensive fighting in Flanders the previous summer and autumn. So much for Lloyd George's simplistic theory of the relative ease and low cost of defensive warfare. What he failed to appreciate was that successful defence is usually less costly than unsuccessful offence; but a defensive failure can be catastrophic.

Not surprisingly, the feud between Lloyd George and Haig hit new heights. The field-marshal evidently expected the prime minister to blame the army for the grim days just passed, and he wasted no opportunity to defend both the BEF and GHQ. On 29 March, when King George visited his headquarters, Haig told His Majesty that

> the Allies were fortunate that the attack has fallen on the British and not on the French because the latter could not have withstood it. I also pointed out that:
> 1. British Infantry in France at the beginning of the Battle were 100,000 less than a year ago!
> 2. We now had three times as many Germans on our front as we had last year.
> 3. We had also extended our line (by order of the British Government) fully 1-5th more than it was last year.[20]

The gentlemanly Haig could no longer conceal his contempt for the prime minister. The field-marshal rode back to GHQ with Lloyd George on 3 April, following the Beauvais conference that confirmed Foch's appointment as generalissimo. Haig commented in his diary: "The P.M. looked as if he had been thoroughly frightened, and he seemed still in a funk.... L.G. is a fatiguing companion in a motor. He talks and argues so! And he appears to me to be a thorough impostor." Later, he added:

> I gathered that L.G. expects to be attacked in the House of Commons for not tackling the manpower problem before, also for personally ordering Divisions to the east at a critical time against the advice of his Military Adviser, viz., the C.I.G.S. (Robertson).... L.G. seems a "cur" and when I am with him I cannot resist a feeling of distrust of him and his intentions.[21]

Haig had good reason to mistrust the prime minister who did, indeed, expect to be attacked in Parliament, as he was. Lloyd George had already prepared an elaborate defence of distortion, half-truth, and outright deception: in other words, it was completely in character for him. Delivering a rambling speech to the House of Commons on 9 April, he claimed that the BEF was substantially stronger at the start of 1918 than it had been a year earlier. Some, like Colonel Repington of the *Morning Post*, revelled in Lloyd George's obvious discomfiture. "This is delicious!" he commented, but he was not fooled by the prime minister's ringing rhetoric. "It is with such tales that L.G. deceives the country. All his line now is to show that we were as strong as the Boches in the West, and expected the attack when it came, and that, *ergo*—he leaves this to be inferred—the soldiers were all born fools."[22]

One of Lloyd George's cabinet ministers, Lord Curzon, made a similar speech in the House of Lords the same day. Curzon stressed what he called "the approximate numerical equality of the opposing forces along the entire Front," and did so, he said,

> because there seems to have been a tendency in some quarters to suppose that, either from a reluctance to tap the available resources of manpower in this country or from a failure to appreciate military advice, the British Army in France had been allowed to decline numerically to a point that was fraught with peril. There is no foundation for such a suspicion; nor were there any apprehensions of such a character either entertained or received. Our Commanders were equally satisfied with the numbers, the equipment, and the morale of their forces.

Concluded Curzon: "The Western Front was well equipped to look after itself; and if it has in any respect failed to do so, the explanation must be sought elsewhere."[23]

These monstrous lies did not go unchallenged. In order to set the record straight, a soldier, Major-General Sir Frederick Maurice, sacrificed his career. Freddy Maurice was upset "that for some time past, the Government has not been telling the truth about the War. Their object is to show that they did everything possible and that the blame rests with the Generals. This is absolutely untrue, and I am one of the few people who know the facts...." After mulling over the matter, Maurice sat down and wrote a letter to various London newspapers, fully realizing that it was, "of course, a breach of military discipline." In his letter, Maurice challenged what he called "certain misstatements which in sum give a totally misleading impression of what happened," and expressed the hope "that Parliament may see fit to order an investigation" of the politicians' claims. The letter was published in *The Times, Morning Post, Daily Chronicle,* and *Daily News* on 7 May.[24]

General Maurice was promptly sacked. His retirement was officially announced on the thirteenth. Though he was a major-general, he was placed on the half-pay of a major, £225 annually, by a vengeful government.

The Maurice case created the biggest political crisis of the war for Prime Minister Lloyd George, and he rose to the occasion. The prime minister loved a good fight, and for two tense days he had one on his hands. As a result of Maurice's charges, a faction of Lloyd George's own Liberal party, fronted by former prime minister Herbert Asquith, openly questioned his leadership. The issue came to a head in the House of Commons on Thursday, 9 May, two days after the Maurice letter appeared in the papers. While Asquith gave a weak and ineffectual speech, Lloyd George responded with a brilliant performance. The whole argument, in his view, centred on the size of the BEF, and all figures provided by the War Office showed that it was bigger in January 1918 than it had been in January 1917. The prime minister admitted that some military men made "a distinction between what are known as 'combatants and non-combatants'," but "I do not accept that distinction."[25] Maurice's bid for a parliamentary inquiry was subsequently voted down. Lloyd George had weathered the storm.

Now, it was the prime minister's turn to go head-hunting. And the head he wanted most was that of Sir Douglas Haig.

The muttering against the field-marshal had resumed with the first German offensive. On 26 March, Lord French, now practically a member of the war cabinet, stayed after a cabinet meeting to talk privately with Lloyd George, Winston Churchill, and Sir Maurice Hankey, who commented in his diary: "French was most bitter about Haig, who, he said, was no judge of men [and] had surrounded himself with stupid people and bad commanders.... He considered Haig had badly let down the Army in shattering it in the hopeless Flanders offensive." French found a most receptive audience for his claims, which events in France appeared to validate. Stubbornly refusing to acknowledge their own culpability, more and more members of the cabinet paid heed to French's complaints regarding Passchendaele. By 8 April, for the first time, Lloyd George's war cabinet openly "discussed the desirability of getting rid of Haig...," noted Hankey. "The difficulty is that there is no obvious successor...."[26]

Even Haig appeared resigned to his fate. On 7 April, the *Morning Post*'s Repington met the disgraced Sir Hubert Gough, who confided "that Haig had told him that he expects to be sent home in a week's time." The uncertainty about his future went on for much more than a week, however. As late as the end of May, Haig confessed to his staff that his job was on the line, as General Charteris commented in his diary: "D.H. says he 'may be wearing a blue suit' in London any day." The only thing he had going for him was that, as Hankey pointed out, there was no obvious replacement. "I think," Haig admitted in a letter to his wife, "that they will find it difficult to find a successor *at this moment*."[27]

Things were seemingly settled in mid-June. On the seventeenth, the CIGS, Sir Henry Wilson, paid Haig a visit. Afterwards, the field-marshal wrote, "The Government has no wish at all to replace me as C. in C. in France." But Haig's faithful subordinate, Charteris, saw Wilson's visit in a very different light:

> He [Wilson] says that the Government "at present" have no wish to replace D.H. as Commander-in-Chief. It is an utterly impossible situation for a Commander-in-Chief to be in—to know that he has only the temporary support of his Government, and that the politicians are only waiting for an opportunity to turn him out. Curiously enough, D.H. does not let it worry him much. He has become almost fatalistic in his outlook on life, and very deeply religious. He seems... quite convinced that he has the especial favour of Providence. I hope he is right.[28]

In fact, Wilson had no business offering Haig such assurances, because Lloyd George and associates were actively looking for a suitable substitute. According to Hankey, the war cabinet's first choice was Sir Hubert Plumer, "in whom the troops are said to have confidence." The only problem, lamented Hankey, was that Plumer was "about as stupid as Haig himself." Another highly regarded choice was Lord Cavan, who had succeeded Plumer in command of the British forces in Italy. On 23 July, Cavan was called to London, ostensibly to outline the situation in Italy, "but really in order to enable the Prime Minister to 'vet' him with a view to his replacing Haig...." But Lloyd George was not impressed, and Cavan's name was removed from the generals' derby.[29]

Even unmistakable success could not divert the prime minister, whose enmity toward Haig grew as the year progressed. In August, the Allies had launched the first of their own great offensives: on the eighth, the Canadian Corps spearheaded a mass tank attack near Amiens, resulting in what Ludendorff hysterically called "the black day of the German Army in the history of the war."[30] It was the beginning of the end. The Allies relentlessly pounded the Germans along the Western Front, forcing them to seek sanctuary behind the vaunted Hindenburg Line, their last line of defence.

Field-Marshal Haig was engineering what would eventually be recognized as "the greatest succession of victories in the British Army's whole history." But he could not escape the spectre of

Passchendaele, even in his moment of glory. London's lack of confidence in him was clearly stated in a telegram from Sir Henry Wilson on 29 August, as the BEF prepared to break through the Hindenburg Line and win the war:

> Just a word of caution in regard to incurring heavy losses in attacks on Hindenburg Line as opposed to losses when driving the enemy back to that line. I do not mean to say that you have incurred such losses, but I know the War Cabinet would become anxious if we received heavy punishment in attacking the Hindenburg Line, without success.

Haig was outraged:

> The object of the telegram is, no doubt, to save the Prime Minister (Lloyd George) in case of any failure. So I read it to mean that I can attack the Hindenburg Line if I think it right to do so.... If my attack is successful, I will remain as C. in C. If we fail, or our losses are excessive, I can hope for no mercy!... What a wretched lot of weaklings we have in high places at the present time![31]

The "weaklings" were still out to get him. On 21 September, Lord Milner, who had replaced Lord Derby as secretary of state for war shortly after the start of the German offensive in the spring, visited Haig at GHQ. Milner had a pessimistic message, Haig noted in his diary: "He states recruiting is very bad, and that if the British Army is used up now there will be no men for next year." Haig was certain that he had the Germans on the ropes—though, in fairness to the politicians, he had been saying the same thing since 1916—and argued that "we ought to do our utmost to get a decision this autumn." Milner was not impressed; Haig's views worried him, as he confessed on his return to London in a meeting with Sir Henry Wilson, who remarked: "He thinks Haig ridiculously optimistic and is afraid that he may embark on another Passchendaele."[32]

At the War Office, planning was under way for a 1919 campaign. Even at this late date, few foresaw an end to the long and bloody conflict. If Lord Milner had his way, Haig would not be around to direct the victory drive next year, because he and Prime Minister Lloyd George had at last selected someone to take the field-marshal's place. Their choice was none other than the man who had helped save Haig's hide by capturing Passchendaele: the commander of the Canadian Corps, Sir Arthur Currie.

21 / Currie: Glory and Tragedy

It was not until after the war that General Currie was told why Passchendaele had to be taken. In Paris for the Versailles peace conference, Currie met Sir Douglas Haig on 12 February 1919 in the lobby of the Hôtel Majestic, the headquarters of the British delegation. Taking Currie aside, Haig explained his reasons for pursuing the Passchendaele operation. Currie later recounted their meeting:

> It was then I learned for the first time the true proportions of the mutiny in the French Army in 1917 and the strength of the Peace Party in France and also in England in that year. He pointed out that after the victories of Vimy and Messines in April and June the British Army had to continue the offensive, in order to keep the enemy from launching an attack against the French.... In order to raise the morale of the French Army and the British Army, and the French Government and the British Government, the Chief decided that the Ridge must be captured.

Currie was not completely convinced. For years afterward, he continued to question "whether it was wise to choose the Ypres district as the battleground," and believed that Passchendaele "may have assumed unduly magnified proportions in the minds of many."[1]

Like most Canadians, Currie was flabbergasted by the British decision to abandon Passchendaele without a fight in the spring of 1918. He felt betrayed, and for a time he allowed his emotions to get the better of him. On 20 April, four days after the ridge was abandoned, General John J. Pershing, commanding the American Expeditionary Force, came to see Currie at Canadian Corps headquarters. General Pershing was impressed with Currie's anger and frustration: "General Currie deplored the fact that the British had so easily given up Passchendaele Ridge, which the year before he had been told must be taken at all costs, and for which the Canadians made the tremendous sacrifice of 16,000 casualties."[2]

Moreover, Currie believed that the crisis facing the BEF in April 1918 was due to high-level negligence and low-level incompetence. Rather unfairly, he lashed out at what he considered to be the poor performance of the British troops. "Many are not fighting," he fumed. "This is what I often claimed in 1917 would be the case. Many of them will not fight and do not fight." He even went so far as to express these uncharitable views to Sir Henry Horne, in whose First Army the Canadians were serving at the time. General Horne,

Currie commented privately, "resented any reflection on [the] fighting ability of British Divisions." An angry Horne complained to Field-Marshal Haig, who noted in his diary: "Currie is suffering from a swollen head, Horne thinks."[3]

The strain between the British and Canadians during 1918 was very real. General Currie was understandably upset, when in late March, GHQ broke up the Canadian Corps, assigning the four Canadian divisions to various British corps, and placing Currie's headquarters in temporary reserve. The arrangement did not last long: when both Currie and the Canadian government protested, Haig reluctantly reunited the Corps. But he could not conceal his annoyance with these upstart colonials: "I could not help feeling that some people in Canada regard themselves rather as allies than as fellow citizens of the Empire."[4] As a result, the Canadians took no direct part in the desperate fighting that spring. However, their contribution was considerable: the Canadians, with less than 10 per cent of the BEF's total strength, held 20 per cent of the British front in northern France. So great was German respect for the Canadians that, while they were dangerously overstretched, theirs was the only major portion of the British lines that was not attacked.

Currie's bitterness had not abated when, in June 1918, he found a forum for his complaints about the British army. At that time, Canada's prime minister, Sir Robert Borden, was in London to attend a meeting of the Imperial War Cabinet—a clever creation of David Lloyd George's, designed to milk more manpower out of the dominions in return for token say in the conduct of the war. On 11 June, Borden listened as Lloyd George related his version of the grim events of March and April on the Western Front. The Canadian leader was shocked at the suggestions of military ineptitude, and he later sought a meeting with Currie, who happened to be on leave with his family in the coastal resort of Bristol. Currie hurried to London the next day.

Prime Minister Borden asked his Corps commander for "the unvarnished truth about the situation at the front," and Currie was happy to oblige.[5]

He launched into a condemnation of Passchendaele. "Currie tells me, and I believe he is right," the prime minister wrote, "that it had no useful result, as the British Army immediately went on the defensive and the campaign ceased for the year. No advantage in position was gained and the effort was wasted," particularly when the ridge was simply handed back to the enemy six months later. It was Currie's opinion, Borden continued, "that the venture was by no means worth the cost; and that it was won to save the face of the British High Command who had undertaken all through the autumn most unsuccessful and highly disastrous attempts."[6]

Warming to the subject, Currie pointed to what he considered to be serious flaws in the BEF's command personnel. He condemned the conduct of several fellow corps commanders, as the prime minister related:

> To give you an example of what work will accomplish and what casual indifference will leave undone; the Canadian Corps put out last autumn and winter 375,000 yards of barbed wire entanglements by which every trench and all supporting trenches were thoroughly protected. At a conference between Currie and three other Corps Commanders, one of them (Portuguese) said that he had put out no barbed wire; one of the British Corps Commanders said that he had put out 30,000 yards, and the other Corps Commander had put out 36,000 yards. A British Officer told Currie that his Corps had no barbed wire protection on any scale as the Canadians and that the men were employed in laying out lawn-tennis courts.[7]

These commanders, Currie knew, were not typical of the British army. But he believed that the BEF boasted too many senior officers who were not equal to the responsibility of their ranks.

Prime Minister Borden promptly reported Currie's comments to the Imperial War Cabinet. At its meeting on 13 June, Borden, who frankly cited Currie as his source, bluntly declared that Passchendaele had not been "worth the candle." He went on to charge "that there has been a conspicuous failure to remove incompetent officers" from senior commands, and that there were too many British divisions "not properly trained, organised or led by competent officers."[8]

The remarks caused a sensation among Borden's fellow prime ministers and associates. Such outspoken questioning of British infallibility was unprecedented. An embarrassed Lord Milner assured Borden "that I would be answered." However, it did not surprise him that "no answer was ever forthcoming for none was available."[9]

Prime Minister Lloyd George joined his colleagues in raising his eyebrows at the Canadian comments. But, far from being distressed, he was delighted. He was also intrigued by the boldness of the soldier Borden credited for his observations. When the cabinet talks adjourned, Lloyd George asked his Canadian counterpart to arrange a meeting with General Currie. They met that very afternoon, and

Lloyd George liked what he saw and heard. "I was greatly impressed with Currie's views," he would remark. "They were, I felt, sane and common-sense. His great ability, his strength of purpose, and his lack of fetishes common to the British officers were most noticeable." An idea was born. "I had not met [Australia's Sir John] Monash at that time," Lloyd George would say, "and my later idea, after I had got to know Monash, was to make him Chief of Staff and Currie Commander-in-Chief."[10]

It was not idle talk on Lloyd George's part. As the summer of 1918 wore on, and no other serious candidates for Haig's job emerged, Currie's attractiveness as a possible successor grew accordingly. Finally, on 14 September, Lord Milner paid a surprise visit to Canadian Corps headquarters. As Currie later recalled, Milner confided "that if the war went into 1919 I would be placed in command of the British Army."[11]

The ironies of the situation are numerous. Lloyd George chose to interpret Currie's comments as criticisms of Sir Douglas Haig; such was not the case. Currie, who admired and respected Haig, had aimed his complaints at the British army as a whole. Currie had come close to talking himself into Haig's job—only the end of the war in November 1918 frustrated Lloyd George's plans for a switch—but the Canadian was not really interested. Indeed, he felt that it would be a mistake to replace the field-marshal, commenting that "it strikes me as a very poor policy to swap horses at this stage." Moreover, Currie did not disagree with Haig's strategical belief that the Western Front was the decisive theatre of operations because it was the location of the main German forces. Currie, too, was well aware of the field-marshal's difficulties in dealing with "those in authority in England who wanted to fight the war in so many places other than the Western front," and he sympathized with the problems presented by politicians who expected Haig "to win battles without casualties." The inevitable conclusion is that, even if Currie had succeeded Haig in 1919, the Canadian would soon have worked his way into Lloyd George's bad books. The British prime minister was looking for a "yes-man," and Currie certainly did not fill the bill.[12]

Whether or not Sir Arthur Currie could have been a successful commander-in-chief of the BEF is a matter of speculation. The odds would have been stacked against him: not only was he a mere colonial, he was a non-professional to boot, and he was much younger than the army commanders who would have reported to him. And, of course, history is full of examples of promising young officers promoted beyond their capabilities. It is a moot point, anyway. The fact that Currie was even considered for the position, and seriously so, is proof of his stature as Canada's greatest soldier—no Canadian, before or since, has ever been so highly regarded—and one of the British Empire's leading commanders.

There is one more irony. If Passchendaele marked Currie as a major military figure, it also precipitated a campaign of vilification against him at home. For it was his misfortune that the fighting in Flanders occurred in the midst of the most bitter election in Canadian history, and Currie was caught in the mud-slinging.

The main issue in the 1917 election was conscription. The passions generated were not unique to Canada, to be sure. Britain had not resorted to conscription until 1916; even then, it was a step taken with the greatest reluctance by the Asquith government and only after long and heated debate in cabinet. In Australia, conscription was twice put to a referendum, and was rejected both times. But the animosity with which Canadians tackled it was unequalled in the Empire. It divided Canada as never before, and rarely since, with Sir Wilfrid Laurier's Liberals and French-speaking Canadians—the majority of them in Quebec—on one side, and Sir Robert Borden's governing Conservatives and most English-speaking Canadians on the other. The ill will engendered during the campaign was exemplified by the pro-conscriptionist claim that "a vote for Laurier is a vote for the Kaiser," and the anti-conscriptionist contention that each vote for Borden "will be a wreath laid on the graves of the boys who have given their lives."[13]

Prime Minister Borden had hoped to avoid a showdown over conscription. He would have preferred to ignore it altogether, but the declining success of voluntary recruitment in early 1917 left him with no alternative: without conscription, Canada could not remain at war. Hoping to introduce it with as little rancour as possible, he proposed to form a coalition with Laurier, but the aging Liberal leader and former prime minister rejected the idea, setting the stage for the subsequent election. Borden responded with an informal coalition, the Union party, composed of his own Conservatives and disenchanted Liberals. On election day, 17 December 1917, the prime minister and his supporters won a sound majority in the House of Commons. Conscription was formally adopted soon afterward.

General Currie had been drawn into the conscription controversy shortly after his appointment as commander of the Canadian Corps in June 1917. Currie had long foreseen the need for compulsory enlistments, fearing that without conscription, it "would... mean the death of the Canadian Corps." At the prime minister's request, the new Corps commander sent to Canada a message endorsing the measure: "It is an imperative and urgent necessity that steps be immediately taken to ensure that sufficient drafts of officers and men are sent from Canada to keep the corps at full strength." A leading Liberal member of Parliament, Frank Oliver, condemned Currie's comments, stating that "when we have a political general in command of our forces, I want to be assured that our battles are not being fought for political effect." It was an absurd suggestion, certainly, but Oliver followed with more criticism of Currie, concerning his conduct of the action at Hill 70 in August. "General Currie," he charged, "has had the honour of directing the operations against the city of Lens: we have suffered greater losses in these operations than in any other undertaking by the Canadian forces at any time since the war began. And we have not yet succeeded in taking Lens."[14]

These kinds of comments were isolated, for a time. But they became more commonplace with the heated feelings over the imminent election. The criticism against Currie escalated with the timely arrival of the casualty lists from Passchendaele. George Waldron, a Liberal candidate in Toronto, won widespread press coverage with his claim that, in the capture of Passchendaele, "the Canadian casualties were excessive and that the conduct of the Army should be inquired into."[15]

Worse followed. In early December, Currie received a letter from his London banker, Dudley Oliver, who told him "that the late Premier, Sir Wilfrid Laurier, in a speech yesterday in Canada stated that you had resigned your position as Commander of the Canadian Corps owing to the losses at Passchendael[e]. I need hardly tell you that no former Premier in Canada ever stooped so low as to make such a false statement in an endeavour to obtain votes for a cause every true Canadian is ashamed of." Currie was equally, if not more, distressed. "I cannot understand," he replied to Oliver, "how a man like Sir Wilfrid Laurier could descend to such false and dishonourable conduct, and could wilfully lie in the hope of getting some advantage for his party."[16]

Some people actually believed Laurier, including a number of newspaper editors who dispatched a telegram to Corps headquarters on 10 December, addressed to "Sir Arthur Currie, or to the Acting Commander of the Canadian Corps." Currie's astonishment gave way to anger. Writing a cabinet minister, Sir George Perley, Currie asked that the government issue a denial of Laurier's claim, "in justice to myself.... To have gone through what anyone who has been here for three years has had to go through, and to have given the very best that is in one to the service of your country, would almost justify one in hoping that your own countrymen would not refer to you as a murderer."[17]

But Currie was to find that, as he put it, "some mud always sticks when thrown." Currie returned from Christmas leave in London in a foul mood. "The air in London I found, as usual, to be filled with rumour and suspicion," he complained. "I learned there...that I was the one who had been proved to be absolutely reckless regarding the lives of Canadians." He believed that there was "an almost organized effort" under way to discredit him, and was angered that at least one high-ranking Canadian officer—Currie believed it to be Lieutenant-General Sir Richard Turner, who commanded the Canadian forces in the United Kingdom—"has been spending most of his time at hospitals and convalescent camps, condoling with the wounded and telling them that casualties in the Corps have been altogether too high, and were unnecessary in many cases."[18]

Few generals have ever been more unfairly castigated. Far from demonstrating his carelessness over casualties, Passchendaele proved Currie's concern for the preservation of the lives of the men under his command; indeed, Currie's actions throughout the war stand as strong evidence of his desire, and ability, to win battles only at the least possible cost. No one knew this better than the senior officers who served with him. Brigadier-General J.E.B. Seely, the sometime commander of the Canadian Cavalry Brigade and onetime British cabinet minister, considered that Currie "had an almost fanatical hatred of unnecessary casualties. Of all the men I knew during four years on the Western Front, I think Currie was the man who took most care of the lives of his troops." His staff officers endorsed this view. It was Currie's habit, according to the Corps counter-battery officer, Andy McNaughton, "to pay the price of victory in shells and not in the lives of men."[19]

These glowing tributes notwithstanding, a lot of Canadians, veterans and conscripts alike, had little regard for General Currie. Passchendaele convinced many of them that victory was his sole consideration. During the last months of the war, when the Canadian Corps spearheaded the BEF's final campaign, it was widely believed in the ranks that Currie was volunteering the Corps for the most difficult tasks. Consider the comment, for example, of Trooper George Hambley of the Canadian Light Horse:

> The majority of men in the corps consider Currie to be the biggest human butcher in the British Army because the Canadians have been mercilessly cut up in the front part of all the recent ad-

vances—Certain it is that he cares nothing whatever for the amount of life wasted so long as the object is attained.[20]

Charges of this nature dogged Currie for much of the rest of his life. Political enemies—and he had many—took up the cry as the war wound down. The most vocal of these was Sir Sam Hughes, a former minister of militia and defence, who was fired for incompetence in late 1916. Hughes, speaking in the sanctuary provided by Parliament, slandered Currie repeatedly in 1919 and 1920, accusing the Canadian commander of deliberately sacrificing the lives of his men in the pursuit of his own personal glory. Currie, who believed that Hughes "is a liar, is at times insane, and apparently is a cur of the worst type,"[21] could do nothing except grind his teeth in frustrated fury. Vindication did not come until 1928, after Currie initiated one of the most celebrated court cases in Canadian history. A small-town Ontario newspaper made the mistake of repeating the accusations made by the now-dead Sam Hughes, and Currie sued for libel. The two-week trial was a traumatic and gruelling experience, but he won. Tragically, he did so at the cost of his health. His death five years later, at the age of fifty-seven, may be attributed, at least indirectly, to the lawsuit.

Such was the harvest of the seeds sown at Passchendaele.

Conclusion

Nothing is so tragic and futile as a life wasted. All war is wasteful, but for seven decades the families of the brave men who fell at Passchendaele have been led to believe that their loved ones died in vain, the victims of their own incompetent generals conducting a hopeless and bloody débâcle. This is the myth that has been perpetuated by feeble-minded historians, vindictive politicians, and overblown military men seeking to portray the British high command as blundering, butchering idiots. In the process, they have detracted from the achievements of the BEF, in general, and the Canadian Corps, in particular.

Much of the controversy that surrounds Passchendaele concerns casualty figures. It has been generally accepted that British losses in the Third Battle of Ypres were, in round numbers, 400,000. For instance, David Lloyd George uses 399,000 in his memoirs; other published estimates range from a low of 300,000 to a high of half a million. However, the actual total is considerably less. In 1948, the British official history tabulated the BEF's casualties as 244,897, which has since been convincingly demonstrated—by John Terraine, the foremost historian of the Great War—to be correct. The hysterical reaction of Passchendaele's legion of detractors is noteworthy. No less an authority than the eminent Sir Basil Liddell Hart denounced the official history's calculation as "preposterous" and "deplorably misleading," and concluded that the figures had been "cooked" by the equally eminent official historian, Sir James Edmonds. Such are the passions aroused by Passchendaele.[1]

Indeed, the emotionally-charged criticism of Passchendaele has masked certain realities. Critics contend that it was a microcosm of all that was wrong with British strategy, that it represented the ultimate in what Lloyd George denounced as a "silly and bloody game of attrition." Lloyd George later argued in his memoirs that Passchendaele proved the futility of the large-scale offensives so favoured by Field-Marshal Haig and represented a kind of bankruptcy of military thinking. The former prime minister concluded that it also justified the alternative strategy proposed by the French commander-in-chief, Pétain, which involved small-scale and strictly limited offensive operations on the Western Front. Indeed, if the war had unfolded as Lloyd George envisaged, this strategy would have been pursued in the second half of 1918, after sitting idly in the first half; 1919, or perhaps 1920, would have been the year of decision. But prolonging the conflict was hardly a method of economizing manpower. One must take into account the grim reality of trench warfare. Casualties were an everyday occurrence: shelling, sniping, and sickness caused enormous losses which acquired the euphemism "normal wastage." According to the War Office, "the average monthly casualties, when there was no severe fighting, was [sic] 35,000" in the BEF alone. Half a year of avoiding major battle on the Western Front, as Lloyd George wished to do, would have cost almost as many casualties as Passchendaele, without bringing the war any closer to a conclusion.[2]

Lloyd George's nonsensical ramblings are typical of his naïveté. He sought, as the much-maligned Sir Hubert Gough perceptibly pointed out, "an easy and cheap way to victory. But...victory can only be won at the cost of heavy fighting and giving proof of superior efficiency, endurance and courage.... It is indeed impossible to win great victories over a powerful enemy without corresponding losses." Gough demolished the prime minister's arguments opposing major battles on the Western Front in favour of his beloved side-show strategy:

> It has been suggested that if all the losses which we suffered during our many battles in the early years of this War had been avoided, we would have been in a much stronger position towards the end of the War to obtain final victory. But would we? This argument overlooks the fact that if we had not fought these battles, our Allies would have fought alone and the Germans would have been saved the terrible losses that we inflicted on them. Their troops also would have been in greater numbers, and in an incomparably higher state of *morale*.... They would have attacked the Allies in some vital direction with the utmost violence and vigour, and then eventually in defending ourselves we would have suffered the same losses that we endured in our offensives, but would have run incomparably greater risks; furthermore the moral ascendancy would have passed to the enemy, and the prospects of an Allied victory been long delayed.[3]

"Attrition" is a cold-blooded word. As Lloyd George disparagingly used it, only military commanders of inferior quality could have considered such a method of winning the war. Oddly, many of the same British writers who condemn Sir Douglas Haig for his policy of wearing down the German army sing the praises of the American general, Ulysses S. Grant, for so effectively employing attrition in his victorious campaign over the great Confederate commander, Robert

E. Lee, in the U.S. Civil War. Attrition was not invented during the Great War of 1914-18, nor did it disappear with that conflict. But attrition was the only practicable way of winning the Great War. The technology which made this the first great modern war and which enabled both sides to kill and maim soldiers in unprecedented numbers had its limitations. The tank is an ideal example. Slow, clumsy, mechanically unreliable, it was undeniably useful in smashing barbed-wire entanglements and snuffing out strongpoints, but it was not a decisive weapon. The generals have been condemned for frittering away their tanks in "penny packets," but penny packets were all that was usually available: it is a fact that there were sufficient numbers of tanks for only two mass attacks in the Great War, Cambrai in November 1917 and Amiens in August 1918, which foreshadowed but could not possibly duplicate the blitzkrieg of the next great war.

Critics of the Western Front consistently overlook the reality that large modern armies, numbering in the millions, can inflict enormous punishment on each other. In World War II, the Russian Front was the equivalent of the Great War's Western Front. Even with huge masses of tanks employed by geniuses in armoured warfare, casualties on the Russian Front in 1941-45 far exceeded those of the Western Front in 1914-18. The fighting see-sawed back and forth across the steppes until attrition intervened: the German army was not vanquished until it was bled white.

Another comparison with World War II is useful in placing Passchendaele in its proper perspective. The Normandy campaign in 1944 provides an interesting contrast; it, like Passchendaele, lasted about three months and involved a million Allied soldiers, roughly the same number as the BEF employed in Flanders. In Normandy, the Allies fought under ideal weather conditions, and with complete control of the air, which severely hampered German ground movement. The Allies also enjoyed an overwhelming superiority in men, tanks, artillery, and other material, and, in the end, won a decisive victory. Despite all these advantages, Allied casualties in Normandy were remarkably similar to those suffered by the BEF, fighting amid horrendous conditions at Passchendaele. The latter lost 244,897, while Allied casualties in Normandy, excluding naval losses, totalled 237,606.[4]

Sir Douglas Haig would later comment that Passchendaele deserves to be ranked "amongst the most glorious of British battles." His antagonists would not be surprised that he would say such a thing, but the basic facts support his contention. For more than three months, the British battled the cream of the German army, virtually alone and unaided, while their French allies did almost nothing.* The opposing forces in Flanders were about equal: the Germans committed eighty-six divisions, the British fifty-one—German divisions, it should be remembered, were smaller than their British counterparts, with only nine battalions to the British twelve, and each German battalion was somewhat weaker, as well. Military theorists reckon that an attacker must have a superiority of two-to-one to have a reasonable chance of success, and three-to-one to ensure success. The British, attacking at even odds, still managed to rock the German army to its very foundations. The Germans suffered a quarter-million casualties, many of them the finest troops in the Reich and, as such, irreplaceable. So mauled was the German army at Passchendaele that, before it could undertake its own offensive operations in 1918, it had to be extensively reorganized into attack and defence divisions. The British official history is therefore justified in contending of Passchendaele: "The wonder is not that complete success was not achieved, but that so much was done by so few to break the spirit and reduce the numbers of the enemy."[5]

The weather was, indisputably, the most important single factor in the Flanders campaign. Haig was quite correct when he claimed that "it was the immense natural difficulties, accentuated manifold by the abnormally wet weather, rather than the enemy's resistance, which limited our progress...."[6] It will be recalled that rain accompanied each and every British operation during August, driving rainstorms that practically paralyzed the attacks. And it was rain that thwarted the Australians and New Zealanders in their efforts to capture Passchendaele on 9 and 12 October. But when the weather was good, as it was for Sir Herbert Plumer's punishing assaults on 20 and 26 September and 4 October, the BEF was irresistible. The Germans were, by their own admission, reeling under these hammer blows, until the rain rescued them from imminent ruin.

History's judgment of Passchendaele has been harsh. Much of it stems, oddly, from Lloyd George's vitriolic vendetta against Haig. The former prime minister used his six-volume *War Memoirs* not only as an excuse for his own reprehensible conduct but also as an instrument to discredit the field-marshal. In Lloyd George's hands, Passchendaele became a club with which to bludgeon Haig's reputation:

---

* The French mounted a pair of diversionary attacks, one in August, the other in October, but neither distracted the Germans from the fighting in Flanders. Moreover, the French forces attached to the BEF for the campaign suffered only 8,500 casualties, which is indicative of how little they contributed.

months later. This is valid comment. The truth is that Germany had lost the war before 21 March 1918, the vital factor being that of manpower and the arrival of the Americans. The Germans would have done well to keep their divisions on the defensive and bargain, still from a position of some strength, for peace.

The suggestion makes for intriguing speculation, in view of the fact that, thanks largely to Lloyd George's interference, the Allies intended to spend most of 1918 on the defensive on the Western Front.[12]

Strategical considerations aside, Passchendaele must also be examined from a tactical viewpoint. As the British official history laments, "'Passchendaele' came to connote not, as it should, a wonderful Canadian success in mud and rain, but a long and persistent struggle under such conditions." The capture of Passchendaele was an achievement of awesome proportions, without equal in Canadian military annals. Applauds the British official historian, Sir James Edmonds: "The capture and retention of the Passchendaele high ground reflects the high standard of the staff work and training of the Canadian Corps and its four divisions. Once again, as at Vimy Ridge and on Hill 70 earlier in the year, the tenacity and endurance of Canada's splendid contribution to the British Imperial Forces were manifest."[13]

The magnitude of the Canadian accomplishment does not seem to be appreciated today. At the time, however, a British officer whose unit relieved the Canadians at Passchendaele marvelled at their exploits. John Nettleton later wrote that

> it was impossible to understand how the Canadians had managed to take it. The valley itself was a morass, due to the small drainage stream at the bottom having been blocked by shell fire and all along the top of the ridge was a line of concrete pill-boxes that completely commanded the slope. It did not seem possible that troops could have struggled through the mud and up the ridge in the face of machine-gun fire from the line of pill-boxes. But they did....[14]

Even some of the Canadian soldiers who were there did not realize at the time what they had done. One was Corporal Will Bird of the 42nd (Royal Highlanders of Canada) Battalion, who returned to Passchendaele fourteen years later. He had to admit amazement. "At one spot I could count fifty-eight pillboxes, and, viewing them, one cannot understand how the enemy was ever routed from his holdings."

> Standing at Bellevue Spur one gets a wonderful view of the Salient.... Stand there and you will realize the immense superiority of the German positions, and the complete observation the enemy had of every move that we made. No person could move above ground without being seen.... German observers could sit snugly on those ridges, marking their maps, talking to gunners over the telephone wires, and register on every crossroad, battery, duckboard track, or new working; could define every foot of parapet and take its measure accordingly. That men survived in those places will always seem an incredible thing....

Of course, many did not survive. A Belgian farmer would tell a Canadian correspondent that "my land is richer than before. It is the best land I have ever seen. My crops are... the biggest yet."[15]

Passchendaele was a triumph, so far as the Canadians were concerned. It was at least the equal of any other victory they won on the Western Front, including Vimy Ridge. Indeed, it may be argued that Passchendaele was a far more impressive achievement than Vimy, which even today stands as the most famous of Canadian battles. At Vimy, the Canadian Corps spent weeks painstakingly preparing for the attack, compared to the few days available at Passchendaele. Moreover, Vimy assumed magnified importance due to the fact that the Canadians were not really expected to take it; they not only captured the ridge, their victory proved to be the only significant success of the Allied offensive in the spring of 1917. It was a truly great achievement by the Canadians, but the Germans minimized the capture of Vimy Ridge by withdrawing a sufficient distance to render it virtually useless to the Allies as an observation post. That fact does not, and cannot, detract from an impressive operation. In the same way, the loss of Passchendaele six months after its capture in no way diminishes a notable feat of arms, overcoming an enemy who enjoyed just about every conceivable advantage. The Canadians were assigned an objective, and they took it, when all others had failed, in the face of appalling battlefield conditions. It was unmistakable testimony to what the Corps commander, Sir Arthur Currie, proudly called "the discipline, training, leadership and fine fighting qualities of the Canadians."[16]

The last word on Passchendaele belongs to General Currie, whose own skills were tested so severely. In the script for a radio address fifteen years after the war, Currie commented:

When the Canadians consolidated Passchendaele Ridge... they consolidated not only the Ridge, not only Douglas Haig's position, but, far more than any of these things, they consolidated the determination of British arms to see the horrible thing through.

That was the result of Canadian sacrifice, Canadian valour, Canadian endurance and Canadian determination. Would that those qualities burned as brightly today![17]

APPENDIX ONE

Order of Battle, Canadian Army Corps

Corps Headquarters

General Officer Commanding: Lieutenant-General Sir A.W. Currie
Brigadier-General, General Staff: Brigadier-General P.P. deB. Radcliffe
Deputy Adjutant and Quartermaster-General: Brigadier-General G.J. Farmar
General Officer Commanding Royal Artillery: Brigadier-General E.W.B. Morrison
Chief Engineer: Brigadier-General W.B. Lindsay

Corps Troops

CAVALRY
Royal Canadian Dragoons
Lord Strathcona's Horse
Fort Garry Horse
Canadian Light Horse
Royal North-West Mounted Police Squadron

ARTILLERY
Royal Canadian Horse Artillery Brigade
8th Army Brigade, Canadian Field Artillery (CFA)
    24th, 30th, 32nd Field Batteries
    42nd Howitzer Battery
"E" Anti-Aircraft Battery

Corps Heavy Artillery
1st Brigade, Canadian Garrison Artillery (CGA)
    1st, 3rd, 7th, 9th Siege Batteries
2nd Brigade, CGA
    1st, 2nd Heavy Batteries
    2nd, 4th, 5th, 6th Siege Batteries
3rd Brigade, CGA
    8th, 10th, 11th, 12th Siege Batteries

Fifth Divisional Artillery
13th Brigade, CFA
    52nd, 53rd, 55th Field Batteries
    51st Howitzer Battery
14th Brigade, CFA
    60th, 61st, 66th Field Batteries
    58th Howitzer Battery

ENGINEERS

MACHINE-GUN CORPS
1st Canadian Motor Machine-Gun Brigade
 "A", "B", Borden, Eaton, Yukon Batteries
1st, 2nd, 3rd, 4th, 5th, 6th, 7th, 8th, 9th, 10th, 11th,
12th, 13th, 14th, 15th, 16th Machine-Gun Companies

ARMY SERVICE CORPS

MEDICAL CORPS
Numbers 1, 2, 3, 6, 7, 8 General Hospitals
Numbers 2, 3, 7, 8, 9, 10 Stationary Hospitals
Numbers 1, 2, 3, 4 Casualty Clearing Stations
7th (Cavalry) Field Ambulance
14th Field Ambulance

Divisional Troops

FIRST CANADIAN DIVISION: Major-General A.C. Macdonell
First Infantry Brigade (Brigadier-General W.A. Griesbach)
    1st (Western Ontario) Battalion
    2nd (Eastern Ontario) Battalion
    3rd (Toronto Regiment) Battalion
    4th (Central Ontario) Battalion
    1st Trench Mortar Battery
Second Infantry Brigade (Brigadier-General F.O.W. Loomis)
    5th (Western Cavalry) Battalion
    7th (1st British Columbia Regiment) Battalion
    8th (90th Winnipeg Rifles) Battalion
    10th (Canadians) Battalion
    2nd Trench Mortar Battery
Third Infantry Brigade (Brigadier-General G.S. Tuxford)
    13th (Royal Highlanders of Canada) Battalion
    14th (Royal Montreal Regiment) Battalion
    15th (48th Highlanders of Canada) Battalion
    16th (Canadian Scottish) Battalion
    3rd Trench Mortar Battery
1st Brigade, CFA
    1st, 3rd, 4th Field Batteries
    2nd Howitzer Battery
2nd Brigade, CFA
    5th, 6th, 7th Field Batteries
    48th Howitzer Battery
1st, 2nd, 3rd Field Ambulances

SECOND CANADIAN DIVISION: Major-General H.E. Burstall
Fourth Infantry Brigade (Brigadier-General R. Rennie)
    18th (Western Ontario) Battalion
    19th (Central Ontario) Battalion
    20th (Central Ontario) Battalion
    21st (Eastern Ontario) Battalion
    4th Trench Mortar Battery
Fifth Infantry Brigade (Brigadier-General J.M. Ross)
    22nd (French Canadian) Battalion
    24th (Victoria Rifles of Canada) Battalion
    25th (Nova Scotia Rifles) Battalion
    26th (New Brunswick) Battalion
    5th Trench Mortar Battery
Sixth Infantry Brigade (Brigadier-General H.D.B. Ketchen)
    27th (Winnipeg) Battalion
    28th (Northwest) Battalion
    29th (Vancouver) Battalion
    31st (Alberta) Battalion
    6th Trench Mortar Battery
5th Brigade, CFA
    17th, 18th, 20th Field Batteries
    23rd Howitzer Battery
6th Brigade, CFA
    15th, 16th, 25th Field Batteries
    22nd Howitzer Battery
4th, 5th, 6th Field Ambulances

THIRD CANADIAN DIVISION: Major-General L.J. Lipsett
Seventh Infantry Brigade (Brigadier-General H.M. Dyer)
    Royal Canadian Regiment
    Princess Patricia's Canadian Light Infantry
    42nd (Royal Highlanders of Canada) Battalion
    49th (Edmonton Regiment) Battalion
    7th Trench Mortar Battery
Eighth Infantry Brigade (Brigadier-General J.H. Elmsley)
    1st Canadian Mounted Rifles
    2nd Canadian Mounted Rifles
    4th Canadian Mounted Rifles
    5th Canadian Mounted Rifles
    8th Trench Mortar Battery
Ninth Infantry Brigade (Brigadier-General F.W. Hill)
    43rd (Cameron Highlanders of Canada) Battalion
    52nd (Ontario) Battalion
    58th (Central Ontario) Battalion
    116th (Ontario) Battalion
    9th Trench Mortar Battery

9th Brigade, CFA
    31st, 33rd, 45th Field Batteries
    36th Howitzer Battery
10th Brigade, CFA
    38th, 39th, 40th Field Batteries
    35th Howitzer Battery
8th, 9th, 10th Field Ambulances

FOURTH CANADIAN DIVISION: Major-General D. Watson
Tenth Infantry Brigade (Brigadier-General E. Hilliam)
    44th (Manitoba) Battalion
    46th (South Saskatchewan) Battalion
    47th (British Columbia) Battalion
    50th (Calgary) Battalion
    10th Trench Mortar Battery
Eleventh Infantry Brigade (Brigadier-General V.W. Odlum)
    54th (Central Ontario) Battalion
    75th (Mississauga) Battalion
    87th (Canadian Grenadier Guards) Battalion
    102nd (Central Ontario) Battalion
    11th Trench Mortar Battery
Twelfth Infantry Brigade (Brigadier-General J.H. MacBrien)
    38th (Ottawa) Battalion
    72nd (Seaforth Highlanders of Canada) Battalion
    78th (Winnipeg Grenadiers) Battalion
    85th (Nova Scotia Highlanders) Battalion
    12th Trench Mortar Battery
3rd Brigade, CFA
    10th, 11th, 12th Field Batteries
    9th Howitzer Battery
4th Brigade, CFA
    13th, 19th, 27th Field Batteries
    21st Howitzer Battery
11th, 12th, 13th Field Ambulances

APPENDIX TWO

Canadian Corps Instructions for the Offensive: Passchendaele No. 1

I. STAGES OF THE ATTACK

The attack (6th phase)* is being resumed by the Second and Fifth Armies on [26 October] on which date the Canadian Corps, in conjunction with the I Anzac Corps on the right and the XVIII Corps on the left, will undertake the 1st stage of the operations for the capture of PASSCHENDAELE.

The objective of the Canadian Corps on "O" [zero] day is the RED Line shown on Map S.19. A pause of 1 hour will be made on the Intermediate Objective (RED DOTTED Line).

The 7th phase (BLUE Line) will probably be carried out on [30 October] and the 8th phase (GREEN Line) on [6 November], but these dates and objectives are subject to alteration according to the progress made in the previous phases.

II. ALLOTMENT OF OBJECTIVES AND TROOPS

The attack of the Canadian Corps RED Line will be carried out by the 4th Canadian Division on the right and the 3rd Canadian Division on the left.

The *4th Canadian Division* is attacking with the 10th Cdn. Inf. Bde., which is employing 1 Battalion in the front line, 2 Battalions in close support, and 1 Battalion in reserve.

The *3rd Canadian Division* is attacking with 2 Brigades, keeping 1 Brigade in divisional reserve.

The *9th Cdn. Inf. Bde.*, on the right, is attacking on a front of 2 Battalions, with 1 Battalion in support, and 1 Battalion in reserve.

The *8th Cdn. Inf. Bde.*, on the left, is attacking on a front of 1 Battalion, with 1 Battalion in support, and 2 Battalions in reserve.

The *7th Cdn. Inf. Bde.* will be in Divisional Reserve in Camp "X".

II(a). ACTION OF THE FLANK CORPS

1. The *I Anzac Corps* has been assigned the task of protecting the right flank of the 4th Canadian Division, and will establish posts for this purpose S. of

---

* This refers to the sixth phase of operations undertaken by the Second Army. The previous phases were those of 20 and 26 September and 4, 9, and 12 October.

the [Ypres-Roulers] Railway, including a strong post well forward on the neck towards ASSYRIA. Facilities will be granted by the 4th Canadian Division for the necessary supports to these posts to move through 4th Canadian Division Area N. of the Railway. The Railway and DECLINE COPSE are inclusive to I Anzac Corps.

2. The objectives (DOTTED RED and RED Lines) of the *XVIII Corps* are shown on Map S.19.

The 63rd [Royal Naval] Division will be attacking on the left of the 3rd Canadian Division and will include SOURCE FARM in its objective.

The XVIII Corps have been asked to neutralize the enemy's positions about VAT COTTAGES (V.29.a.5.9.) during the advance, and specially during consolidation.

III. BOUNDARIES AND HEADQUARTERS
Divisional and Brigade boundaries are shown on Map S.19.

Canadian Corps H.Q.	TEN ELMS
Canadian Corps H.A. H.Q.	VLAMERTINGHE CHATEAU
3rd Canadian Division	YPRES, Canal Bank
7th Cdn. Inf. Bde.	CAPITOL
8th Cdn. Inf. Bde.	KANSAS HOUSE
9th Cdn. Inf. Bde.	CAPITOL
4th Canadian Division	YPRES, MENIN GATE
10th Cdn. Inf. Bde.	BOETHOEK
11th Cdn. Inf. Bde.	YPRES
12th Cdn. Inf. Bde.	BRANDHOEK AREA

IV. GERMAN DISPOSITIONS AND DEFENCES
1. Dispositions
There is no very definite information available regarding the enemy's dispositions, but judging from the present situation, and from the enemy's usual dispositions in this battle area, it may be assumed that each Division in the Line has three companies in front, with one company in close support.

The Support Battalions would be about 500 to 1,000 yards, and the Reserve Battalion 2,000 to 3,000 yards, in rear of the front line according to the nature of the ground.

A notable feature in this area is the enemy's habit of defending Forward Positions by machine guns, which are located not necessarily in concrete dug-outs, but frequently in small portions of trench sheltered by pieces of canvas or corrugated iron, and which are fired from the nearest shell hole.

It is thought that the troops opposite us at present are the

* 238th Division, which has relieved the 220th Division, holding the line from E.13.a.0.0. to WOLF COPSE inclusive.

The order of battle of the regiments of this Division is not known.

It appears that the front line of this Division runs from about E.13.a.0.0. through VIENNA COTTAGES in D.12.d. to DECK WOOD in D.11.b. to the Southern edge of HAALEN COPSE in D.11.b. There is then a gap on account of the marshy ground and the line continues from North of FRIESLAND about SNIPE HALL along the road crossing the BELLEVUE SPUR to SOURCE TRENCH in V.28.c. Confirmation of this line is required. In front of this line there are machine gun posts at DECLINE COPSE in D.18.a., on the PASSCHENDAELE ROAD about D.11.d.90.15., in DAD TRENCH, and the BELLEVUE Defences, and probably one or two posts about 200 yards North of WOLF COPSE. The BELLEVUE Defences form a strong defended locality, well organized for machine gun defence.

The position of Support Battalions is not clear, but they are probably on the line DETECT CROSSING in D.12.d.—CREST FARM in D.6.c. to MEETCHEELE.

* Since writing the above prisoners of the 11th Bavarian Division have been captured on our front. It appears therefore that this Division is now in the Line (23-10-17).

The Reserve Divisions are possibly in ENCORE WOOD in E.1.d.-EXERT COPSE in E.1.a. and WRAP COPSE in W.19.d. The 238th Division has been resting and re-fitting for some time, and is probably in good fighting condition.

North of the 11th Bavarian Divn. is the 111th Division, which came into the line on the night 20th/21st in relief of the 5th Bavarian Reserve Divn. Their order of battle from N. to S. is—

76th Infantry Regiment.

73rd Fusilier Regiment.

164th Infantry Regiment.

Each regiment has one battalion in front with 3 companies in the front line, on[e] company in close support. One battalion in support on the line TOURNANT FARM in V.28.b. to CAMERON HOUSE in V.21.a. One battalion in reserve just West of the PASSCHENDAELE-WESTROOSEBEKE ROAD.

Troops available for counter-attack appear to be the 220th Division, which may still be round VIERKAVENHOEK in W.28.b.

16th Bavarian Division, round ROULERS.

5th Bavarian Reserve Division, round OOSTNIEUWKERKE.

It is doubtful whether these troops will be employed in the forthcoming operation, since the limits of our objective are comparatively short and our attack would probably be met by the Divisions in the line.

2. *Defences*

The enemy's defences in this area consist principally of isolated posts in short lengths of trench which are connected by wire entanglements. Many of these isolated posts are round concrete "Pill Boxes." These "Pill Boxes" appear to have been constructed usually only for protection and not for defensive purposes (though some recently captured have loopholes for enfilade fire), the machine gun garrisons coming out from them to take up their positions in shell holes nearby. There is no definite trench line in the area opposite this Corps, and there are no signs of very recent activity, except in the repair and construction of wire entanglements in D.4. and D.10.b.

3. *Artillery*

The Artillery opposed to this Corps belongs principally to three Groups, one Group East of PASSCHENDAELE, one Group round MOORSLEDE and one Group round WATERDANHOEK. There has been an increase in the enemy's artillery activity lately, probably owing to the more settled conditions under which he has been operating.

If the attack is expected and the enemy considers that our objective will not be too limited, it is probable that some of the heavy artillery batteries will be withdrawn and will not come into action until the situation after our attack has been cleared up. As soon as the enemy knows the situation these batteries will take up position in the open near roads which are passable for artillery, concentrating on area shoots, without registration.

V. TACTICAL CONDITIONS

The conditions in the present area of operations differ widely from those experienced by the Canadian Corps in previous fighting this year. The following are some of the main features:

(i) The nature of the soil does not permit of the construction of deep dug-outs, consequently the Germans have had recourse to concrete structures known as "Pill Boxes" erected usually inside buildings. Every house or farm must therefore be looked upon as a possible strong point or machine gun emplacement, and special measures taken to deal with each one. These concrete structures present a small target and are very difficult actually to destroy with even the heaviest artillery. The destructive bombardment of these "Pill Boxes" should accordingly be arranged to take place not more than 24 or 36 hours before zero with the object of shell-shocking the garrison, who must then be prevented from being relieved by intense and systematic harassing fire of field artillery and machine guns. In the assault the infantry must keep very close to the barrage and work rapidly round the flanks.

Every "Pill Box" will probably be of value to us after reaching the objective, as affording the only cover to be had.

(ii) The enemy has no longer any well defined trench system, but relies on a system of defence in depth, particularly by machine guns in "Pill Boxes" and strong points, with troops held ready for immediate counter-attack. Recently owing to our policy of making short advances with very limited objectives he has modified his former plan of holding the front system lightly and employing large formations for immediate counter-attack. The German tendency now is to thicken up the garrisons of his front system, bringing up the machine guns of reserve units, with the object of breaking up our advance at the outset. This gives us a chance of inflicting heavy loss on him by systematic bombardment of the forward area in conjunction with a comprehensive system of harassing fire to isolate the forward garrisons.

The immediate counter-attack by reserve battalions of regiments in the line is still to be expected, but large formations such as counter-attack divisions are not likely to be employed as a whole until after the enemy has had time to clear up the situation and to organize thorough preparation.

(iii) The systematic mopping up of areas and the advance by the "leap-frog" system are more than ever essential. In view of the heavy going the only way to give the troops destined for the final objective a fair chance of defending it successfully against counter-attack is to spare them all possible fighting before they get there.

(iv) Present conditions call for a large degree of initiative and resource on the part of all unit commanders. To enable them to use their initiative all such commanders from the platoon upwards must have a reserve in their own hands capable of being quickly put in to fill a gap, to form a front to a flank or to work round the flank of some hostile centre of resistance which is holding up the advance of their own or an adjoining unit.

(v) A feature of the recent fighting here has been the comparatively limited use of hand grenades. One bomb per man is usually sufficient—but rifle grenades have been specially valuable, also smoke rifle grenades (No. 27) for blinding machine guns while working round their flank.

On the other hand the rifle and Lewis gun have much more opportunity than previously, and efforts should be made to get as much S.A.A. [small arms ammunition] forward as possible. Wire in unexpected or concealed positions, round "Pill Boxes" etc., is likely to be met with and will be very difficult to detect previously owing to the churned up ground. It is important that as many men in each platoon should be equipped and trained in the use of the wire breakers (rifle attachment) in accordance with instructions issued for the operations against LENS. Precautions should be taken to preserve these and to make up the number after each fight.

(vi) Much of the ground in front of us is very boggy and almost impassible [*sic*]. This is the case in practically every valley such as the RAVEBEEK, where the stream has been clogged by shell fire and has no outlet. This makes it imperative for the main advance to be made along the high ground, the number of men sent through the low ground being only sufficient to investigate and mop up any "Pill Boxes" or strong points known to exist there.

(vii) Special attention is directed to the valuable "Notes on Operations" previously circulated by Second Army Headquarters, which should be carefully studied by all Officers.

VI. ARTILLERY

The Artillery plan and instructions for bombardments and barrages have already been issued by G.O.C.R.A. [General Officer Commanding Royal Artillery], Canadian Corps (Artillery Order No. 91 dated 21-10-17). The attack will be made under a creeping barrage, the initial line of which will be put down 150 yards in front of our front line and move forward by lifts of 50 yards at a rate of 100 yards in 8 minutes. It is essential to adopt lifts of 50 yards in view of the heavy nature of the ground which prevents the infantry closing up to the barrage after each lift sufficiently quickly to stop machine guns etc. coming to life in between lifts if the latter are 100 yards each. The protective barrage will lift off the Intermediate Objective (DOTTED RED Line) at Z plus 156 minutes.

If the wind is favourable smoke will be used to obscure the enemy's observation and machine guns about CREST FARM and MEETCHEELE.

During the practice barrages on the days previous to "Attack Day" Divisions will take special note of the localities on which the enemy's retaliatory barrage falls, with a view to the subsequent assembly and movement of troops.

VII. MACHINE GUNS

Preliminary instructions for machine gun barrage etc. have been issued under Canadian Corps G.817/2520-3 dated 20th October, 1917.

The complete scheme will be issued shortly.

The machine guns available will allow of 1 to 30 yards of barrage front.

VIII. ROYAL FLYING CORPS

1. A contact patrol aeroplane will be furnished by No. 21 Squadron RFC to fly and call for flares at Zero plus 4 hours. The contact aeroplane will be marked as follows:

In addition to the ordinary Squadron marking (a dumb-bell on the fusilage behind the national marking, and a big "A" in front of the national marking) contact machines will have a small black rectangular plaque extending behind the lower plane on each side.

2. The most advanced infantry will signal their position on the aeroplane calling by Klaxon horn or showing white lights by lighting WHITE flares and signalling with Watson fans. Flares must be lit in the bottom of trenches or in the bottom on shell-holes. The extreme importance of communicating their position must be impressed upon all units as one of the chief difficulties in the present type of fighting is the accurate location of our own front line, and unless the Infantry make their position know[n] they cannot expect effective support from our artillery in case of emergency.

3. In addition to the contact aeroplane a patrol will be furnished to fly at ZERO plus one hour and remain in the air the whole day for the special purpose of locating and informing the artillery of any signs of counter-attacks. This machine has no special markings.

4. When the contact patrol machine has got all possible information, messages and maps will be dropped at SALVATION CORNER (I.6.d.0.8.) for the 3rd Canadian Division, and on the MAIN SQUARE, YPRES (I.8.c.5.9) for the 4th Canadian Division, and a full report will be wired to Headquarters as soon as possible after the landing at the aerodrome followed by a written report. Contact patrol observers will visit both Divisional Headquarters previous to "Attacking Day" to ensure that they are precisely informed as to the situation and objectives of our own troops and are provided with accurate and up-to-date maps of the area.

IX. CONSOLIDATION

1. The main objects to be kept in view in organizing the consolidation in each stage of the PASSCHENDAELE operations are:

(i)   To provide the best defence against counter-attack.
(ii) To secure the best line from which to start the next advance.

2. The limits of the RED objectives do not permit of depriving the Germans of their observation over our back area—but the main line of defence should be sited so as to be out of sight of the enemy's direct observation and machine gun fire—from CREST FARM and MEETCHEELE in particular. This would appear to indicate the best line as being roughly from DECLINE COPSE along the RED DOTTED line with outposts pushed as far out in front as possible. On the right flank the outpost line should not be further over (i.e. East of) the Crest of the Main BROODSEINDE-PASSCHENDAELE Ridge than will just secure observation into the Valley of the BROUBEEK.

3. It is above all necessary that wherever the most advanced line of posts is situated it should be definitely located by the personal reconnaissance of Brigade or Divisional Staff Officers, and Commanders are responsible that this is done at the earliest opportunity. If the lower formations can not give a satisfactory report it becomes the duty of the superior Staff to find out for themselves.

4. The construction of communication trenches is difficult and should be confined to exposed localities such as forward slopes which are in full view. Elsewhere their places must be taken by bath-matted tracks. The rapid pushing forward of these is of extreme importance and plans for them should be included in all schemes for consolidation.

5. The establishment of forward dumps required for the next advance must be undertaken at the earliest possible moment.

6. The principles of anti-aircraft defence laid down in Canadian Corps G.810/2520-1 dated October 20th, 1917, will be applied in the plan of consolidation.

X. ANTI-AIRCRAFT DEFENCE

The scheme for anti-aircraft defence of the area has already been issued in Canadian Corps G.810/2520-1, dated 20th October, 1917.

It must be clearly understood that the duty of defending themselves against low flying aircraft rests with the Infantry. Our own aeroplanes cannot effectively deal with them but recent experience on this front has conclusively proved that rifle and machine gun fire from the ground is most effective for the purpose. Four or five hostile machines have been brought down by these means in one day.

XI. LIGHT SIGNALS

1. S.O.S. Signal

On the Second Army front the S.O.S. is a rifle grenade signal showing three parachute lights, viz. RED over GREEN over YELLOW. This signal will remain in force on the Canadian Corps front until further orders.

The S.O.S. on the Fifth Army front is a succession of rifle grenade signals bursting into two RED and two GREEN simultaneously.

2. Signal to Denote Capture of Objective

Three WHITE Very Lights will be fired in quick succession to denote the capture of the intermediate objective and of the RED Line. These lights will be fired only on the order of a Company Commander.

3. It has been found advisable to establish S.O.S. Relay Posts to repeat the signal from the front line back to Supporting Battalions and Artillery.

XII. COMMUNICATIONS

The Details of the system in the Corps Area are given in Appendix "A" [not reproduced here].

1. Buried Cable

Map S.19 (a) shows the existing buried cable system and proposed extensions. It is hoped that the bury will be completed to DAB trench before Attack (6) day, and it is important that it should be pushed on thence up to the main ridge as fast as possible in order to ensure communication with OP's. covering the valleys to the East.

2. Visual Signalling

Very good results have been obtained with the Lucas lamp in recent operations on this front, and all arrangements should be made for their employment to the fullest extent.

3. Pigeons

Good results have been obtained from Pigeons.

4. Runners

Runners have had great difficulty in working over this ground, and special means to assist them have been found necessary in the shape of laying tapes or otherwise making tracks along the best routes for their use.

5. Telephone Restrictions

Attention is directed to the instructions with regard to the use of telephones, issued with Canadian Corps G.823/3-12 dated 21st October, 1917. Too much care cannot be taken to ensure secrecy with regard to impending operations as to which the enemy has on more than one occasion received warning from indiscreet talk on the telephones.

XIII. SYNCHRONIZATION OF WATCHES

Watches will be synchronized in accordance with instructions given in Canadian Corps G.872/2520-10 dated 22nd October, 1917.

XIV. ENGINEER SERVICES AND WORKING PARTIES

The programme of engineer work on roadways, tramways, supply, etc., together with the working parties required from Divisions has been issued separately under Canadian Corps G.859/2520-11 dated 21st October, 1917.

Acknowledgments

Legacy of Valour is the product of considerable co-operation and assistance by numerous individuals and institutions. These include Hurtig Publishers: Mel Hurtig, his editor-in-chief, Elizabeth Munroe, and my editor, Jean Wilson. Also, special recognition must go to the Alberta Foundation for the Literary Arts and its executive director, George Melnyk. Much of my research was undertaken with the help of a grant provided by the Foundation. I consider myself most fortunate to live in a province that does so much for the literary arts.

The research for this book took me right across Canada, and I must thank the helpful and courteous staff members of the following institutions: Provincial Archives of British Columbia; Glenbow Museum; City of Edmonton Archives; Provincial Archives of Alberta; Saskatchewan Archives Board; Provincial Archives of Manitoba; Archives of Ontario; Provincial Archives Canada; Archives nationales de Québec; Provincial Archives of New Brunswick; Public Archives of Prince Edward Island; Public Archives of Nova Scotia. In addition, I wish to recognize the assistance of the Imperial War Museum in London.

One outstanding source of material, and one that deserves more credit than it generally gets, is the 1964 Canadian Broadcasting Corporation radio series, "Flanders Fields," a seventeen-part program produced by J. Frank Willis. It is a treasure trove of first-person recollections of the Great War of 1914-1918. My thanks to Dido Mendl and Gail Donald of the CBC Program Archives in Toronto.

Another excellent source of oral recollections is housed at the Saskatchewan Archives Board in Regina. The interviews of veterans of the 46th (South Saskatchewan) Battalion formed the basis of *The Suicide Battalion* (Hurtig, 1978), by James L. McWilliams and R. James Steel.

I also wish to thank Patricia Robertson of Victoria, for permission to quote from the unpublished memoirs of her grandfather, Brigadier-General George Tuxford. Similarly, Mrs. R.D. Hall of Calgary kindly provided me with a portion of the unpublished memoirs of her father, Sergeant-Major Donald Patterson, who served at Passchendaele with the 39th Battery, Canadian Field Artillery.

George Sassoon of Warminster, Wiltshire, England, was kind enough to grant permission for the use of an excerpt from Siegfried Sassoon's poem, "Memorial Tablet."

And, last but not least, thanks to some special people: my family, for their interest and encouragement, and my friend, Carolyn Stout, for her moral support during difficult times.

Notes

Published sources are identified in the Notes by author and, if necessary, by a brief description of the title of the work, followed by the page number. A Roman numeral preceding the page number indicates the volume number, where applicable. For full details, refer to the Bibliography.

Unpublished sources involve lengthier entries. For the sake of brevity, however, collection numbers are not listed. The following abbreviations are used for the institutions that house the collections, in alphabetical order:

 AO   Archives of Ontario (Toronto)
 CBC   Canadian Broadcasting Corporation, Program Archives (Toronto)
 GM   Glenbow Museum (Calgary)
 PAA   Provincial Archives of Alberta (Edmonton)
 PABC Provincial Archives of British Columbia (Victoria)
 PAC   Public Archives Canada (Ottawa)
 PAM   Provincial Archives of Manitoba (Winnipeg)
 PANS Public Archives of Nova Scotia (Halifax)
 SAB   Saskatchewan Archives Board (Regina)

INTRODUCTION
 1 Lloyd George IV/2110; Churchill *1916-1918* 333; Taylor *World War* 194; Liddell Hart *Real* 361.
 2 Terraine *Haig* 345, 370.

PART ONE

Chapter 1
 1 Charteris *GHQ* 169.
 2 Lloyd George II/866-67.
 3 Rowland 387.
 4 Taylor *Lloyd George* 102; Hankey 555.
 5 Riddell 141, 156, 157.
 6 Rowland 343; Riddell 189; Hankey 556.
 7 Taylor *Lloyd George* 108; McCormick 108.
 8 Owen 327; Taylor *Lloyd George* 117; Riddell 218; Lloyd George VI/3423; Rose 201.
 9 Lloyd George I/372-78.
 10 Spears *Prelude* 33, 34; Blake 122; Robertson *Soldiers* I/256; Repington I/449-50, 457.
 11 Blake 122; Repington I/504, 514.
 12 Robertson *Private* 248; *Soldiers* I/198-203.
 13 Blake 96; Charteris *Haig* 185-86.
 14 Ibid., 35.
 15 Duncan 23; Charteris *GHQ* 135, 189.

16 Duff Cooper I/327–28; Duncan 122.
17 Ibid., 65; Terraine *Road* 275.
18 Charteris *GHQ* 11, 50, 122.
19 Charteris *Haig* 65, 152, 387–88.
20 Ibid., 40, 54; Terraine *Road* 290.
21 Charteris *GHQ* 7.
22 Blake 217; Duff Cooper II/429; Duncan 90.
23 Blake 157–58; Lloyd George II/874.
24 Taylor *Lloyd George* 118, 121, 139.
25 Richard Lloyd George 171; Lloyd George IV/2266–67, VI/3383.
26 Riddell 174, 297; Lloyd George II/543, 779, 782.
27 Blake 126, 166, 195; Gough *Fifth* 174.
28 Blake 166–67.
29 Ibid., 251; Robertson *Soldiers* I/185.

Chapter 2
1 Falls *Appendices* 1.
2 Blake 122.
3 Ibid., 184.
4 Churchill *1915* 30.
5 Charteris *Haig* 77; Terraine *Road* 10; Charteris *GHQ* 74; Blake 120.
6 Charteris *GHQ* 132.
7 Terraine *Road* 14.
8 Lloyd George IV/2119–20, 2116–17; Blake 181.
9 Spears *Prelude* 31; Duff Cooper II/13.
10 Lloyd George III/1379; Robertson *Soldiers* II/203; Duff Cooper II/20; Hankey 594; Blake 246.
11 Roskill 351.
12 Spears *Prelude* 41.
13 Falls *Appendices* 4–6.
14 Charteris *GHQ* 181.
15 Falls *Appendices* 13–15.
16 Ibid.
17 Blake 191, 195.
18 Ibid., 192.
19 Bean IV/ii; Edmonds 11; Lloyd George III/1497–98; Duff Cooper II/32.
20 *See* Falls *Appendices* Appendix 8.
21 Spears *Prelude* 46; Blake 193, 194.
22 Roskill 361.
23 Spears *Prelude* 516.
24 Taylor *Lloyd George* 139.
25 Duff Cooper II/41; Charteris *Haig* 243.
26 Taylor *Lloyd George* 146.
27 Duff Cooper II/44.
28 Ibid.
29 Ibid., 45, 46.

30 Hankey 615-16.
31 Spears *Prelude* 143; Duff Cooper II/46; Robertson *Soldiers* II/211.
32 Roskill 362-63.
33 Duff Cooper II/47.
34 Ibid., 48; Hankey 616.
35 Ibid.
36 Falls *Appendices* 65; Duff Cooper II/58.
37 Lloyd George VI/3398; Blake 204.
38 Duff Cooper II/57, 60; Blake 203.
39 Duff Cooper II/78; Spears *Prelude* 149.
40 Ibid., 547; Blake 203.
41 Spears *Prelude* 550, 558; Charteris *GHQ* 202.
42 Terraine *Road* 56.
43 Spears *Prelude* 565, 569.
44 Hankey 628; Lennox 114.
45 Spears *Prelude* 189; Duff Cooper II/66.
46 Ibid., 73.
47 Ibid., 74; Roskill 368.
48 Spears *Prelude* 369.
49 Lennox 120.
50 Charteris *GHQ* 219; Terraine *Road* 72.
51 Ibid., 73.
52 Taylor *Lloyd George* 157; Lloyd George III/1518; Duff Cooper II/105.
53 Lloyd George III/1538-41; Roskill 385.
54 Terraine *Haig* 292-93.
55 Duff Cooper II/105.
56 Robertson *Soldiers* II/235.
57 Blake 228; Duff Cooper II/107.
58 Edmonds 23; Blake 230.
59 Ibid., 227.
60 Ibid., 232; Duff Cooper II/112-13.
61 Spears *Two Men* 87, 97.
62 Blake 234, 244, 245; Duff Cooper II/118; Charteris *GHQ* 225.
63 Blake 112, 125, 246.
64 Repington I/440.
65 Duff Cooper II/101.
66 Ibid.; Blake 222; Edmonds 24-25.

Chapter 3
1 Gilbert 60, 60fn; Riddell 249; Hankey 735.
2 Robertson *Soldiers* I/313.
3 Repington I/455.
4 Blake 233-34.
5 Terraine *Road* 117; Blake 238.
6 Ibid., 130.
7 Ibid., 239.

8 Ibid., 236-37.
9 Ibid., 237-38.
10 Terraine *Road* 137-40, 145.
11 Lloyd George IV/2158; Terraine *Haig* 333.
12 Lloyd George IV/2192; Terraine *Road* 115, 126.
13 Lloyd George IV/2168, 2170, 2174, 2197.
14 Blake 240; Duff Cooper II/125; Robertson *Soldiers* II/242fn.
15 Patterson 173.
16 Lloyd George IV/2162; Blake 240; Hankey 632, 679.
17 Duff Cooper II/129; Robertson *Soldiers* II/248.
18 Ibid.; Hankey 683.
19 Lloyd George IV/2204, 2287-89.
20 Terraine *Road* 203; Blake 246-47.
21 Terraine *Road* 203; Blake 247.

PART TWO

Chapter 4
1 Duff Cooper I/206.
2 Terraine *Haig* 250; Falls *Military Operations* 21.
3 Terraine *Road* 137-38.
4 Duff Cooper II/121.
5 Ibid., 102.
6 Terraine *Road* 185-87.
7 Edmonds 17, 406, 408.
8 Wolff 102; Lloyd 154.
9 Terraine *Haig* 337; Repington II/606; Edmonds 127fn.
10 Ibid.
11 Gough *Fifth* 192.
12 Ibid., 193-94.
13 Terraine *Haig* 338-39.
14 Edmonds 127fn.
15 Hankey 409.
16 Bean IV/700; Duguid 174.
17 Terraine *Haig* 340.
18 *See* Terraine *Impacts* 106.
19 Terraine *Road* 207, 211.
20 Blake 249.
21 Charteris *GHQ* 236-38.

Chapter 5
1 Macdonald 110-11.
2 Blake 249; Gough *Fifth* 201.
3 Farrar-Hockley 222; Blake 250; Charteris *GHQ* 241.
4 Charteris *Haig* 272; Terraine *Road* 205.
5 Boraston 116; Terraine *Road* 216.
6 Ibid., 220.

7 Fuller *Tanks* 38.
8 Wolff 108; Swinton 263; Liddell Hart *Reputations* 135.
9 Terraine *Road* 240; Gough *Fifth* 205, 215.
10 Ibid., 202.
11 Macdonald 187-88.
12 Ibid., 124, 186-87, 211.
13 Gibbs 475, 476.
14 Ibid., 477.
15 Ibid., 473, 485.
16 Gough *Fifth* 205, *Soldiering* 140.
17 Terraine *Road* 228-29, 236.
18 Lloyd George IV/2212fn; Duff Cooper II/144.

Chapter 6
1 Riddell 263.
2 Blake 251.
3 Terraine *Road* 228.
4 Duff Cooper II/145; Terraine *Road* 237.
5 Lloyd George IV/2292-93.
6 Robertson *Soldiers* I/270.
7 Blake 251-52, 256.
8 Hankey 693.
9 Blake 253.
10 Duff Cooper II/153.
11 Ibid., 157-58, 162; Hankey 697; Lloyd George IV/2222-23.
12 Owen 401; Hankey 697.
13 Robertson *Soldiers* II/253-54.
14 Duff Cooper II/158.
15 Fuller *Decisive* II/360.
16 Terraine *Road* 217, 230, 237-38.
17 Blake 315; Duff Cooper II/156.
18 Charteris *GHQ* 250; Terraine *Road* 221-22; Bean IV/726.
19 Edmonds iv.
20 Bean IV/878; Terraine *Road* 274.
21 Gough *Fifth* 212; Charteris *GHQ* 257.
22 Blake 256.
23 Ibid., 259.
24 Bean IV/877fn.
25 Terraine *Road* 281.
26 Ibid., 282.
27 Blake 257; Terraine *Road* 283.

Chapter 7
1 Terraine *White Heat* 220.
2 Charteris *GHQ* 258-59; Bean IV/884.
3 Boraston 127-28.

4 Lloyd George IV/2141, 2215.
5 Charteris *GHQ* 77, 136.
6 Macdonald 112.
7 Charteris *Haig* 89, *GHQ* 233.
8 Duff Cooper II/198-99.
9 Blake 256, 257.
10 Ludendorff II/89-92, 101-2.
11 Blake 258-59.
12 Ibid.; Lloyd George IV/2102; Rowland 413.
13 Bean IV/928; Blake 257-58.
14 Charteris *GHQ* 259.
15 Blake 260; Boraston 129.
16 Terraine *Road* 297-98.
17 Bean IV/912.
18 Cutlack 202; Bean IV/890, 931.
19 Ibid., 881.
20 Birdwood 318.
21 Boraston 130; Blake 260; Terraine *Road* 305.
22 Duff Cooper II/134, 165; Davidson 115; Spears *Two* 126; *See* Terraine *Road* 349-50 and *To Win* 11-12.
23 *See* Repington II/98-103.
24 Terraine *Road* 301; Second Army/Canadian Corps, 13/10/17, Canadian Corps Records (hereafter Corps Records), PAC.

PART THREE

Chapter 8
1 Currie/J.G. Rattray, 22/4/20, A.W. Currie Papers (hereafter Currie Papers), PAC.
2 Currie/A. Fraser, 16/9/20, loc. cit.; Dancocks 18.
3 McKenzie 109.
4 Diary, 3/5/17, Currie Papers, PAC.
5 Dancocks 285.
6 "First Canadian Division Report on the Vimy Ridge-Willerval-Arleux-Fresnoy Operations, April 9-May 5, 1917," Currie Papers, PAC.
7 Currie/J.G. Rattray, 22/4/20, loc. cit.
8 Urquhart 170; Dancocks 106.
9 Urquhart 158; Currie/McGillicuddy, n.d., Currie Papers, PAC.
10 Currie/J.L. Ralston, 9/2/28, loc. cit.; Dancocks 99.
11 Currie/J.G. Rattray, 22/4/20, Currie Papers, PAC.
12 Terraine *Road* 234.
13 Currie/J.L. Ralston, 9/2/28, Currie Papers, PAC; Duff Cooper II/149.
14 Currie/J.G. Rattray, 22/4/20, Currie Papers, PAC.
15 Dancocks 110.
16 Currie/F. Livesay, 26/1/33, Currie Papers, PAC; Currie/J.G. Rattray, 22/4/20, loc. cit.

17 Blake 257.
18 Gough *Fifth* 151.
19 Currie/F. Livesay, 26/1/33, Currie Papers, PAC; script for radio address, 9/11/33, loc. cit.; Goodspeed *Vimy* 114; Urquhart 174.
20 Macdonell/H. Cameron, 27/10/34, A.C. Macdonell Papers, AO.
21 Ibid.

Chapter 9
1 Nicholson *CEF* 314.
2 Radcliffe/division commanders, 16/10/17, Corps Records, PAC.
3 Report on operations, 16/11/17, Currie Papers, PAC.
4 "Causes of Success and Failure," 20/11/17, Corps Records, PAC.
5 Radcliffe/GOCRA et al., 16/10/17, loc. cit.
6 Urquhart 173-74.
7 Pope 59.
8 Swettenham *McNaughton* 111.
9 Diary, 17/10/17, Currie Papers, PAC.
10 McKenzie 110.
11 Canadian Corps/Fourth Division, 15/10/17, Corps Records, PAC.
12 McKenzie 111; diary, 30/10/17, Currie Papers, PAC.
13 McWilliams 108; Corrigall 153.
14 Hamilton 129.
15 Currie/F. Livesay, 17/4/20, Currie Papers, PAC; Dancocks 113.
16 A.C. Macdonell/H. Cameron, 27/10/34, A.C. Macdonell Papers, AO.
17 Barnes 73; A.F. Duguid/H.W. Timmins, 2/9/25, Corps Records, PAC.
18 Canadian Corps Artillery report, n.d., loc. cit.
19 Ibid.
20 Ibid.; McWilliams 110; unpublished memoirs, courtesy Mrs. R.D. Hall, Calgary.
21 Ibid.
22 Second Division Artillery report, 30/10/17, Corps Records, PAC.
23 Canadian Corps Artillery report, n.d., loc. cit.
24 Debney taped interview, PAA; "Flanders Fields," Production 10, produced by J. Frank Willis, 1964 (hereafter "Flanders Fields"), CBC.
25 Unpublished memoirs, G.S. Howard Papers, SAB; A.F. Duguid/J.E. Edmonds, 20/11/45, Corps Records, PAC.
26 Currie/C. Swayne, 23/1/18, Currie Papers, PAC.
27 First Division Engineers' report, n.d., Corps Records, PAC.
28 Kerry 140; Macdonald 217.
29 Duguid 161.
30 Nicholson *CEF* 313.
31 Warren 102; MacDonald 112.
32 Hazlewood/father, 10/11/17, F.N. Hazlewood Papers, PAC.
33 "Flanders Fields," CBC.
34 Duguid 162.
35 Unpublished ms, J. Swettenham Papers, PAC; Moir 27, 28.

36 "Flanders Fields," CBC.
37 Macphail 101.
38 Keegan 266.
39 Ibid., 264-66.
40 Macphail 105, 109; Hutchinson 135.
41 Unpublished memoirs, W. Bapty Papers, PABC; Reid 162.

Chapter 10
1 Currie/Second Army, 16, 17/10/17, Corps Records, PAC.
2 Dancocks 144.
3 Currie/J.G. Rattray, 22/4/20, Currie Papers, PAC; Currie/F. Livesay, 26/1/33, loc. cit.; Urquhart 178.
4 Currie/J.G. Rattray, 22/4/20, Currie Papers, PAC.
5 Currie/F. Livesay, 26/1/33, loc. cit.
6 Currie/W. Beattie, 8/2/28, loc. cit.
7 Ibid.
8 Dancocks 114.
9 Currie/W. Beattie, 8/2/28, Currie Papers, PAC; Fraser 78.
10 McKerchar taped interview, SAB.
11 Bird *Ghosts* 73; McWilliams 109.
12 "Flanders Fields," CBC.
13 Unpublished memoirs, A. Turner Papers, GM.
14 Kilpatrick/parents, 6/11/17, G. Kilpatrick Papers, PAC; Barry 31.
15 Bird *Thirteen* 11; "Flanders Fields," CBC; McWilliams 108.
16 Diary, H. McGill Papers, GM.
17 Macdonald 212.
18 Diary, H. McGill Papers, GM.
19 Diary, 30/10/17, L.V. Shier Papers, AO; Kilpatrick/parents, 6/11/17, G. Kilpatrick Papers, PAC; Adamson/M. Adamson, 23/10/17, A. Adamson Papers, PAC; Roy *Bravery* 55.
20 Unpublished memoirs, G.S. Tuxford Papers, SAB; scrapbook, P. Villiers Papers, PAC.
21 Burns taped interview, SAB; "Flanders Fields," CBC.
22 McWilliams 111; "Flanders Fields," CBC.
23 Quelch/mother, 25/11/17, J.W. Quelch Papers, PAM.
24 Bennett 74.
25 "Flanders Fields," CBC.
26 *Letters* 295.
27 Bean V/676.

Chapter 11
1 McWilliams 114.
2 Third Division report, 5/12/17, Corps Records, PAC.
3 Nicholson *CEF* 319; artillery order 93, 24/10/17, Corps Records, PAC.
4 Unpublished memoirs, A. Turner Papers, GM; J. Quelch/father, 29/10/17, J.W. Quelch Papers, PAM.
5 Toronto *Daily Star* 14/3/19; Bennett 75.

6 Ibid., 79; 4th CMR report, n.d., Corps Records, PAC; "Flanders Fields," CBC.
7 Ibid.
8 Ibid.
9 Bennett 85.
10 *See* Mathieson 123-25.
11 Bennett 86; McFarland/E.W. McQuay, 4/11/17, 23/12/17, E.W. McQuay Papers, AO.
12 "Flanders Fields," CBC.
13 52nd Battalion war diary, 26/10/17, PAM.
14 Hill/V. Odlum, 30/10/17, V. Odlum papers, PAC.
15 McKerchar taped interview, SAB.
16 46th Battalion report, n.d., Corps Records, PAC; McWilliams 114.
17 Ibid.
18 Ibid., 115.
19 Burns taped interview, SAB.
20 McWilliams 118.
21 McKerchar taped interview, SAB.
22 McWilliams 119.
23 Ibid.; unpublished memoirs, A. Turner Papers, GM.
24 McWilliams 119.
25 Tenth Brigade report, 1/11/17, Corps records, PAC; McWilliams 123.
26 44th Battalion report, 30/10/17, Corps Records, PAC.
27 Russenholt 122.
28 Ibid.
29 47th Battalion report, n.d., Corps Records, PAC.
30 44th Battalion report, 30/10/17, loc. cit.
31 Diary, 26/10/17, Currie Papers, PAC; Second Army/Canadian Corps, 27/10/17, Corps Records, PAC.
32 Gough *Fifth* 213-14.
33 Terraine *Road* 313.
34 Quelch/father, 29/10/17, J.W. Quelch Papers, PAM.
35 Corps medical report, 28/10/17, Corps Records, PAC; Eleventh 83; 3rd Canadian Field Ambulance report, 15/11/17, Corps Records, PAC.
36 Eleventh 83; unpublished memoirs, A. Turner Papers, GM.
37 Gunn 81-83.
38 McGill/E. Griffis, 28/10/17, H. McGill Papers, GM.

Chapter 12
1 Nicholson *CEF* 320.
2 Hahn 48.
3 Diary, 29/10/17, Currie Papers, PAC.
4 McKenzie 169.
5 Hayes 89.
6 85th Battalion report, n.d., Corps Records, PAC.
7 Ibid.; "Flanders Fields," CBC.

8 Ibid.; 78th Battalion report, n.d., Corps Records, PAC; Kirkaldy/J.H. MacBrien, 4/11/17, loc. cit.
9 McEvoy 82.
10 Ibid., 79.
11 72nd Battalion report, n.d., Corps Records, PAC.
12 McEvoy 83.
13 72nd Battalion report, n.d., Corps Records, PAC.
14 McEvoy 83.
15 Twelfth Brigade report, 17/11/17, Corps Records, PAC.
16 Adamson/G.C. McDonald, 5/11/17, A. Adamson Papers, PAC; Hodder-Williams 254.
17 Adamson/G.C. McDonald, 5/11/17, A. Adamson Papers, PAC; Hodder-Williams 257.
18 "Flanders Fields," CBC.
19 Hodder-Williams 273; Williams *PPCLI* 24.
20 PPCLI report, 4/11/17, Corps Records, PAC.
21 Adamson/M. Adamson, 2,8/11/17, A. Adamson Papers, PAC.
22 49th Battalion report, 4/11/17, Corps Records, PAC.
23 Stevens 101-2.
24 49th Battalion report, 4/11/17, Corps Records, PAC.
25 Ibid.
26 Edmonton *Journal* 12/8/85.
27 Mathieson 187; Roy *Bravery* 57.
28 Mathieson 188.
29 Ibid., 187.
30 Ibid., 188.
31 Ibid., 189.
32 Ibid.
33 Ibid.; Roy *Bravery* 59-60, 63.
34 Ibid., 60.
35 2nd CMR report, n.d., Corps Records, PAC.
36 "Flanders Fields," CBC; Mathieson 190-91.
37 McNeil 209.
38 A.F. Duguid/J.E. Edmonds, 20/11/45, Corps Records, PAC.
39 "Causes of Success and Failure," 20/11/17, loc. cit.
40 Corps medical report, 2/11/17, loc. cit.; "Flanders Fields," CBC.
41 Diary, A.I.M. Taylor Papers, PANS.

Chapter 13
1 Nicholson *CEF* 323.
2 Gough *Fifth* 214; diary, 30/10/17, Currie Papers, PAC.
3 Second Army/Canadian Corps, 1/11/17, Corps Records, PAC; Blake 262; Terraine *Road* 314-15.
4 "Causes of Success and Failure," 20/11/17, Corps Records, PAC.
5 *Canada in the Great World War* 240.
6 Diary, 30/10/17, L.V. Shier Papers, AO.
7 Diary, 3/11/17, R. Smith Papers, PAC.

8 Roy *Fraser* 16-17.
9 McKenzie 113-14.
10 Kilpatrick/parents, 6/11/17, G. Kilpatrick Papers, PAC.
11 Ninth Brigade report, 5/11/17, Corps Records, PAC.
12 Bird *Ghosts* 79.
13 "Flanders Fields," CBC.
14 Diary, 3/11/17, Currie Papers, PAC.
15 *Canada in the Great World War* 239.

Chapter 14
1 McGill/E. Griffis, 6/11/17, H. McGill Papers, GM.
2 Goodspeed *Battle* 203-4.
3 Ibid., 206, 209.
4 First Division report, n.d., Corps Records, PAC.
5 First Brigade report, 15/11/17, loc. cit.; 1st Battalion report, 13/11/17, loc. cit.
6 Ibid.
7 Macdonell/H. Macdonald, 14/11/17, A.C. Macdonell Papers, AO.
8 "Flanders Fields," CBC; Barry 32; 26th Battalion report, 26/11/17, Corps Records, PAC.
9 Barry 32.
10 "Flanders Fields," CBC.
11 Hewitt 22.
12 Calder 161; *Canada in the Great World War* 243.
13 Sixth Brigade report, 20/11/17, Corps Records, PAC.
14 Ibid.
15 Badger/A. Ross, 5/2/18, 28th Battalion report, loc. cit.
16 Calder 159.
17 Gould *26th* 29.
18 "Flanders Fields," CBC.
19 MacDonald 118.
20 *Canada in the Great World War* 255.
21 Diary, 6/11/17, Currie Papers, PAC; Hopkins 176.
22 Macdonald 229.
23 Currie/W. Beattie, 8/2/28, Currie Papers, PAC.
24 Second Army/Canadian Corps, 7/11/17, Corps Records, PAC; Blake 264.
25 Charteris *GHQ* 266.

Chapter 15
1 Terraine *Road* 321.
2 Calder 162-63.
3 Ibid., 163.
4 "Flanders Fields," CBC.
5 Fetherstonhaugh *13th* 213; Lapointe 74-75.
6 Diary, 8/11/17, Currie Papers, PAC.
7 Second Brigade report, n.d., Corps Records, PAC.

8 Ibid.
9 Ibid.
10 Ibid.
11 Fourth Brigade report, n.d., loc. cit.
12 Second Brigade report, n.d., loc. cit.
13 Diary, 10/11/17, Currie Papers, PAC.
14 Nicholson *CEF* 326; diary, 10/11/17, Currie Papers, PAC; Bean IV/935.
15 *Canada in the Great World War* 257; Reid 165.
16 Toronto *Daily Star* 23/5/19.

Chapter 16
1 Terraine *Road* 328.
2 Nicholson *CEF* 327; Edmonds 359; Currie/J.G. Rattray, 22/4/20, Currie Papers, PAC.
3 Hutchison 116; RCR report, n.d., Corps Records, PAC; Fetherstonhaugh *24th* 184; Duguid 504; Gould *Baisieux* 72.
4 Fetherstonhaugh *13th* 214.
5 Gunn 89; Corrigall 165.
6 "Flanders Fields," CBC; Jenner taped interview, SAB; Gunn 95-96.
7 Allen/mother, 29/12/17, Alma Russell Papers, PABC; Quelch/mother, 9/11/17, J.W. Quelch Papers, PAM; unpublished memoirs, D.E. McIntyre Papers, PAC; unpublished memoirs, A. Turner Papers, GM; Nicholson *Gunners* 306; "Flanders Fields," CBC.
8 Anderson, Bagley, Johnson taped interviews, GM.
9 "Flanders Fields," CBC.
10 *Letters* 242; "Flanders Fields," CBC.
11 Gunn 94.
12 *Letters* 245.
13 Stevens 105; "Flanders Fields," CBC.
14 Unpublished memoirs, A. Turner Papers, GM.
15 *Canada in the Great World War* 227; Armstrong/Currie, 12/11/17, Currie Papers, PAC.
16 *World War* 1198; Currie/J.J. Creelman, 30/11/17, Currie Papers, PAC; Currie/C. Swayne, 23/1/18, loc. cit.; Currie/F.B. McCurdy, 31/1/18, loc. cit.
17 Currie/J.G. Rattray, 22/4/20, loc. cit.
18 Currie/G. Perley, 3/12/17, loc. cit.

Chapter 17
1 McKenzie 180.

PART FOUR

Chapter 18
1 Duff Cooper, II/175; Terraine *Road* 328, 346-47.
2 Bean IV/941; Ludendorff II/164; Edmonds xiii.
3 Ludendorff II/106; Terraine *Road* 329; Edmonds xv.

4 Ludendorff II/106, 161, 163, 164, 165.
5 Ibid., 165; Duff Cooper II/247.

Chapter 19
1 Terraine *To Win* 27; Blake 261.
2 Ibid.
3 Callwell II/18.
4 Lloyd George IV/2384; Robertson *Soldiers* II/257.
5 Terraine *Road* 297.
6 Roskill 446-47; Lloyd George IV/2378.
7 Callwell II/7, 10.
8 Hankey 695; Owen 431.
9 Charteris *GHQ* 262-63; Hankey 718.
10 Roskill 451.
11 Hankey 716, 719.
12 Lloyd George IV/2393.
13 Ibid., 2402-3; Repington II/132.
14 Charteris *GHQ* 267.
15 Duff Cooper II/186-87; Owen 433.
16 Duff Cooper II/185-86; Blake 264.
17 Duff Cooper II/203.
18 Repington II/132; Riddell 294.
19 Williams *Byng* 175; Byng lecture, 26/2/18, Currie Papers, PAC.
20 Ibid.; Lloyd George IV/2255-56, V/2442.
21 Charteris *GHQ* 246.
22 Lloyd George V/2614; McCormick 124.
23 Duff Cooper II/183.
24 Gilbert 204; Hankey 739.
25 Maurice 94; Lloyd George IV/2242-44.
26 Charteris *GHQ* 274; Lloyd George V/2619.
27 Owen 445-46.
28 Lloyd George V/2634.
29 Repington II/180.
30 Ibid., 197.
31 Gilbert 233; Robertson *Soldiers* I/319.
32 Terraine *To Win* 34.
33 McCormick 134.
34 Richard Lloyd George 188; Robertson *Soldiers* I/317; Ludendorff I/214; Gilbert 222.
35 Duff Cooper I/196, II/210; Lloyd George V/2834; Charteris *Haig* 294.
36 Duff Cooper II/208.
37 Davidson 62.
38 Robertson *Soldiers* I/324-25.
39 Ibid., 323-24.
40 Maurice 64.
41 Lloyd George II/1034-35.

42 Robertson *Soldiers* II/270.
43 Ibid., 286-87.
44 Duff Cooper II/221; Robertson *Private* 315; Repington II/237.
45 Maurice 66, 68.
46 Robertson *Private* 328, 335.
47 Ibid., 336-37.
48 Blake 90, 290; Hankey 830, 831.
49 Repington II/246; Blake 284; Lloyd George V/2792-93, 2821.
50 Rose 205-6.
51 Blake 283.
52 Charteris *GHQ* 268; Blake 272; Duff Cooper II/198.
53 Farrar-Hockley 239.
54 Duff Cooper II/200.
55 Blake 271.
56 Lennox 239; Roskill 470, 484, 485.
57 Ibid., 387; Hankey 756.

Chapter 20
1 Maurice 71-75.
2 Blake 292.
3 Maurice 139.
4 Duff Cooper II/229; Blake 291.
5 Duff Cooper II/229, 237.
6 Blake 294.
7 Maurice 76.
8 Blake 296.
9 Ibid., 297.
10 Ibid., 297, 298.
11 Owen 436.
12 Blake 297; Duff Cooper II/222.
13 Blake 298, 300.
14 Charteris *GHQ* 294.
15 Ludendorff II/232.
16 Charteris *GHQ* 301.
17 Blake 302, 303, 313-14.
18 Terraine *To Win* 50; Maurice 81.
19 Blake 267-68; Lloyd George IV/2241.
20 Blake 298-99.
21 Ibid., 300, 301.
22 Repington II/272-73.
23 Maurice 120-22.
24 Ibid., 60, 97-99.
25 Ibid., 127.
26 Hankey 787; Roskill 521.
27 Repington II/270; Charteris *GHQ* 312; Blake 309.
28 Ibid., 315; Charteris *GHQ* 314.

29 Roskill 521; Hankey 828.
30 Ludendorff II/326.
31 Terraine *To Win* xvi; Blake 325, 326.
32 Duff Cooper II/378; Blake 324.

Chapter 21
1 Currie/W. Beattie, 8/2/28, Currie Papers, PAC.
2 Pershing 3.
3 Diary, 11,14/4/18, Currie Papers, PAC; Blake 303.
4 Dancocks 135.
5 Borden 138.
6 "Memorandum Respecting the Late Sir Arthur Currie" (hereafter Currie memo), R.L. Borden Papers, PAC.
7 Ibid.
8 Stacey 557-58.
9 Currie memo, R.L. Borden Papers, PAC.
10 Urquhart 226-27.
11 Currie/McGillicuddy, n.d., Currie Papers, PAC.
12 Urquhart 206; Currie/W. Beattie, 8/2/28, Currie Papers, PAC.
13 English 153.
14 Currie/D. Oliver, 30/11/17, Currie Papers, PAC; *Canada in the Great World War* 118; *Canadian Annual Review, 1917* 521; Urquhart 188.
15 *Canadian Annual Review, 1917* 521.
16 Oliver/Currie, 6/12/17, Currie Papers, PAC; Currie/Oliver, 9/12/17, loc. cit.
17 Currie/Perley, 10/12/17, loc. cit.
18 Ibid.; Currie/F.O.W. Loomis, 27/1/18, loc. cit.; Currie/A. Fraser, 7/12/18, loc. cit.
19 Seely 226; Swettenham *McNaughton* 160.
20 Diary, 18/9/18, G.H. Hambley Papers, PAM.
21 Currie/A. Fraser, 7/12/18, Currie Papers, PAC.

CONCLUSION

1 Lloyd George V/2245. *See* Terraine *Haig* 371-72; Terraine *Road* 345.
2 Lloyd George II/1035; Terraine *Road* 345.
3 Gough *Fifth* 175.
4 *See* Carlo D'Este *Decision in Normandy* (New York: E.P. Dutton, 1983) 517.
5 Boraston 136; Edmonds 380.
6 Boraston 135.
7 Lloyd George IV/2265-66; Edmonds iv.
8 Boraston 319.
9 Ibid., 320.
10 Ibid.
11 Ibid., 321.
12 Middlebrook 308, 342-43.

13 Edmonds iv, 359.
14 Nettleton 114.
15 Bird *Thirteen* 13–15.
16 Currie/W. Hearst, 14/11/17, Currie Papers, PAC.
17 Script, 9/11/33, loc. cit.

Bibliography

Barnes, Leslie W.C.S. *Canada's Guns*. Ottawa: Canadian War Museum, 1979.
Barry, A.L. *Batman to Brigadier*. n.p., n.d.
Bean, C.E.W. *Official History of Australia in the War of 1914-1918*. Volumes IV, V. Sydney: Angus & Robertson, 1943.
Bennett, S.G. *The 4th Canadian Mounted Rifles, 1914-1919*. Toronto: Murray, 1926.
Bird, Will R. *Thirteen Years After*. Toronto: Maclean, 1932.
———. *Ghosts Have Warm Hands*. Toronto: Clarke, Irwin, 1968.
Birdwood, Sir William. *Khaki and Gown*. London, Melbourne: Ward, Lock, 1941.
Blake, Robert, ed. *The Private Papers of Douglas Haig, 1914-1919*. London: Eyre & Spottiswoode, 1952.
Boraston, J.H., ed. *Sir Douglas Haig's Despatches*. 1919. Reprint. London: J.M. Dent, 1979.
Borden, Henry, ed. *Robert Laird Borden: His Memoirs*. Volume II. Toronto: McClelland & Stewart, 1969.
Brice, Beatrix. *The Battle Book of Ypres*. London: John Murray, 1927.
Burns, E.L.M. *General Mud*. Toronto: Clarke, Irwin, 1970.
Calder, D.G.S., ed. *The History of the 28th (Northwest) Battalion, CEF*. Regina: Regina Rifle Regiment, 1961.
Callwell, Sir C.E. *Field-Marshal Sir Henry Wilson*. Volumes I, II. London: Cassell, 1927.
Canada in the Great World War. Volume IV. Toronto: United, 1919.
Canadian Annual Review, 1917. Toronto: Canadian Annual Review Limited, 1918.
Charteris, John. *Field-Marshal Earl Haig*. London: Cassell, 1929.
———. *At G.H.Q.* London: Cassell, 1931.
Churchill, Winston. *The World Crisis, 1915*. Toronto: Macmillan, 1923.
———. *The World Crisis, 1916-1918*. Volume II. London: Thornton, Butterworth, 1927.
Corrigall, D.J. *The History of the Twentieth Canadian Battalion*. Toronto: Twentieth Battalion, 1935.
Cutlack, F.M., ed. *War Letters of General Monash*. Sydney: Angus & Robertson, 1935.
Dancocks, Daniel G. *Sir Arthur Currie*. Toronto: Methuen, 1985.
Davidson, Sir John. *Haig, Master of the Battlefield*. London: Peter Nevill, 1953.
Duff Cooper, A. *Haig*. Volumes I, II. Toronto: Macmillan, 1935-36.
Duguid, A.F. *History of the Canadian Grenadier Guards, 1760-1964*. Montreal: Gazette, 1965.
Duncan, G.S. *Douglas Haig as I Knew Him*. London: George Allen & Unwin, 1966.

Edmonds, Sir James. *Military Operations, France and Belgium, 1917*. London: His Majesty's Stationery Office, 1948.
Eleventh Canadian Field Ambulance. *Diary of the Eleventh*. n.p., n.d.
English, John. *Borden*. Toronto: McGraw-Hill Ryerson, 1977.
Falls, Cyril. *Military Operations, France and Belgium, 1917*. London: Macmillan, 1940.
―――. *Military Operations, France and Belgium, 1917: Appendices*. London: Macmillan, 1940.
Farrar-Hockley, Anthony. *Goughie*. London: Hart-Davis, McGibbon, 1975.
Fetherstonhaugh, R.C. *The 13th Battalion, Royal Highlanders of Canada: 1914-1919*. Royal Highlanders of Canada, 1925.
―――, ed. *The 24th Battalion, C.E.F., Victoria Rifles of Canada, 1914-1919*. Montreal: Gazette, 1930.
―――. *The Royal Canadian Regiment, 1883-1933*. 1936. Reprint. Fredericton: Centennial, 1981.
1st Canadian Pioneers. Calgary: 1st Pioneers' Association, 1938.
Fraser, David. *Alanbrooke*. London: Collins, 1982.
Fuller, J.F.C. *Tanks in the Great War*. London: John Murray, 1920.
―――. *The Decisive Battles of the Western World*. Volume II. St. Alban's: Paladin, 1975.
Gibbs, Philip. *Now It Can Be Told*. New York, London: Harper, 1920.
Gilbert, Martin. *Winston S. Churchill*. Companion Volume IV. Part I. London: Heinemann, 1977.
Goodspeed, D.J. *The Armed Forces of Canada, 1867-1967*. Ottawa: Queen's Printer, 1967.
―――. *The Road Past Vimy*. Toronto: Macmillan, 1969.
―――. *Battle Royal*. Toronto: Royal Regiment of Canada Association, 1979.
Gough, Sir Hubert. *The Fifth Army*. London: Hodder & Stoughton, 1931.
―――. *Soldiering On*. London: Arthur Baker, 1954.
Gould, L. McLeod. *From B.C. to Baisieux*. Victoria: Thos. R. Cusack, 1919.
Gould, R.W., and S.K. Smith. *The Story of the Fighting 26th*. Saint John: Saint John News, n.d.
Graves, Sandham. *The Lost Diary*. Victoria: Charles F. Banfield, 1941.
Gunn, J.N., and E.E. Dutton. *Historical Records of Number 8 Canadian Field Ambulance, 1915-1919*. Toronto: Ryerson, 1920.
Hahn, J.E. *The Intelligence Service Within the Canadian Corps, 1914-1918*. Toronto: Macmillan, 1930.
Hamilton, Nigel. *Monty*. Volume I. London: Hamish Hamilton, 1981.
Hankey, Lord. *The Supreme Command, 1914-1918*. Volume II. London: George Allen & Unwin, 1961.
Hayes, Joseph. *The Eighty-fifth in France and Flanders*. Halifax: Royal, 1920.
Hewitt, G.E. *The Story of the Twenty-eighth (North-West) Battalion, 1914-1917*. London: Canadian War Records Office, 1918.
Hodder-Williams, Ralph. *Princess Patricia's Canadian Light Infantry, 1914-1919*. Volume I. London, Toronto: Hodder & Stoughton, 1923.

Hopkins, J. Castell. *Canada at War, 1914-1918.* Toronto: Canadian Annual Review Limited, 1919.
Hutchinson, Wood. *The Doctor in War.* Boston, New York: Houghton, Mifflin, 1918.
Hutchison, Paul. P. *Canada's Black Watch.* Montreal: The Black Watch of Canada, 1962.
Johnston, G. Chalmers. *The 2nd Canadian Mounted Rifles.* Vernon: Vernon News, n.d.
Keegan, John. *The Face of Battle.* New York: Viking, 1976.
Kerry, A.J., and W.A. McDill. *The History of the Corps of Royal Canadian Engineers.* Volume I. Ottawa: Military Engineers Association of Canada, 1962.
Lapointe, A.J. *Soldier of Quebec.* Montreal: Editions Edouard Garand, 1931.
Lennox, Lady Algernon Gordon, ed. *The Diary of Lord Bertie.* Volume II. London: Hodder & Stoughton, 1924.
Letters from the Front. Volume I. Toronto: Canadian Bank of Commerce, 1920.
Liddell Hart, B.H. *Reputations Ten Years Later.* Boston: Little, Brown, 1928.
———. *The Real War.* London: Faber & Faber, 1930.
Lloyd, Alan. *The War in the Trenches.* London: Hart-David, McGibbon, 1976.
Lloyd George, David. *War Memoirs.* Volumes II, III, IV, V. London: Ivor Nicholson & Watson, 1933-36.
Lloyd George, Richard. *Lloyd George.* London: Frederick Muller, 1960.
Ludendorff, Erich. *Ludendorff's Own Story.* Volumes I, II. 1920. Reprint. Freeport, N.Y.: Books for Libraries Press, 1971.
MacDonald, J.A., ed. *Gun-Fire.* Toronto: Greenway, n.d.
Macdonald, Lyn. *They Called It Passchendaele.* London: Michael Joseph, 1978.
Macphail, Sir Andrew. *Official History of the Canadian Forces in the Great War, 1914-1919: The Medical Services.* Ottawa: King's Printer, 1925.
Marshall-Cornwall, James. *Haig as Military Commander.* New York: Crane, Russak, 1973.
Mathieson, William. *My Grandfather's War.* Toronto: Macmillan, 1981.
Maurice, Nancy, ed. *The Maurice Case.* London: Leo Cooper, 1972.
McCormick, Donald. *The Mask of Merlin.* London: Macdonald, 1963.
McEvoy, Bernard, and A.H. Finley. *History of the 72nd Canadian Infantry Battalion, Seaforth Highlanders of Canada.* Vancouver: Cowan & Brookhouse, 1920.
McKenzie, F.A. *Canada's Day of Glory.* Toronto: William Briggs, 1918.
McNeil, Bill. *Voice of the Pioneer.* Volume II. Toronto: Macmillan, 1984.
McWilliams, James L., and R. James Steel. *The Suicide Battalion.* Edmonton: Hurtig, 1978.
Middlebrook, Martin. *The Kaiser's Battle.* London: Allen Lane, 1978.
Moir, J.S., ed. *History of the Royal Canadian Corps of Signals.* Ottawa: Corps Committee, Royal Canadian Corps of Signals, 1962.

Murray, W.W. *The History of the 2nd Canadian Battalion.* Ottawa: The Historical Committee, 2nd Battalion, CEF, 1947.
Nettleton, John. *The Anger of the Guns.* London: William Kimber, 1979.
Nicholson, G.W.L. *Canadian Expeditionary Force, 1914-1919.* Ottawa: Queen's Printer, 1964.
———. *The Gunners of Canada.* Volume I. Toronto, Montreal: McClelland & Stewart, 1967.
———. *Seventy Years of Service.* Ottawa: Borealis, 1977.
Owen, Frank. *Tempestuous Journey.* London: Hutchinson, 1954.
Patterson, A. Temple. *The Jellicoe Papers.* Volume I. London: Navy Records Society, 1968.
Pershing, John J. *My Experiences in the World War.* Volume II. New York: Frederick A. Stokes, 1931.
Pitt, Barrie, ed. *Great Battles of the 20th Century.* London: Phoebus, 1977.
Pope, Maurice A. *Soldiers and Politicians.* Toronto: University of Toronto Press, 1962.
Reid, Gordon. *Poor Bloody Murder.* Oakville: Mosaic, 1980.
Repington, C. *The First World War.* Volumes I, II. Boston, New York: Houghton, Mifflin, 1920.
Riddell, Lord. *Lord Riddell's War Diary, 1914-1918.* London: Ivor Nicholson & Watson, 1933.
Roberts, T.G., et al. *Thirty Canadian V.Cs.* London: Canadian War Records Office, 1918.
Robertson, Sir William. *From Private to Field-Marshal.* London: Constable, 1921.
———. *Soldiers and Statesmen.* Volumes I, II. London: Cassell, 1926.
Rose, Kenneth. *King George V.* New York: Alfred A. Knopf, 1984.
Roskill, Stephen. *Hankey, Man of Secrets.* Volume I. 1970. Reprint. London: Collins, 1978.
Rowland, Peter. *Lloyd George.* London: Barrie & Jenkins, 1975.
Roy, Reginald, H. *For Most Conspicuous Bravery.* Vancouver: University of British Columbia Press, 1977.
———. *The Journal of Private Fraser.* Victoria: Sono Nis Press, 1985.
Russenholt, E.S. *Six Thousand Canadian Men.* Winnipeg: Forty-fourth Battalion Association, 1932.
Scudamore, T.V. *A Short History of the 7th Battalion, CEF.* Vancouver: Anderson & Odlum, 1930.
Seely, J.E.B. *Adventure.* London: Heinemann, 1930.
Sixsmith, E.K.G. *British Generalship in the Twentieth Century.* London: Arms and Armour Press, 1970.
———. *Douglas Haig.* London: Weidenfeld & Nicolson, 1976.
Smithers, A.J. *Sir John Monash.* London: Leo Cooper, 1973.
Spears, E.J. *Prelude to Victory.* London: Jonathan Cape, 1939.
———. *Two Men Who Saved France.* London: Eyre & Spottiswoode, 1966.
Stacey, C.P. *Historical Documents of Canada.* Volume V. Toronto: Macmillan, 1972.

Stevens, G.R. *A City Goes to War*. Brampton: The Loyal Edmonton Regiment Associates, 1964.
Swettenham, John. *To Seize the Victory*. Toronto: Ryerson, 1965.
———, ed. *Valiant Men*. Toronto: Hakkert, 1973.
———. *McNaughton*. Volume I. Toronto: Ryerson, 1968.
Swinton, Sir Ernest D. *Eyewitness*. Garden City, N.Y.: Doubleday, Doran, 1933.
Tascona, Bruce, and Eric Wells. *Little Black Devils*. Winnipeg: Royal Winnipeg Rifles, 1983.
Taylor, A.J.P., ed. *Lloyd George: A Diary by Frances Stevenson*. London: Hutchinson, 1971.
———. *The First World War*. Penguin, 1977.
Terraine, John. *Douglas Haig, the Educated Soldier*. London: Hutchinson, 1963.
———. *Impacts of War, 1914 & 1918*. London: Hutchinson, 1970.
———. *The Road to Passchendaele*. London: Leo Cooper, 1977.
———. *To Win a War*. New York: Doubleday, 1981.
———. *White Heat*. London: Sidgwick & Jackson, 1982.
Topp, C. Beresford. *The 42nd Battalion, C.E.F., Royal Highlanders of Canada*. Montreal: Gazette, 1931.
Urquhart, Hugh M. *Arthur Currie: The Biography of a Great Canadian*. Toronto, Vancouver: J.M. Dent, 1950.
Warren, Arnold. *Wait for the Waggon*. McClelland & Stewart, 1961.
Williams, Jeffrey. *Princess Patricia's Canadian Light Infantry*. London: Leo Cooper, 1972.
———. *Byng of Vimy*. London: Leo Cooper, 1983.
Wolff, Leon. *In Flanders Fields*. London: Readers Union/Longmans, Green, 1960.
Woodward, Sir Llewellyn. *Great Britain and the War of 1914-1918*. London: Methuen, 1967.
World War, The. Volume II. New York: Grolier, 1920

Index

Note: In most cases, ranks and titles are those held at the time of Passchendaele.

ABBREVIATIONS

FM	Field-Marshal
Gen.	General
Lt.-Gen.	Lieutenant-General
Maj.-Gen.	Major-General
Brig.-Gen.	Brigadier-General
Col.	Colonel
Lt.-Col.	Lieutenant-Colonel
Maj.	Major
Capt.	Captain
Lieut.	Lieutenant
2nd.-Lieut.	Second-Lieutenant
Sgt.-Maj.	Sergeant-Major
Sgt.	Sergeant
Cpl.	Corporal
L.-Cpl.	Lance-Corporal
Pte.	Private
Gnr.	Gunner
Tpr.	Trooper

Adamson, Lt.-Col. Agar, 121, 146, 147, 148–49
Aisne, River, 32, 34
Albon, C.J., 179
Aldershot, 11
Alderson, Lt.-Gen. Sir E.A.H., 90
Allen, Cpl. Fred, 179
Allenby, Gen. Sir Edmund, 203, 204, 209
Amiens, 35, 57fn, 212, 214, 216, 220, 233
Anderson, E.O., 180
Anderson, Maj. Percival, 142
Annan, Lieut. Jim, 68
Anthoine, Gen. Paul, 35, 58, 61
Ardennes, 54
Arleux, 90, 91
Armentières, 215
Armstrong, Charles, 182
Arras, 19, 32, 34
Asquith, Herbert, 5, 6, 19, 219
Asquith, Margot, 7
Austria-Hungary, 3, 8, 39, 44

Bacon, Vice-Admiral Sir Reginald, 18, 19
Badger, Pte. H., 168
Bagley, G.A., 180
Baker, Cpl. H.C., 170
Baker, Stanley, 124
Baker-Carr, Brig.-Gen. C.D., 65
Bapty, Walter, 114
Barron, Cpl. C.F., 164
Barry, Lieut. A.L., 119, 166
Barton, Pte. N.O., 179
Beauvais, 214, 217
Becelaere, 58
Belgian army, 23, 78
Belgium, ix, 3, 18, 29fn, 154; coast of, 17–18, 19, 22, 31, 37, 42, 52, 54, 73. *See also* Flanders.
Bellevue Spur, 83, 106, 131, 132, 140, 160, 238; described, 125
Bertie, Lord, 30, 32, 208
Bethune, 215
Birch, Lt.-Gen. Sir Noel, 93, 103
Bird, Cpl. Will, 118, 119, 160–61, 237–38
Birdwood, Lt.-Gen. Sir William, 84fn, 140
Birks, 2nd-Lieut. H.L., 67
Borden, Prime Minister Sir Robert, 94fn, 223–24, 226
Bottrill, Lieut. W.A., 172
Boulogne, 76–77, 197, 206
Briand, Aristide, 14, 25, 30, 31
Brice, Sgt. John, 181
British Expeditionary Force (BEF), 9, 35, 38, 51, 208, 209, 224, 225, 228; role in 1917, 17, 23; in Flanders, 63–178 *passim,* 231–34; demoralization of, 67–68, 200; manpower shortage, 197–200, 202; and German offensives, 210–17

Armies
First, 18, 92, 95, 210, 222
Second, 40, 74, 78, 96, 99, 103, 115, 116, 136, 158, 210; continues Flanders offensive, 75–76, 77, 82–83, 86; Canadians join, 96
Third, 95, 195–96, 210, 212, 214

279

Fifth, 57, 58–59, 75, 78, 95, 116, 136, 140–41, 158; launches Flanders offensive, 63–64; resumes attacks, 65–66, 74; and German offensives, 210–12, 214

Corps
I, 51
II, 158
VIII, 178
X, 136
XIV, 136
XVIII, 136, 140, 158
I Anzac, 84fn, 136, 140
II Anzac, 82, 83, 99
Canadian. *See* Canadian Army Corps.
Tank, 65, 67, 80, 195–96

Divisions
1st, 176
16th (Nationalist), 68
36th (Ulster), 68
51st (Highland), 68
63rd (Royal Naval), 150
3rd Australian, 83–84, 99, 101
New Zealand, 83, 99, 101

Brigades
3rd, 176
190th, 150

Battalions
1/9th Royal Scots Regiment, 68
2/8th Lancashire Fusiliers, 82
10th Royal Fusiliers, 67
38th Australian, 83
Artists' Rifles, 150–51
East Lancashire Regiment, 68
Royal Munster Fusiliers, 176
Royal Newfoundland Regiment, 184
South Staffordshire Regiment, 67
South Wales Borderers, 176
See also General Headquarters.
Broodseinde, *ix*fn, 58, 73, 77
Brooke, Maj. Alan, 117

Brown, Pte. Archie, 142
Brown, Pte. Gordon, 105, 134
Bruges, 54
Brussels, 54
Buckle, Maj.-Gen. C.R., 103
Bulgaria, 3
Burns, Pte. Pat, 122, 125, 133, 134
Burstall, Maj.-Gen. H.E., 91–92, 159, 162, 166
Butler, Maj.-Gen. Sir Richard, 207
Byng, Gen. Sir Julian, 86, 90, 95, 195–96, 210, 211, 212

Cadorna, Gen. Luigi, 71
Calais: conference, 25–27, 34; agreement, 27–31
Cambrai, 57fn, 86, 195–96, 233
Cameron, Lieut. J.A., 167
Caporetto, Battle of, 192, 194, 212fn
Canadian Army Corps, 32, 51, 52, 86, 90, 91, 190, 195, 210, 220, 221; Currie commands, 92, 93; at Hill 70, 92–93, 94–95; moves to Flanders, 98; efficiency of staff, 115; offensive operations at Passchendaele, 125–177 *passim;* departs Flanders, 178; casualties, 178, 178fn; and German offensives, 222–24; achievement at Passchendaele, 237–39

Divisions
First, 90, 94, 108, 115, 123, 158, 162, 165–66, 172
Second, 92, 94, 105, 115, 158, 162, 166, 170
Third, 92, 115, 125, 132, 140, 145, 158
Fourth, 92, 100, 115, 125, 132, 140, 158, 180

Brigades
First, 159, 162
Second, 173
Third, 121
Fourth, 173, 180
Fifth, 166
Sixth, 166, 168

Seventh, 145
Eighth, 125, 145
Ninth, 125, 129, 130, 131, 132, 159
Tenth, 125, 135
Twelfth, 141

Battalions
1st (Western Ontario), 162, 164-66
2nd (Eastern Ontario), 162, 164-66
3rd (Toronto Regiment), 162, 164
4th (Central Ontario), 172
5th (Western Cavalry), 121, 176
7th (1st British Columbia Regiment), 173-74, 176
8th (90th Winnipeg Rifles), 173, 174-76
10th (Canadians), 174, 176, 177
13th (Royal Highlanders of Canada), 172, 179
16th (Canadian Scottish), 180
18th (Western Ontario), 110
19th (Central Ontario), 110, 124, 177
20th (Central Ontario), 102, 120, 157, 174, 177
22nd (French Canadian), 172
24th (Victoria Rifles of Canada), 178
25th (Nova Scotia Rifles), 179
26th (New Brunswick), 119, 166
27th (Winnipeg), 166, 168-69
28th (Northwest), 166, 167, 168-69, 170, 171
31st (Alberta), 119, 166, 167, 167fn
42nd (Royal Highlanders of Canada), 118, 119, 121, 122, 153, 159, 160, 161, 178, 237
43rd (Cameron Highlanders of Canada), 125, 130-31
44th (Manitoba), 123, 135-36, 137, 141, 179
46th (South Saskatchewan), 102, 105, 117, 118, 120, 122, 125, 132-35, 178, 179
47th (British Columbia), 135-36

49th (Edmonton Regiment), 145, 146, 149, 160, 178, 180, 181
50th (Calgary), 119, 125, 126, 133, 135, 138, 180, 182
52nd (Ontario), 131
54th (Central Ontario), 124, 180
58th (Central Ontario), 125, 130
72nd (Seaforth Highlanders of Canada), 105, 122, 141, 144-45
78th (Winnipeg Grenadiers), 118, 124, 141, 142-44, 145
85th (Nova Scotia Highlanders), 136, 141-42, 145, 154
87th (Canadian Grenadier Guards), 110, 179
102nd (Central Ontario), 114, 179
1st Canadian Mounted Rifles, 129
2nd Canadian Mounted Rifles, 152
4th Canadian Mounted Rifles, 125, 126-30
5th Canadian Mounted Rifles, 114, 121, 145, 150-53, 180
Princess Patricia's Canadian Light Infantry, 110, 121, 145-49, 160, 181
Royal Canadian Regiment, 148, 149, 178, 179

Other Services
Army Service Corps, 109-10
Artillery, 103-7, 111, 126
  10th Field Battery, 107
  15th Field Battery, 107
  18th Field Battery, 107
  32nd Field Battery, 106
  39th Field Battery, 105
  23rd Howitzer Battery, 110
Cavalry: Canadian Cavalry Brigade, 228
  Canadian Light Horse, 228
Engineers, 109, 156-57; and road construction, 107-8
Machine-Gun Corps: 7th Company, 147
  10th Company, 134

Medical Corps, 111-14, 122-23, 137-39; stretcher-bearers, 137-38, 153, 171
   3rd Field Ambulance, 138
   5th Field Ambulance, 120, 139
   8th Field Ambulance, 138, 179
  Pioneers, 108fn
   107th Pioneer Battalion, 108
Carmichael, Lieut. G., 173
Casualties: Verdun, 4; Somme, 4, 14; spring of 1918, 215, 216-17; Third Ypres:
  German, 61, 63, 187
  French, 248fn
  British, 66, 75, 77, 82, 86, 216, 231
  Canadian: Currie estimates, 96
   26-28 October, 137
   30 October, 153
   6 November, 170
   10 November, 177
   total, 178, 178fn
   artillery, 107
   engineers, 109
   infantry, (3rd Battalion) 164, (24th Battalion) 178, (28th Battalion) 170, 171, (42nd Battalion) 178, (46th Battalion) 135, 178, (49th Battalion) 149, 178, (72nd Battalion) 145, (78th Battalion) 145, (85th Battalion) 145, (87th Battalion) 179, (102nd Battalion) 179, (4th CMR) 130, (5th CMR) 152-53, (PPCLI) 147-48, (RCR) 178
Cavan, Lt.-Gen. the Earl of, 220
Central Powers, 3, 44
Chantilly, 17, 19
Charteris, Brig.-Gen. John, 21, 29, 74, 85, 192-93, 198, 214, 219-20; impressions of Haig, 11-13; favours Flanders, 18; on French mutinies, 36; anxieties about offensive, 61-62, 76, 79, 83; and rain, 63-64; Lloyd George's opinion of, 79-80; influences Haig, 79-81; view of offensive, 170; victim of Lloyd George's vendetta, 206-7

Churchill, Winston, ix, 8, 18, 18fn, 199-200, 201, 219; appointed to cabinet, 39
Clark, Lt.-Col. J.A., 144
Clemenceau, Georges, 85
Cloth Hall, 118
Cohen, Lieut. M.T., 161
Conscription: Australia, 226; Britain, 39, 226; Canada, 226-27
Constantinople, 8
Crest Farm, 133, 140, 144-45
Currie, Lt.-Gen. Sir A.W., 86, 158; character and background, 89-91, 94fn; and Hill 70, 92-93, 94-95; relationship with Haig, 93-94; ordered to take Passchendaele, 86, 95-98; Gough's opinion of, 96fn; oversees preparations, 99-103, 107, 112; talks to troops, 102, 159; draws up plans, 115-17; clashes with Gough, 115-16, 140-41; and trench foot, 123; pleased with operations, 136; opposes withdrawals, 153; angered by British failures, 155, 176; revises plans, 155-56; mixed feelings about success, 169-70; approves final attack, 172; leaves salient, 178; pride in Canadians, 182-83; decorated by Belgians and French, 183; selected as Haig's successor, 221-26; told reasons for Passchendaele, 222; critical of British, 222-23; complains to Borden, 223-24; meets Lloyd George, 224; and conscription, 226-27; criticism of, 227-29; opinion of Passchendaele, 222, 223-24, 238-39
Curzon, Lord, 41, 71, 218

Daily Chronicle, 182, 218
Daily Express, 182
Daily News, 218
Dardanelles, 8
Davidson, Maj.-Gen. Sir John, 85
Davies, Lt.-Col. R.D., 135, 136
Davis, Capt. W.H., 129-30

Dawson, Lt.-Col. Herbert, 132, 133, 135
Debney, Philip, 106-7
Decline Copse, 126, 132, 135-36, 141
Decoteau, Alec, 149fn
Derby, Lord, 42, 72, 86fn, 195, 205, 207, 221
Donaldson, Lt.-Col. H.S., 138
Dorais, Pte. Crosby, 174
Doullens, 37, 213
Duck Lodge, 146, 147
Dunkirk, 54
Dyer, Brig.-Gen. Hugh, 145

Edinburgh, 11
Edmonds, Sir James, 231, 237
Elmsley, Brig.-Gen. J.H., 145

Farmar, Brig.-Gen. G.J., 115
Fiset, Maj.-Gen. Sir Eugène, 94fn
Fisken, Capt. A.D., 174
Flanders, 9, 10, 21-22, 36, 38; strategic importance, 17-19, 42-43, 52-54; topography, 51. *See also* Belgium.
Foch, Gen. (*later* Marshal) Ferdinand, 15, 72, 212fn, 236; named generalissimo, 213-14; angers Haig, 215-16
Francis, Lt.-Col. M., 135-36
Fraser, L.-Cpl. Donald, 157-58
French army: at Verdun, 4, 17; and spring 1917 offensive, 32; mutinies, 35-36, 43-44, 84-85; and Flanders offensive, 23, 38, 78, 85; Haig's opinion of, 215-16

Formations
First Army, 35, 58
See also Grand Quartier General; Joffre; Nivelle; Pétain.
French, FM Sir John (*later* Lord), 9, 11, 190-91
Fresnoy, 90-91
Fuller, J.F.C., 73, 80
Furst Farm, 149, 160

Gallipoli, 8
Gas. *See* poison gas.
Gas gangrene, 113-14
General Headquarters (GHQ), 13, 18, 61, 63-65, 70, 72, 76, 81, 198, 209, 214, 217, 221, 223; target of Lloyd George's vendetta, 206-8
George V, King, 11, 27, 86fn, 206fn, 217
Gericht, 4. *See also* Verdun.
German army: invasion of France and Belgium, 3, 51; and Verdun, 4, 19; withdrawal to Hindenburg Line, 29; effect of Flanders offensive on, 81, 84, 187-89, 234, 236-37; respect for Canadians, 124, 169

Formations
Fourth Army, 60
11th Bavarian Division, 124, 140
4th Infantry Division, 161, 173fn
11th Infantry Division, 161, 173fn
238th Infantry Division, 141
44th Reserve Infantry Division, 173fn
See also casualties; Hindenburg Line; Ludendorff; Oberste Herrseleitung; Rupprecht.
Gheluvelt, 58, 78, 136
Ghent, 54
Gibbs, Philip, 68
Gillis, Pte. P.M., 144
Glencorse Wood, 65
Godeswaersvalde, 61
Godley, Lt.-Gen. Sir Alexander, 83
Gold, Lt.-Col. E., 64
Goodspeed, D.J., 162
Gotha bombers, 123-24
Goudberg, 162, 164, 170
Gough, Gen. Sir Hubert, 30, 75, 79, 84, 219, 232; given responsibility for Flanders offensive, 57-60; postpones attack, 61; launches offensive, 63-64; appalled at conditions, 66-67; loses confidence of men, 68; favours halt, 68, 76, 137; shunted aside, 73-74; Currie refuses to serve under, 95-96;

283

opinion of Currie, 96fn; asks for change in Currie's plan, 116, 140–41; admits difficulties, 136–37, 155; role in Flanders ends, 158; and German offensive, 210–12; sacked, 214
Graf House, 146–47, 161, 165, 178
Grand Quartier Général (GQG), 44, 190, 214, 215
Gravenstafel, 108, 121, 158
Griesbach, Brig.-Gen. W.A., 159, 162
Gun, Lt.-Col. J.N., 138–39, 179

Haalen Copse, 144
Haig, FM Sir Douglas: views on war, 10–11, 12,13, 40, 81–82; background and character, 11–13; opinion of Lloyd George, 15, 28, 71, 217, 221; and politicians, 12; opinion of allies, 12, 36, 61, 215–16; and Joffre, 17; attraction to Flanders, 18, 21–22, 29, 34, 37, 42–43, 52–54; and Nivelle, 20, 21–24, 28fn, 28–32; Lloyd George's opinion of, 14; and Calais conference, 25–28; and Pétain, 35, 212–13; pleads for manpower, 40–42; and war policy committee, 41–46; on "side-shows," 47; gets cabinet approval for offensive, 47; at First Ypres, 51; plans for Flanders, 54–59; troubles with Gough, 59–60; and start of offensive, 63–64; undeterred by rain, 68–70; revises plans, 73–76, 78; loses confidence in Robertson, 41–42, 76–77; persists with campaign, 79–82, 83, 84–86; influenced by Charteris, 79–81; relationship with Currie, 93–94, 96, 97–98; impressions of Canadians, 95; gives Currie extra guns, 103-4; visits Currie's headquarters, 116, 117; Currie sympathizes with, 116–17; congratulates Currie, 136, 155, 170; renewed optimism, 137; opinion of Crest Farm attack, 144; halts offensive, 178; suspicious of Lloyd George, 190; target of Lloyd George's intrigues, 191–210; plans to renew Flanders offensive in 1918, 196–97; opinion of Wilson, 205fn, 205–6; prepares for German offensive, 210–11; urges Foch as generalissimo, 213–14; special order, 216; expects to be attacked by Lloyd George, 217, 219–20; angered by Wilson, 221; opinion of Passchendaele, 233, and justification for, 235–36
Haig, Lady, 64, 84, 86fn, 206, 211, 220
Haldane, Lord, 11
Hambley, Tpr. George, 228–29
Hankey, Lt.-Col. Sir Maurice, 6, 20, 24, 31, 45–46, 71–72, 191–93, 197, 205fn; and Calais conference, 26–27; defends Haig, 30; seeks successor to Haig, 208; on replacing Haig, 219–20
Hanotaux, Gabriel, 183
Harper, Maj.-Gen. G.M., 68
Harris, Pte. Ernie, 120, 132–33
Hazebrouck, 216
Hazlewood, Gnr. Frank, 110
Hell Fire Corner, 118
Hellings, Pte. Percy, 122, 132
Higgins, Gnr. D.C., 181
Hill, Brig.-Gen. F.W., 130, 132
Hilliam, Brig.-Gen. Edward, 135
Hill 52, 173–74
Hill 70, 92–93, 94–95, 94fn, 106, 124, 227, 237
Hindenberg, FM Paul von, 45fn
Hindenburg Line, 29, 30, 32, 220, 221
Holder, G.K.K., 166
Holland, 29fn, 52
Holmes, Pte. Tommy, 128–29
Honnebeek, 108
Hooglede, 78
Hope, Maj. John, 134–35
Horne, Gen. Sir Henry, 90, 92–93, 95–96, 210, 222–23
Horse-trains, 110, 157–58. *See also* mule-trains; work parties.

284

Hôtel de la Gare Maritime (Calais), 25
Hôtel Majestic (Paris), 222
Hôtel Meurice (Paris), 183
House of Commons: British, 193, 213fn, 217, 219; Canadian, 226, 229
House of Lords, 218
Houthulst Forest, 58, 74, 78
Howard, Sgt. Gordon, 107
Hughes, Sir Sam, 94fn, 229
Hunter-Weston, Lt.-Gen. Sir Aylmer, 178

Imperial War Cabinet, 223-24
Inverness Copse, 65
Ironside, Lt.-Col. Edmund, 100, 100fn
Irwin, L.-Cpl. S., 144-45
Isonzo, Eleventh Battle of, 3, 71
Italy, 3, 20, 39, 41, 44, 47, 70, 72, 188, 196, 202; and Caporetto débâcle, 192-93

Jacob, Lt.-Gen. Sir Claud, 158
Jellicoe, Admiral Sir John, 37, 45, 45fn
Jenner, Pte. Ernie, 179
Jericho, 209-10
Jerusalem, 20, 203
Joffre, Gen. (*later* Marshal) Joseph, 17, 18-20
Johnson, Pte. James, 114, 180

Kaiserschlact, 189, 236
Keegan, John, 112
Kemp, Sir Edward, 94fn
Kennedy, Capt. William, 134
Kennedy, Lieut. H., 167
Ketchen, Brig.-Gen. H.D.B., 166
Kiggell, Lt.-Gen. Sir Launcelot, 56-57, 170, 193, 195; sacked, 207
Kilpatrick, Maj. George, 119, 121, 153, 159, 161
Kindermord, 51
King, Lieut. Paddy, 68
Kinross, Pte. C.J., 149
Kirkaldy, Lt.-Col. J., 144
Kitchener, Lord, 4, 6

Knight, Lieut. E.R., 181
Kuhl, Gen. Hermann von, 61, 94, 187-88

Lamkeek, 133
Langemarck, Battle of, *ix*fn
Lansdowne, Lord, 4-5
Lapointe, Pte. A.J., 172
Laurier, Sir Wilfrid, 226, 227
Law, A. Bonar, 41, 71, 73, 210
Lens, 38, 92, 227
Liddell Hart, Sir B.H., ix, 231
Lipsett, Maj.-Gen. L.J., 91-92, 125, 145
Lloyd George, Prime Minister David, 69, 76, 81, 189, 196, 199fn, 205fn, 212fn, 213fn; opinion of Passchendaele, ix, 190, 198, 235; background and character, 5-7; appointed prime minister, 7, 17; and conduct of war, 6, 7-9, 22, 231-32; opinion of Asquith, 6; opinion of Haig, 14, 79; opinion of Robertson, 14-15, 70-71; and Nivelle, 20-21, 24; and "side-shows," 7-9, 20, 39-42, 46, 70, 73, 191-93, 202-4, 209-10, 224-25; wants to sack Haig, 24, 30, 72, 190, 208, 219-21; and Calais conference, 25-28; on Nivelle's failure, 33; manpower concerns, 39, 197-200; forms war policy committee, 41; argues against Flanders offensive, 43-45, 46-47; tries to halt offensive, 70-73, 82; opinion of Charteris, 79-80; "irregular warfare" against Haig and Robertson, 190-95, 197-201, 202-10; defends government's role, 217-18; and Maurice crisis, 218-19; meets Currie, 224-25
Lloyd George, Richard, 200
London, 5, 20, 29, 43, 77, 80, 94fn, 115, 139, 182, 205, 219, 220, 223, 227, 228; conferences, 22-23, 30-31, 70, 72
Longstaffe, Pte. P.H., 108
Loomis, Brig.-Gen. F.O.W., 173-74

Ludendorff, Gen. Erich, 45fn, 81, 187–89, 201, 202, 220; impressed by Canadians, 188
Lyautey, Louis, 25, 30
Lys, River, 215

MacBrien, Brig.-Gen. J.H., 141
Macdonald, Lyn, 120
Macdonell, Maj.-Gen. A.C., 91–92, 97–98, 103, 158, 162, 166
MacIntyre, D.E., 180
MacKenzie, Capt. Ross, 141
MacKenzie, Lieut. Hugh, 147
MacKenzie, John, 122
Macphail, Sir Andrew, 113
Macpherson, Capt. M.M., 146
Maurice, Maj.-Gen. Sir Frederick, 43, 202, 204, 209–10, 216; sacrifices career, 218–19
Maxse, Lt.-Gen. Sir Ivor, 140
Maxwell, Lt.-Gen. Sir Richard, 207
McCormick, Donald, 200
McEwan, Maj. John, 142
McFarland, Maj. G.F., 130
McGill, Capt. Harold, 120, 139, 162
McKenzie, F.A., 101, 159
McKerchar, Pte. Don, 117, 132, 134
McKnight, Pte. G., 166
McNaughton, Lt.-Col. Andrew, 100, 106, 228
Meetcheele, 140, 146, 147, 148
Menin Gate, 118
Menin Road, 118
Menin Road Ridge, *ix*fn, 75
Mesopotamia, 8. *See also* Middle East; Palestine.
Messines Ridge, 38, 40–41, 51, 57, 59
Middlebrook, Martin, 126
Middle East, 8, 204. *See also* Mesopotamia; Palestine.
Miles, Pte. Charlie, 67
Milner, Lord, 41, 194, 221, 224, 225
Molyneux, Pte. A., 151–52
Monash, Maj.-Gen. (*later* Lt.-Gen. Sir) John, 84, 225

Mons, 188, 189
Montgomery, Capt. B.L., 102–3
Moorslede, 58, 78
Mordy, Maj. Arnott, 180
Morning Post, 199fn, 205, 218, 219
Morrison, Brig.-Gen. E.W.B., 100
Moser, Gen. Otto von, 188
Mosselmarkt, 131, 161, 162, 164–65, 170
Mount Sorrel, Battle of, 52, 90
Mule-trains, 110, 140. *See also* horse-trains; work parties.
Mullin, Sgt. George, 147

Naylor, Lieut. J.W., 67
Nettleton, John, 237
New Statesman, 235
Nicholas II, Czar, 3
Nieuport, 54
Nivelle, Gen. Robert, 34, 39, 43, 47, 57, 60; succeeds Joffre, 20; Lloyd George's opinion of, 20–21; plans for 1917, 21–24; and Calais conference, 25–28; clashes with Haig, 28–30; failure of offensive, 31–32; sacked, 32
Niven, Maj. H.W., 148
Nonne Boschen, 65

Oberste Heerseleitung (OHL), 77–78, 171, 188–89
Odlum, Brig.-Gen. V.W., 94fn
Oise, River, 17
O'Kelly, Capt. Christopher, 131
Oliver, Dudley, 227
Oliver, Frank, 227
O'Neill, Joe, 124
Orpen, Sir William, 13
Ostend, 18, 19, 22, 23, 45, 47, 54, 58
Overseas Military Forces of Canada, 94fn

Page, Lt.-Col. Lionel, 119
Page, Walter, 5
Painlevé, Paul, 31, 76–77
Palestine, 8, 203, 209–10. *See also* Mesopotamia; Middle East.
Palmer, Lt.-Col. R.H., 149
Papineau, Maj. Talbot, 148

Paris, 17, 20, 30, 64, 183, 193, 194-95, 208, 213, 222; conferences, 34-35, 47
Passchendaele, First and Second Battle of, *ix*fn. *See also* Ypres, Third Battle of.
Passchendaele (ridge), 54, 56, 58, 73, 75, 77, 83, 84, 86, 89-182 passim; becomes primary objective, 74, 78, 86; abandoned by British, 216
Passchendaele (village), 51, 83, 120, 133, 145, 147, 155, 161, 166, 173; captured by Canadians, 162, 168-69, 170
Patterson, Lt.-Col. W.R., 128-29
Patterson, Sgt.-Maj. Donald, 105
Pearkes, Maj. George, 121, 150-52
Perley, Sir George, 94fn, 227
Pershing, Gen. J.J., 222
Pétain, Gen. Henri, 32, 33, 34, 38, 72, 76, 85, 197, 212fn, 231; and Haig, 35-36; approves of Flanders, 35, 44; panics, 212-13
Philpott, Gnr. Elmer, 180
Pilckem, Battle of, *ix*fn
Pillboxes, 66-67, 159-60
Plumer, Gen. Sir Herbert, 40-41, 56-58, 75, 79, 82, 84, 103, 170, 210, 220; put in charge in Flanders offensive, 74; changes tactics, 74-75; launches attacks, 75-77; Currie appeals to, 96; sides with Currie, 116; congratulates Currie, 136; sent to Italy, 193
Poelcappelle, Battle of, *ix*fn
Poincaré, President Raymond, 28fn, 36
Poison gas, 51, 90, 114
Polygon Wood, *ix*fn, 65, 75
Poperinghe, 100, 101
Potijze, 157

Quelch, Pte. Jack, 123, 137, 179-80
Quinton, Lieut. Stanley, 124

Radcliffe, Brig.-Gen. P.P. deB., 99, 115

Rapallo, 193, 194
Rattray, Pte. Thomas, 177
Ravebeek, 120, 125, 145, 153, 167
Rawlinson, Gen. Sir Henry, 56-57, 75, 214
Reece, Sgt.-Maj. Lewis, 93
Repington, Lt.-Col. Charles, 10, 37, 39fn, 57-58, 193, 195, 199fn, 205, 219; critical of Lloyd George, 199, 217-18
Ribot, Premier Alexandre, 31
Rice, Maj.-Gen. Sir Robert, 207
Riddell, Sir George, 6, 7, 70
Robertson, Gen. Sir William ("Wully"), 25, 57-58, 80, 82, 201, 206-7, 208, 217; background and character, 9; and politicians, 9-10, 71; opinion of allies, 10; views on war, 10; opinion of Lloyd George, 16, 23, 28; and Flanders, 19; Lloyd George's opinion of, 14-15; and Calais conference, 25-28; on Nivelle's failure, 32; and 1917 strategy, 34; and U-boats, 37; wavers on offensive policy, 41-42; and war policy committee, 41-46; thwarts Lloyd George's "side-shows," 70-71, 73; loses Haig's confidence, 41-42, 76-77, 197, 205; clashes with Lloyd George, 190-91, 192-93, 198-99, 202-5; ceases to serve, 205, 206fn
Robertson, Pte. James, 168
Romania, 3
Rome, 20
Ross, Brig.-Gen. J.M., 166
Ross, Col. A.E., 111
Ross, Lt.-Col. Alex, 167, 171
Roulers, 52, 54, 56, 58, 59, 78
Royal Flying Corps: 21 Squadron, 106
Royal Navy, 37, 45
Rupprecht, Crown Prince of Bavaria, 61, 82, 84, 187
Russia, 3, 8, 81, 189

Sallaumines Hill, 95
Salonika, 8, 202

Sauvigny, Bertier de, 24
Scott, Lieut. Stewart, 118-19
Seely, Brig.-Gen. J.E.B., 228
Shankland, Lieut. Robert, 130-31, 131fn
Shields, Sgt. T.T., 110
Shier, Lieut. L.V., 120, 157
Slodgett, Lt.-Gen. Sir Arthur, 207
Smith, Maj. Richard, 157
Smuts, Lt.-Gen. Jan, 33, 41, 43, 71, 208
Snipe Hall, 146
Somme, Battle of, 15fn, 21, 34, 44, 46, 56, 61, 215, 235; casualties, 4, 14; origins of, 18-19; tanks at, 64; Canadians at, 90
Somme, River, 4, 17, 19, 212
Source Farm, 151, 152
Sparling, Maj. Walt, 165
Staff College, 9, 11, 92
Stamfordham, Lord, 206fn
Stevens, Lieut. G.R., 181
Stevenson, Frances, 6, 14, 24
Stewart, Col. J.S., 180
Submarines. *See* U-boats.
Sulivan, Maj. H.E., 148
Supreme War Council, 199fn, 203, 204, 205fn, 212fn, 213fn; origins of, 191-92; creation of, 193
Sutherland, Lieut. Howard, 110
Swettenham, John, 111
Swinton, Col. Ernest, 65
Syrett, Pte. Vic, 118

Tanks, 57, 57fn, 64-65, 195-96, 220
Taylor, A.J.P., ix
Taylor, L.-Cpl. W.J., 161
Taylor, Pte. Alexander, 154
10 Downing Street, 7, 18, 20, 22, 71, 210
Ten Elms, 101-2, 103, 116
Terraine, John, x, 43, 56, 57, 190, 200, 231
Thourout, 52, 54, 56, 78
Tiber House, 133
Times, The, 10, 37, 39fn, 57, 82, 195, 199, 199fn, 218; opinion of Passchendaele, 182

Trench foot, 122-23
Triple Entente, 3
Turkey, 3, 8, 44, 73, 203
Turner, Lt.-Gen. Sir R.E.W., 228
Turner, O.J., 180
Turner, Pte. Arthur, 119, 126, 138, 180, 182
Turner, Pte. W.E., 169
Tuxford, Brig.-Gen. G.S., 121

U-boats, 19, 37, 45
United States of America, 3, 19, 37, 189

Vapour Farm, 140, 150-52
Venture Farm, 174
Verdun, Battle of, 4, 19, 20, 24, 34, 188
Versailles, 193, 203, 204, 205, 222
Vienna Cottage, 140
Villiers, Maj. Paul, 121
Vimy Ridge, 17, 25, 32, 86, 90, 91, 106, 124, 178, 181, 210, 237, 238
Vindictive Crossroads, 173
Vine Cottage, 150, 151, 164
Vlamertinghe Mill, 138

Wade, Maj. George, 67
Waldron, George, 227
War cabinet, 25, 30-31, 41, 42, 45, 202, 221; approves Nivelle offensive, 23; approves Flanders offensive, 47; congratulates Haig, 190; and manpower for BEF, 200; ignores attack warnings, 209; discusses replacement of Haig, 219
War Office, 6, 24, 80, 115, 197, 202, 209, 219, 221, 232
War policy committee, 41-46, 77, 80
Watson, Maj.-Gen. David, 91-92, 94fn, 125, 141
Western Front: origins, 3-4, 51; Lloyd George's views of, 7-8, 22; Haig's views of, 10-11, 40; Robertson's views of, 10; average monthly British casualties on, 232
Wieltje, 121

Wilhelm II, Kaiser, 3
Wilson, Gen. Sir Henry, 30, 44, 190-91, 193, 204, 209, 212, 220; succeeds Robertson, 205-6; Haig's opinion of, 205fn; warns Haig about casualties, 221
Wilson, President Woodrow, 192
Woodland Plantation, 129
Work parties, 105, 108, 109, 110, 140, 156-57, 172. *See also* horse-trains; mule-trains.
Wytschaete, 51

Youngman, Ed, 110
Ypres, Battles of:
  First, 51, 213
  Second, 51, 90, 114, 121
  Third, ix-x; origins and preparations, 17-19, 23-24, 37, 43-46, 52-53, 54-59, 60; preliminary bombardment, 61; offensive, 31 July-12 November, 63-178 passim; results, 187-89, 197-208, 231-39
Ypres (salient), 56, 60; origin, 51; importance, 52-54
Ypres (town), 29, 31, 51, 52, 99, 101, 118, 169
Ypres-Roulers railway, 120, 126, 161

Zeebrugge, 18, 19, 22, 33, 45, 52, 54
Zonnebeke, 59